Race in Modern Irish Literature and Culture

To Conor, Owen and Laura

Race in Modern Irish Literature and Culture

John Brannigan

Edinburgh University Press

© John Brannigan, 2009

Edinburgh University Press Ltd
22 George Square, Edinburgh

www.euppublishing.com

Typeset in Sabon and Futura
by Servis Filmsetting Ltd, Stockport, Cheshire, and
printed and bound in Great Britain by
CPI Antony Rowe, Chippenham and Eastbourne

A CIP record for this book is available from the British Library

ISBN 978 0 7486 3883 3 (hardback)

The right of John Brannigan
to be identified as author of this work
has been asserted in accordance with
the Copyright, Designs and Patents Act 1988.

Contents

Illustrations

Acknowledgements

This book could not have been written without a lot of help. The time necessary to research and write the book was generously provided by the President's Research Fellowship of University College Dublin in 2007–8, which provided one year's leave from teaching and administrative duties. Some of the ideas articulated in the book also benefited greatly from 'trial runs' as papers or articles, and for the opportunities to do so, I am very grateful to Anne Fogarty of the *Irish University Review*, Peter Nichols of *Textual Practice*, Elizabeth Gilmartin and Eileen Reilly for the Grian conferences on race and cosmopolitanism at New York University, Borbála Faragó and Moynagh Sullivan for the 'Double Vision' conference in University College Dublin, Graham Huggan and Ian Law for the 'Racism, Postcolonialism, Europe' conference in Leeds University, and Colin Graham for the invitation to speak at NUI Maynooth. For her immediate interest and unequivocal support for the book, I would like to thank especially Jackie Jones at Edinburgh University Press, and for their invaluable work in preparing the book for publication, Sarah Hall, James Dale, Máiréad McElligott, and Claire Abel. I am also thankful to the two readers of the proposal, Colin Graham and John Waters, who provided wise counsel as well as much valued encouragement.

I owe many thanks, as well as cups of tea and biscuits, to my mentors, colleagues and friends in University College Dublin, especially to Susan Cahill, Ron Callan, Andrew Carpenter, Danielle Clarke, Mary Clayton, Mary Daly, Nicholas Daly, Fionnuala Dillane, Eamonn Dunne, Anne Fogarty, Adam Kelly, Declan Kiberd, P. J. Mathews, Frank McGuinness, Gerardine Meaney, Anne Mulhall, Chris Murray, Vike Plock, Tony Roche, Brian Thomson, and Nerys Williams, all of whom provided helpful prompts, advice, support, camaraderie, and encouragement at various stages of the project. I have also been extraordinarily privileged to have good and helpful companionship

wherever the research and writing of the book took me. I owe many
debts of gratitude to those who provided me with invaluable assistance
in numerous libraries and archives: Mairead Delaney, Abbey Theatre
Archives; Scott Krafft, McCormick Library of Special Collections,
Northwestern University Library, Illinois; Donal Maguire and Roisin
Kennedy, National Gallery of Ireland; Pat Kervick, Peabody Museum
of Archaeology and Ethnology, Harvard University; Seamus Helferty
and Antoinette Doran in UCD Archives; Katherine McSharry and
Eugene Roche in UCD Special Collections; as well as the librarians and
archivists of the National Archives of Ireland, the National Library
of Ireland, the British Library, the British Newspaper Library at
Colindale, and the Billy Rose Theatre Collection in New York Public
Library. I benefited also from the expertise of Anne Fogarty, Marilyn
Reizbaum, and Paul K. Saint-Amour in fruitful conversations on Joyce
studies, from the encyclopedic knowledge of Irish theatre shared by
Chris Murray, Tony Roche, and Beth Mannion, from Paul Durcan's
comments on allusions in his own work, from Thérèse Smith's advice
regarding Irish music and the historical provenance of the banjo, and
from generous suggestions by John Waters and Omaar Hena concerning scholarship on blackface minstrelsy and Irish America. From these
companions and conversations, and many more, I have learned a great
deal, but the shortcomings and errors of this book are mine alone.

Much of this book was written in the comforts of my home in
Belfast, in which I was able to enjoy the love, support, and distractions
of my family. I owe my greatest debt to my wife, Moyra, who has been,
as always, generous and patient in her love, advice, and her support,
and she remains my first and most assiduous reader. My mother-in-law,
Maisie, and my parents, Peter and Maureen, were also indispensable in
the love, support, and time they have constantly given to me and my
family. This book is dedicated to my three children, Conor, Owen, and
Laura, who were always ready to provide the necessary distractions
and relief from the work of writing the book, and who make it easy to
believe in a brighter future.

Credits

Newspaper Archives and Independent News and Media gave kind permission to reproduce the 'Golden Blush' advertisement from the *Irish Independent*, January 1922; The Peabody Museum of Archaeology and Ethnology of Harvard University kindly gave permission to quote from the papers of Earnest A. Hooton (#995–1) and the Harvard Irish Study records, as well as to reproduce some materials from Earnest A. Hooton and C. Wesley Dupertuis, *The Physical Anthropology of Ireland*, Papers of the Peabody Museum of Archaeology and Ethnology, vol. 30, no. 1, 1955; UCD Archives kindly gave permission to quote from the papers of Eoin MacNeill [LA1/J/82 and LA1/F/235], Michael Hayes [P53/143, P53/145, and P53/151], and Eamon de Valera [P150/1603 and P150/1605], and to include the photograph of the Irish Race Congress, taken from the Tierney/MacNeill photograph collection [LA30/PH/394]; The British Library kindly gave permission for the reproduction of the photograph of *Zulus* from *New Spotlight* magazine, 22 April 1972, from its newspaper collection; Getty Images provided the licence agreement for the reproduction of the photograph of Phil Lynott, published by the *Evening Standard*, from the Hulton Archive collection. The Yeats estate, c/o DACS, kindly gave permission for the reproduction of Jack Yeats's paintings.

Every effort has been made to establish the identity of or to establish contact with copyright holders; where this has not been possible I hope this general acknowledgement will be taken as sufficient.

Introduction

Quite suddenly, or so it seemed, Ireland became a multi-cultural society. It happened in or around 1996, and caught everyone by surprise. The television comedy series, *Father Ted*, dramatised this moment in an episode first screened in March 1998. Father Ted, to relieve the boredom of having to clean the house, gives Father Dougal a knowing smile, puts a 'coolie' lampshade on his head, pulls back the skin on either side of his eyes to narrow them to a slit, peels his upper lip back over his teeth, and then proceeds to mimic a Chinese pidgin-English accent, saying 'Oh! Ho! I am Chinese if you please'.[1] The audience laughs, and Father Ted goads Dougal for appearing rather dumbstruck by his 'Ching Chong Chinaman' impression, but Ted's cheeky grin soon disappears when he turns to find three Chinese people looking at him through his window. Ted looks aghast to Dougal for an explanation, and is told that the Chinese people are the Yin family living in 'that whole Chinatown area'. 'There's a Chinatown in Craggy Island?', gasps Ted, and then admonishes Dougal for not telling him this: 'Dougal, I wouldn't have done a Chinaman impression if I'd known there was going to be a Chinaman there to see me doing a Chinaman impression . . . . They'll think I'm a racist'.[2]

Ted's 'Chinaman' impression belongs, of course, to an extensive and familiar Western tradition of comic racial stereotypes, which has its origins in the same music hall and theatrical contexts that saw blackface minstrelsy emerge in the 1830s in the United States, and can be traced further back to the ways in which cultural and racial differences had been used within English comedies since Shakespeare's time. According to Krystyn Moon, 'yellowface minstrelsy' developed from the 1850s onwards, and comprised 'dialect, makeup, posture, and costuming', which 'marked the Chinese body as inferior and foreign', and which emerged as an expression of American anxieties about Chinese migration into California in the 1850s.[3] It has remained since that time as a recurrent and controversial trope in Western culture, most recently in a 'slit-eyed' gesture adopted by the Spanish basketball team for an advertisement photograph prior to their participation in the 2008 Beijing Olympics.[4] When the audience begins to laugh as soon as Ted places the 'coolie' lampshade on his head, it is an indication that the cultural codes of racial mimicry have already been recognised, that the conventions of the 'Chinaman' impression are already familiar. To ask what the audience is laughing at (acknowledging, of course, that the laughter 'track' is edited for the television programme), is to ask a complex question not just about the mechanics of racism and comic racial stereotypes, but also about the relationship between cultural codes and their performance. What forms of cultural identification are being articulated in Ted's performance of the 'Chinaman', and in the audience's laughter? In Homi Bhabha's terms, what 'processes of subjectification' are made possible and plausible through such a performance?[5]

The audience's laughter intensifies when Ted turns to discover his Chinese spectators, suggesting that the audience not only identifies with Ted's comic performance, but also with his 'culture shock' at having suddenly realised that in an increasingly multi-cultural, and rapidly changing society, his racial caricature is likely to cause offence. It is clear, in other words, that the 'joke' depends upon the seemingly illicit, perhaps even nostalgic, desire to 'enjoy' racial caricatures, as well as the open disparagement of racism as unacceptable in a liberal, multi-cultural society. The comedy also depends, of course, upon the telescoping of the much publicised social changes in Irish society in the 1990s into the already parodic setting of 'Craggy Island', arguably a metonym for the old, rural, poor Ireland, defined by conservative Catholic nationalism. That Craggy Island becomes the scene of Ireland's 'new racial geography', to use Steve Garner's phrase,[6] enables the writers to visually juxtapose the old and the new, pitting nostalgia for the 'small, knowable community', with its familiar and cosy cultural codes, directly against satisfaction with the liberalism and modernity of the new Ireland, including its increasingly 'cosmopolitan' population.

The suddenness of the change from the old to the new Ireland has been widely noted, if perhaps even caricatured. In 1996, Ireland experienced net immigration, and continued to do so over the next ten years, reaching record levels of inward migration in 2006–7.[7] 'Comparing Ireland to other EU countries underlines its rapid changes', argues Martin Ruhs:

> During 1990–1994, Ireland was the only country among the member states of the EU-15 with a negative net migration rate. In contrast, between 1995 and 1999, Ireland's average annual net migration rate was the second highest in the EU-15, surpassed only by that of Luxembourg.[8]

Unprecedented economic prosperity and economic growth rates were, of course, the main determinants of Irish migration trends during this period, with the bulk of immigrants arriving to fill labour shortages, followed by a significant proportion of refugees. A sizeable percentage of the net immigration figures also comprised returning Irish migrants, but, as Bryan Fanning has argued, media attention was devoted largely to the 'new phenomenon' of racism, particularly in response to 'asylum seekers'.[9] Fanning's pioneering sociological study has done much to show that racism has a longer history in the Irish state and society than media representations in the 1990s would suggest. If one lesson of the *Father Ted* scene discussed above is that racist caricatures of Chinese people were already affective within Irish culture before significant numbers of Chinese migrants arrived in Ireland, a further lesson from the work of Fanning and others over the past decade has been that the Irish state has never been a 'monoculture', immune from racial conflicts, not least in relation to its 'internal others', especially Protestant, Jewish, and traveller peoples. Racism did not simply arrive with the immigrants in 1996, but emerged in different forms, and in response to different contexts and anxieties, long before.

What is new about immigration in Irish society is the scale of contemporary migratory movement, the fact that migration to contemporary Ireland has resulted in the formation of particular ethnically perceived communities, and the degree to which Irish governments since the 1990s have felt compelled to react with political and legal measures either to limit immigration or to dictate the terms of 'integration', although as we shall see in Chapter 3, these responses are not without precedent. Towards the end of the first decade of the twenty-first century, the joke in *Father Ted* about a 'whole Chinatown area' is not so far-fetched, although admittedly the emerging 'Chinatown' district in Parnell Square in Dublin is still somewhat remote from 'Craggy Island'. Adjacent to the 'Chinatown' district, for perhaps ten years now there has existed an area east of Parnell Street known as 'Little Africa', largely a collection of African shops which not only offer goods, especially foods, distinctive to some African cultures, but also serve as a focal point for African communities in Dublin. Not far away, one can find shops selling Polish and Lithuanian goods, and, in 2005, the *Evening Herald* began to publish a weekly supplement in Polish. Migrants have also begun to participate actively in Irish politics too, with Portlaoise electing a Nigerian national, Councillor Rotimi Adebari, as its mayor in 2007. The story of the host society's response to Ireland's new immigrant communities, of course, has been partly one of integration and acceptance, but sadly it has also been characterised by exclusion, hostility and violence.

The signs of such hostility were early, public, and highly symbolic, when some of the first GAA players from ethnically mixed backgrounds such as Jason Sherlock and Seán Óg Ó hAilpín were greeted with racial taunts from opposing fans. In one such incident in 1995, the reporter from the *Sunday Independent* recorded that Sherlock was subjected to chants of 'little nigger', 'little Chink', and 'slanty-eyed f****r', which led the reporter to ask 'is abuse like this part of what we are?'[10] Since the foundation of the GAA in 1884, as Steve Garner argues, 'a body of writing has sought to make Gaelic games a privileged depository of racialised Irishness', an argument also central to Mike Cronin's examination of the history of the GAA.[11] That Gaelic sport provided the setting for some of the earliest and most public forms of racist abuse against those from ethnically mixed, or ethnically different backgrounds in the 'new Ireland', suggests a problematic relationship between the 'racialised Irishness' produced through cultural nationalist institutions, and the racialisation of immigrants in contemporary Irish society. The racist abuse of sportsmen, however, is only the most public face of a more pervasive and injurious racism, which at its worst has been responsible for violent crimes targeted in specific and vocal ways against perceived racial 'others'.

The evidence of racist violence and abuse in the 'new Ireland' against immigrants and those perceived to be ethnically non-Irish followed hard on a renewed awareness in Irish public discourse of the legacies of the 'Irish diaspora'. Indeed, it was only under the presidency of Mary Robinson (1990–7) that the term 'Irish diaspora' gained popular currency, and the modern history of mass Irish emigration became more widely discussed as a social and cultural phenomenon (rather than simply an economic necessity and political embarrassment). Given such a history, the evidence of both 'popular' and institutional forms of racism in Irish society against its own immigrants came as a kind of 'culture shock' itself, and arguably has inspired many of the sociological and historical studies which have attempted to situate Irish forms of racism in relation to wider and deeper social and historical contexts. The work of Bryan Fanning, Ronit Lentin, Jim McLaughlin, Steve Garner, Robbie McVeigh, Bill Rolston, Dermot Keogh, Cormac Ó Gráda, Gretchen Fitzgerald, Paul Cullen, and others, has begun the task of exploring the history and sociology of racist practices in modern Ireland, either generally or in relation to specific social groups.[12] Such studies frequently express the hope that the historical experience of racism against the Irish, both as colonial subjects in Ireland and as emigrants to Britain, the USA, and Australia, might equip them to understand and counter the racialisation and racist abuse of Ireland's recent immigrants, but it is a hope often tempered by the recognition of racist practices in recent Irish social history.

The aim of this study is partly to build further upon such work in showing the history of the instrumentalisation of race and racism within the Irish state, but with a specific focus upon the interaction between social phenomena and cultural representations. As Garner suggests, for some time now Irish literary and cultural studies have been inspired by some of the most renowned modern theorists of race and colonialism (such as Fanon, Said, and Bhabha), but, citing the work of Gibbons, Kiberd, and Lloyd in particular, Garner argues that 'it is already clear that the problem of "race" in Irish history has been approached from only one direction', that of 'the historical racialisation of the Irish *per se*'.[13] Understanding the histories of how Irish peoples have been racialised, either in Ireland or overseas, is an important context for examining contemporary racist practices in Ireland, of course, but I agree with Garner that it is only one side of a multi-faceted problem, and arguably, what is occluded in such work is the agency of '"White" Irish communities (with all their internal distinctions) . . . in the process of racialising other groups in Ireland'.[14] To foreground this sense of agency, this book takes as its focus the cultural history of the Irish state, concentrating specifically on the period from 1922 to the 1980s, that is from the foundation of the state through to the period just prior to Ireland's 'sudden change' to a prosperous, confident, 'multi-cultural' society. It does not pretend to be comprehensive either as a history of racism in the state, or as a survey of cultural production. Although state borders are obviously both artificial and porous, the Irish state (as the Irish Free State, 1922–49, and its successor, the Republic of Ireland, 1949–), is the basic geo-political unit of analysis, primarily so as to attend to the relationship between legislative authority, cultural productions and racial ideologies and practices. The risk of such tightly defined legislative parameters is to give the impression that the public sphere of cultural representations is regulated entirely, or even effectively, by the state, but, as I hope the chapters of this book show, it is precisely this relationship between legislative authority and cultural expression which is a primary site of contest in modern Irish cultural history.

The argument of this book is that racial ideologies and racist practices have not only undergirded the Irish state and its defining cultural institutions and policies, often in muted and insidious forms, but have been central to the ways in which official discourses of 'Irishness' have been negotiated and contested in the cultural sphere. 'Race' is also a central figure in the debates concerning the location and provenance of Irish studies, and yet, perhaps because of its insinuative forms, it remains relatively underexplored as an affective agent in Irish culture. This lacuna in Irish studies might be related to the supposed newness of theoretical and cultural criticism in Ireland, which clearly motivates Claire Connolly's collection, *Theorizing Ireland*, which itself does not include any consideration of race.[15] In this, Connolly's collection is not alone among recent surveys of Irish cultural studies. *The Cambridge Companion to Modern Irish Culture* also includes scant discussion of race or ethnicity, and then only in relation to 'the creation of an Irish ethnic identity' in Britain and the United States.[16] *Reinventing Ireland: Culture and the Celtic Tiger*, a collection of essays designed to interrogate the role of culture as a site of resistance to the rise of neo-liberal market capitalism in the 'new Ireland', also contains little discussion of race or racism, and leaves Garner with the impression that race is not considered important in Irish cultural studies, 'unless it is in the nationalist project of consolidating the metanarrative of unbroken and unchanging discrimination across time'.[17] The fault for the relative lack of attention to race as an affective agent in modern Irish culture lies not simply with individual ideological commitments to nationalism, however, nor indeed with the presumptuous sense that theoretical and cultural criticism is a new phenomenon in Ireland.

There are two reasons for the relative absence of considerations of race and racism from studies of modern Irish culture which I want to explore briefly here. The first is a structural and theoretical legacy of the post-colonial paradigms which have influenced the course of much recent Irish cultural criticism, that racism is routinely understood within post-colonial theories as an instrument of colonial discourses of control, developed, according to Bhabha 'in order to justify conquest and to establish systems of administration and instruction'.[18] In Gibbons's work, for example, such an understanding of the colonial system of racial representation and administration certainly enables a persuasive explanation of how Irishness was produced as a form of racial otherness in nineteenth-century colonial discourses, but racial modes of nationalist representation in the twentieth century are merely seen as extensions of colonialism, the lingering shadows of residual colonial ideologies cast over the founding structures of cultural nationalism.[19] In David Lloyd's work, too, the recurrent allure of racial identifications in Irish culture is understood to be the product of the arrested economic and social structures of a 'classical post-colonial situation'.[20] As such, then, racial ideologies and racist expressions within modern Irish culture (that is, since 1922) are merely overlooked as the secondary, or belated, signifiers of an effectively redundant colonial interpretative regime. They appear to require no explanation, since the colonial discourses which produced them in the first place have already been explained. One intention of this book is to show that this is not the case, that although racial ideologies within Irish cultural nationalism are inevitably intermeshed with their colonial origins, they need to be examined at the point of their iteration in order to understand fully the specific historical conditions, forms, objects and effects of racial ideologies and racist expressions within modern Irish culture. Each of the chapters of this book alights on very specific moments in the histories of race and racism in Irish culture, which are both clearly indebted to pre-existent structures and forms of racial thinking, and at the same time, evidently the product of the particular social and ideological conditions of that moment in Irish cultural history. None of the forms of racial or racist expression examined here is exceptional either as a historically or culturally specific experience in western modernity, but each shows clearly that we must take seriously, and examine closely, the evidence of Irish cultural and political investments in the wages of racism.

The lack of attention to race in Irish studies might also be closely related to what Cheryl Herr observed more generally in Irish culture as a 'social repression of the body', and more specifically an erosion 'in the sphere of representations that constitute social identity, [of] a comfortable sense of the body'.[21] This observation has particular ramifications for my attempts to read the epidermal and corporeal figurations of racial identity in Irish cultural productions, for it is obviously the body which is the site of racial figurations, and which proves to be the object of fascination and denial in Irish representations of racial difference. To read 'race' in Irish writing and culture, then, is arguably an attempt to read what Herr calls the 'erotics of Irishness'. It is to focus on the rhetorical strategies of Irish literary and cultural representations of the racialised body, whether 'Irish' or 'foreign'. If Irish significations of racial difference are to be understood as cultural productions, then one central point of this book is to encounter those acts of cultural production in historically informed close readings, to explicate their meanings, and to situate them socially and culturally. The aim of such a strategy is not simply to identify positive and negative representations of Irishness or otherness in racialised terms, but to reach an understanding of how cultural productions construct and contest the social meanings of race in modern Ireland. To study cultural productions in this way can illuminate the insidious roles of racial and racist ideologies in securing and maintaining political legitimacy, and particularly in masking anxieties about, and deficits in, political legitimacy. Jürgen Habermas attributes a particular facility for ideological critique to cultural productions for this reason, since, he argues, 'The procurement of legitimation is self-defeating as soon as the mode of procurement is seen through'. Habermas depicts the role of culture in the public sphere specifically as one of securing and contesting legitimacy: 'the public realm . . . has above all the function of directing attention to topical areas – that is, of pushing *other* themes, problems and arguments below the threshold of attention, and thereby of withholding them from opinion-formation'.[22] However, because there is no fully effective means to control cultural production (despite the various means of censorship, suppression and co-option available to state authorities), cultural representations retain an equal facility for contesting, as well as corroborating, the instrumentality of racial ideologies in the public sphere.

In contemporary political and media representations of racism, it is frequently claimed that racism persists at a popular or folk level, despite the averred commitments of state authorities and political representatives to multi-culturalism and anti-racism. It should be clear from the outline of my aims above that this book does not subscribe to this perception. To begin with, as Ronit Lentin has pointed out, the state commitment to anti-racism is not only weak, but is frequently contradicted by the state's 'racializing technologies' of immigration controls, citizenship definitions, and cultural policies which ignore 'intra-ethnic heterogeneities and contestations'.[23] Although the state is responsible for policing and prosecuting racially motivated crimes, it is also instrumental in generating some of the terms within which racialised categories are made effective within the social sphere, most obviously in conceiving of immigration solely as a social problem, and adopting a rhetoric of crisis and alarm in response to particular groups of immigrants. Lentin cites the notorious case of Irish government ministers repeatedly arguing that new citizenship legislation was required in 2004 in order to stop the 'flood' of 'refugees and asylum seekers', particularly from Africa, arriving in the late stages of pregnancy to give birth in Ireland, simply to claim citizenship.[24] Such arguments obviously fuel anxieties concerning the social, cultural, and economic impact of immigration, and give licence to public perceptions of racialised groups of immigrants as parasitic upon state resources. While government actions, policies and rhetoric are culpable for fostering racism in Irish society, however, the popularity of measures taken to curb immigration and deny immigrants the same rights and privileges of citizenship are undeniable. The citizenship referendum of 2004, which explicitly targeted the right to citizenship of children born in the Irish Republic to 'non-national' parents, was resoundingly endorsed by the voting public (79 per cent). Clearly, then, the responsibility for racialised distinctions within Irish society is neither wholly the result of state action, nor is it merely the preserve of a recalcitrant xenophobic minority. Nor is racism explicable solely or convincingly in relation to economic terms, since the contemporary resurgence of racist violence and abuse in Irish society coincides exactly with the period of greatest prosperity, lowest unemployment, low levels of emigration, and relative stability in terms of income, inflation, and all other measures of economic welfare. Instead, in order to understand the role of race and racism in contemporary Ireland, we must first understand neither simply its colonial antecedence nor its correspondence to the legislative demands of 'fortress Europe', but also the cultural history of racial and racist ideologies in the Irish state. If, as David Lloyd argues in his reading of Fanon's work, 'culture itself constitutes the formal principles of racist discourse', since racism is a function of the normative structures of the public sphere,[25] then it is crucial that we attend to the interaction between political and cultural discourses of identity formation, to the interpellation of the subject, in order to grasp what Paul Gilroy describes as 'the lore that brings the virtual realities of "race" to dismal and destructive life'.[26]

In Britain and France, the persistence of derogatory racial stereotypes and racist rhetoric in the contemporary period is commonly explained as the consequence of imperial history, transmitted into insular forms in response to cultural changes influenced by immigration, and although this explanatory model is limited in its capacity to understand racism in those countries, it presents a further problem for Ireland as a European nation founded upon a cultural narrative of resistance to imperialism. The circulation of similar racial stereotypes in Irish culture after 1922, and throughout a period in which Ireland experienced low levels of immigration, especially from non-Western countries, appears to have neither purpose nor object. Father Ted's 'Chinaman' impression may serve to illustrate the point. According to Bhabha, such performed or articulated stereotypes constitute 'metonymies of presence' within colonial discourse, which impede 'the circulation and articulation of the signifier of "race" as anything other than its *fixity* as racism'.[27] Seemingly far removed from the social contexts which gave rise to 'yellowface minstrelsy', however, or indeed the colonial discourse theorised in Bhabha's work, Father Ted's mimicry of the racial stereotype of the 'Chinaman', and the audience laughter it evinces, raises the question about what forms of authority and power license the reproduction of this particular metonym of racial difference in the 'Ireland' symbolised by 'Craggy Island'. It raises the question of how, in the apparent absence of Chinese migrants, or their descendants, such a racist stereotype could find affective expression within Irish society. It was in an attempt to understand the role of racism in a society which largely believed it contained no significant racial differences, and to understand the currency of racial ideologies within a nominally post-colonial Ireland, that the research for this book was undertaken.

As David Theo Goldberg suggests, the 'renewable currency' of race lies in its 'embeddedness' in prevailing social and cultural discourses, in its apparent referentiality, and thus even academic studies of race and racism which are motivated by anti-racism frequently run the risk of reifying race.[28] Kenan Malik's recent book on the 'race debate' indeed argues specifically that anti-racist campaigners are as much responsible for perpetuating a racial view of the world in espousing the importance of 'difference' and 'diversity' as avowedly racist movements.[29] It is important at the outset of this study to make it clear what is meant by 'race' and 'racism', and how my analysis aims to isolate 'race' as what Henry Louis Gates calls 'a dangerous trope' rather than reifying it as somehow a natural or objective phenomenon.[30] 'Race' has no basis in scientific or biological fact, but by arrogating to itself the apparent historical evidence of genetic continuity, linguistic and cultural traditions, skin pigmentation and phenotypology, racial discourse masquerades as 'common sense'.

Racial ideologies have been central to the mechanics of modern subjectivity, and appear to provide observable or discernible indices to invented typologies of human identity, perhaps most frequently in relation to visible differences of skin colour. They have been most notoriously the tools of colonial and fascist regimes, which sought to justify slavery, exploitation, genocide, and all sorts of other heinous crimes and injustices on the basis of supposedly observable marks of racial difference and inferiority. But 'race' is dangerous also when it is less obviously a tool of political manipulation, when it almost silently underlies the sense of commonality which binds into a self-consciously cohesive identity the disparate members, or more simply, the majority groups, of a nation, state, or region. 'Race' in this context supplies the meaning, the illusion of historical and biological basis, for a collective identity which, stripped of such illusion, is only bound by a common adherence to certain laws, a common dependence upon certain trade or market centres, or perhaps more bleakly, a defensive response to the alienation and anonymity of modernity. It is less recognisably dangerous in this context because of the apparently positive sense of civic unity which may flow from this notion of a shared history, culture and character. The notion of Ireland as the embodiment of a single, harmonious culture dominated the cultural nationalist agenda for much of the late nineteenth and early twentieth centuries, and was frequently attacked by writers and artists after independence as an impoverished and destructive ideal. What sociologists have increasingly recognised in recent years is the extent to which this ideal was expressed and produced within the Irish state to the detriment of individuals and groups who were deemed to be 'others' and 'outsiders', and, I would add, to the detriment also of what ought to bind any society together, namely an inclusive sense of common welfare. The dangers of 'race' are not only that it manifests itself in racist violence and abuse, that it denies to those who find themselves defined as 'others' the rights to a common humanity, but that it also works to inure a society to all kinds of discrimination and injustice. The critique of the dangers of race and racism in Irish society did not begin with contemporary sociologists, however, for I argue here that many writers and artists, whether they were themselves adherents or critics of racial ideologies, exposed the functional dependence of the Irish nation-state upon race, in various guises, from its foundations.

This brings us to one of the key questions at the heart of this book, about the relationships between racism and nationalism. I argued above that one reason why racism in modern Irish culture has largely been ignored by contemporary cultural critics is because of the tendency to explain racism as the product of colonialism. As a correlative to that argument, or perhaps as an alternative formulation, it might be said that the association of racism and nationalism is obscure in the Irish situation, since Irish nationalism is often seen as a movement of liberation from colonialism, and therefore from the racial ideologies underpinning colonialism. Thus, in a crude summary of this view, there are bad nationalisms and good nationalisms, ones which are founded upon racism and ones which are founded upon anti-racism. The episode of *Father Ted* discussed above plays out this distinction to its comic extreme, of course, when Father Ted, through a series of accidents, finds himself associated with Nazism, as if racism is inevitably synonymous with its most notorious, supra-national expression. This comic conflation of racism and Nazism is nevertheless a revealing insight into the extent to which 'racist' has become perhaps the ultimate term of political abuse and moral denunciation in Western liberal societies, but in its crudity, of course, it fails to account for the very dependence of every form of nationalism upon some racial and racist basis. This is merely to reiterate Etienne Balibar's reminder that Nazism not only created a greater awareness of the potential consequences of racism, but also a 'prohibition', a necessity for contemporary racist discourse to present itself as thoroughly different from Nazism. Nazism is, in some senses, then, an alibi, an obscene marker of 'the place of racism in history', which allows us too easily to overlook the ways in which racisms are 'ever active formations, part conscious and part unconscious, which contribute to structuring behaviour and movements emerging out of present conditions'.[31] Thus, the fact that the Irish state took democratic rather than fascist form in 1922, or that 'the Blueshirts' were neither as successful nor as extreme as their counterparts in Germany, Italy and Spain in the 1930s, are not evidence of the absence of racial ideologies and racist practices in Irish society.

The political nationalisms of the early twentieth-century Ireland, which found institutional form in the establishment of the Irish Free State in 1922, frequently expressed themselves in relation to an imagined Irish race, and through the form of racial and racist distinctions from other peoples. A racial distinction between the Irish and the English was arguably crucial to the ideological impetus of nationalist movements, but it is also perhaps surprising now to recognise the extent to which these movements also expressed themselves in racist distinctions from other colonised and racialised peoples. This is partly the subject of Chapter 1, which examines the centrality of racial ideologies to the founding moments of the state, and how this relationship between racism and the new state forms a key theme in Joyce's *Ulysses*. It is also widely assumed that, since Irish nationalism was founded upon resistance to colonialism, that the state which emerged from it would somehow express antipathy towards racial ideologies. Chapter 2 re-examines the relationship between the 'sciences' of racial typology in the 1930s and Irish political and cultural discourses, and argues that the relationship between typologies of the Irish 'race' and state nationalism may be a more important context for certain forms of late modernist writing and art in Ireland than has hitherto been acknowledged. Chapters 3 and 4 analyse the ways in which, from the 1930s to the 1970s, a suspicion of the cosmopolitan and the foreign manifested itself in deep-rooted forms in Irish politics and culture, and that the cultural politics of the racialised body became a central figure in literary and artistic dialogues with the state. In these later chapters, in particular, it becomes more and more evident that what Lentin calls the 'crisis racism' of 'Celtic Tiger' Ireland had precedents in the history of the state, and that racism is not simply a new phenomenon within Irish society and politics, but is and has been rather more deeply imbricated in the structures and mechanics of the nation-state. This realisation obviously has consequences for the study of ideologies of race and racism in contemporary Ireland, which I outline in the conclusion. As Robert Miles argues,

> Ideologies are never only received but are also constructed and reconstructed by people responding to their material and cultural circumstances in order to comprehend, represent and act in relation to those circumstances.

Ideological reproduction is therefore a consequence of a transaction between historical legacy and individual and collective attempts to make sense of the world.[32]

Races do not have any basis in scientific or biological fact, yet in terms of how human beings understand their social and cultural surroundings, racial and racist explanations clearly thrive. This paradox has stimulated the interest of sociologists and cultural theorists, in particular, in working to understand how race retains a persistent allure in contemporary cultural discourse, and for whom the term 'racialisation' has come to mean the discursive and cultural process whereby human beings have instrumentalised race as a fundamental principle of social organisation.[33] Thus far in Irish studies, the historical legacy of 'racialisation' has largely been understood as the history of English colonialism in Ireland, or the history of Irish emigrant conflicts with other racialised groups, but one key argument of this book is that we need to also examine the process of 'self-racialisation', whereby Irish political and cultural actors have generated their own lexicon of racial understanding, and their own stigmata of otherness. It is to the task of exploring and attempting to explain the historical and cultural legacy of ideologies of race and racism in Ireland since 1922 that I turn in the chapters to follow.

Notes

1. 'Are You Right There, Father Ted?', Series 3, Episode 1, *Father Ted: The Complete Series*, DVD 2002. The episode was originally aired on Channel 4 on 5 March 1998.
2. Maureen Reddy also discusses this *Father Ted* episode in her essay, 'Talking the Talk: Codes of Racialization', in Faragó and Sullivan (eds), *Facing the Other*, pp. 220–31, particularly to emphasise the 'racial codes' underpinning Father Ted's anxiety that he might be labelled a 'racist'. Reddy goes on to argue that the episode 'underscores absurdity rather than opening the possibility of serious engagement with racism' by satirising racism against Chinese people, because 'there was virtually no public consciousness of Chinese as possible targets of racism' in the late 1990s (p. 222). This is to underestimate the currency of anti-Chinese racism in Irish society, I would argue, and indeed more widely against immigrants, students and tourists from south-east Asia.
3. Krystyn R. Moon, *Yellowface*, pp. 2–4.
4. 'Olympics: Spain's eye-catching faux pas', *The Guardian: Sports section*, 11 August 2008, p. 9.
5. Homi Bhabha, *The Location of Culture*, p. 67.
6. Steve Garner, *Racism in the Irish Experience*, p. 227.

7. See the annual 'Population and Migration Estimates' for 1996–2008, published by the Central Statistics Office, Dublin: http://www.cso.ie/releasespublications/pr_pop.htm

8. Martin Ruhs, 'Ireland: A Crash Course in Immigration Policy', *Migration Information Source*: http://www.migrationinformation.org/Profiles/display.cfm?ID=260

9. Bryan Fanning, *Racism and Social Change in the Republic of Ireland*, p. 1.

10. 'Inside Left: Terrace Abuse for Jason Sherlock', *Sunday Independent*, 16 July 1995, p. 25L.

11. Garner, *Racism in the Irish Experience*, p. 152. See Mike Cronin, *Sport and Nationalism in Ireland*.

12. See Gretchen Fitzgerald, *Repulsing Racism*, Liam Greenslade, 'White Skins, White Masks', pp. 201–25, Jim McLaughlin, *Travellers and Ireland*, Noel Ignatiev, *How the Irish Became White*, Ethel Crowley and Jim MacLaughlin (eds), *Under the Belly of the Celtic Tiger*, Dermot Keogh, *Jews in Twentieth-Century Ireland*, Ronit Lentin, *The Expanding Nation*, Paul Cullen, *Refugees and Asylum-Seekers in Ireland*, Bryan Fanning, *Racism and Social Change in the Republic of Ireland*, Robbie McVeigh and Ronit Lentin (eds), *Racism and Anti-Racism in Ireland*, Bill Rolston and Michael Shannon, *Encounters*, and Steve Garner, *Racism in the Irish Experience*.

13. Garner, *Racism in the Irish Experience*, p. 244.

14. Ibid., p. 244.

15. Claire Connolly (ed.), *Theorizing Ireland*.

16. Joe Cleary and Claire Connolly (eds), *The Cambridge Companion to Modern Irish Culture*. See Mary Hickman's chapter, 'Migration and Diaspora', concerning Irish ethnic identifications in Britain and the USA, pp. 117–36.

17. See Peadar Kirby, Luke Gibbons and Mike Cronin (eds), *Reinventing Ireland*. Garner's allusion to the nationalist project of unbroken and unchanging oppression is keyed specifically to Gibbons' chapter on race in his *Transformations in Irish Culture*, which he develops further, but along the same lines, in *Gaelic Gothic*. Gibbons in particular has been instrumental in examining how theories of racial inferiority were used by British imperial powers to consolidate colonial rule over the Irish, but at no point in his work is the adoption of racial theories within Irish nationalist discourse considered as anything other than a knee-jerk reaction to colonial racism.

18. Bhabha, *The Location of Culture*, p. 70.

19. Gibbons, *Transformations in Irish Culture*, p. 156.

20. David Lloyd, *Anomalous States*, pp. 17–18.

21. Cheryl Herr, 'The Erotics of Irishness', p. 6.

22. Jürgen Habermas, *Legitimation Crisis*, p. 70.

23. Ronit Lentin, 'Ireland: Racial State and Crisis Racism', p. 611.

24. Ibid., 621–2.

25. David Lloyd, 'Race Under Representation', p. 265.

26. Paul Gilroy, *Between Camps*, p. 11.

27. Bhabha, *The Location of Culture*, p. 75.

28. David Theo Goldberg, *Racist Culture*, p. 89.
29. Kenan Malik, *Strange Fruit*, passim.
30. Henry Louis Gates, Jr (ed.), *"Race," Writing and Difference*, p. 5.
31. Etienne Balibar and Immanuel Wallerstein, *Race, Nation, Class*, p. 40.
32. Robert Miles, *Racism*, p. 132.
33. Goldberg argues that the lexicon of racial theory may indeed have become too successful, and blames the 'culturalist turn' of the last decades of the twentieth century for adopting terms like 'racialisation' too casually, with the result that contemporary cultural discourse appears to have an 'infatuation with racial identities'. This may be true of the humanities in the USA, but has not been the case in Irish studies, in which race has been conspicuously absent as a critical focus. See David Theo Goldberg, *The Racial State*, pp. 1–2.

Chapter 1

1922, *Ulysses*, and the Irish Race Congress

The advertisement for *Golden Blush* cigarettes which took up the front page of the *Irish Independent* on 4 January 1922 offers a revealing graphic narrative of Ireland's passage into industrialised modernity. In contrast to the well-worn themes of colonial oppression, mass emigration, and economic underdevelopment, the sequential illustrations bring us from the raw materials in plantation fields in Virginia, controlled by the Irish manufacturers, through to the cathedral-like cigarette factory in Dublin, and on to the happy male consumers who symbolise an Irish public, mature and contented with its own modernity. Embroidered with a Celtic interlace design, the illustrations are thus branded with allegiance to the cultural nationalism of the revival period, and announce the arrival of a specifically Irish industrial modernity. In doing so, it proffers a political vision more optimistic than was possible for the provisional government ushered into place just three days later, on 7 January 1922, when the Dáil ratified the Anglo-Irish treaty, and thus paved the way for the establishment of the Irish Free State later that year. The advertisement envisions industrial development, profitable on the back of cheap foreign raw materials, and skilled employment in manufacturing, distribution, and sales in a city characterised by social harmony, prosperity, and a thriving consumer culture. That this story of national triumph is concerned with tobacco, a product with historic associations with colonial and capitalist exploitation of black labour, is itself significant and revealing of the ideological complexities of this marriage of counter-colonial nationalism and industrial modernity. Yet this takes on even more poignancy given the pastoral vision of Virginian tobacco fields in which we are invited to identify not with the black plantation workers, who are invisible and seemingly irrelevant, but with the white planter.[1] The exclusion of black labour from this story is, of course, a necessary masking of the real, ugly workings of capitalist exploitation, of the real reason for the 'low price' and 'high quality' of Virginian

Figure 1.1 'Golden Blush' advertisement, *Irish Independent*, 4 January 1922, reproduced by kind permission of Irish Newspaper Archives and Independent News and Media

tobacco. The tobacco industry was dependent globally on a racialised economy, initially based upon slavery, and later upon a racially divided workforce in which black labour was always devalued. The absence of black workers in the image of the plantation is not just a mask of capitalist exploitation, however, for it is also a form of racial inscription or affiliation. The advertisement figures a declaration of allegiance within this racialised economy of tobacco production, emphatically occluding the history of colonial domination and servitude by identifying Ireland's emergent modernity with the white plantation owner. To follow the footprints of Ireland's march to national self-determination, or at least one tobacco company's evidently self-interested version of this story, takes us to a primal scene of racial and colonial oppression, the plantation, as iconic of oppression and displacement in Irish colonial history as it is in African-American and Caribbean histories. Thus, what this advertisement celebrates is not liberation from colonialism, so much as a switching of hierarchical positions within the racialised economy of colonialism. The independence negotiated in the Anglo-Irish treaty enables Ireland to 'takes its place among the nations of the earth', in Robert Emmet's famous words, to do what other modern, western nations do, that is.[2] More specifically, one could also argue that what this advertisement implicitly celebrates in its occlusion of the black plantation workers, and its triumphal narrative of Irish national becoming, is the assimilation of the Irish into white, western modernity, or, to use Steve Garner's phrase, the 'instrumentalisation of whiteness' by the Irish 'both as a means of achieving, and an outcome of, unequal power relations with black and other Third World people'.[3]

Perhaps this is to read 'too much' into an advertisement designed merely to sell cigarettes to Irish consumers, but in this chapter I argue that such racial figurations, either of the Irish as a race, or of other peoples as races, were pervasive and played a key role in the foundational moments of Irish political and cultural modernity in 1922. The untold story of Ireland's emergence into formal statehood in 1922 is the extent to which racial discourse pervaded the language of its culture and politics. In telling this story, I follow the lead of Tom Garvin in his book, *1922: The Birth of a Democracy*, in making a virtue of historical untidiness by referring to the 'Long 1922', running roughly from the truce of 11 July 1921 to the end of the civil war in May 1923.[4] The 'Long 1922' encapsulates many significant and evidently divisive moments in Irish history, including the treaty negotiations and ratification, the appointment of a provisional government, the formal establishment of the Irish Free State, and, of course, the civil war. These events were crucial in defining the boundaries of the emergent nation-state, and in shaping the political and cultural future of the state. In literary and cultural studies, 1922 is also a landmark year, most famously for the publication of James Joyce's *Ulysses*, which it has been argued brings the Irish literary revival to a close,[5] and which, along with T. S. Eliot's *The Waste Land*, makes 1922 the defining year of literary modernism in English.[6] As Terence Brown once observed, however, the coincidence of chronology that saw two of the greatest works of literary experiment published and the political experiment of the Irish Free State brought into being 'ought to have stimulated more reflection than it has'.[7] That no such work has been undertaken, Brown argues, has much to do with the apparent incommensurability of the cosmopolitan, radically internationalist vision of literary modernism and the antithetical tendencies of nationalist revolution. I shall be arguing here for the necessity of revisiting this relationship between the cosmopolitanism of *Ulysses* and the political (and racial) experiment of the Irish Free State, and more specifically, that *Ulysses* addresses a number of problematic questions concerning race, culture and the state which are both appropriate and sensitive to the time of its production in 1922.

The reasons for the lack of research on the relationship between *Ulysses* and the Irish Free State in 1922 are also more complex than Brown suggests, more complex because they are tied to methodological problems in the critical reception to Joyce's great novel. In *Marxism and Form*, Fredric Jameson asked a question of *Ulysses* which in many senses, despite the wealth of Joyce criticism, remains largely unanswered: 'in what sense can *Ulysses* be said to be part of the events which took place in 1922?'[8] Much of the historicist work on *Ulysses*, in ways which are counter-intuitive to our approaches to other literary texts, focuses on what the novel tells us about its setting, in 1904, rather than how the novel connects with the events and concerns of 1922. Jameson observes that this is part of the problem with an historical approach to any literary work, that literature invariably 'resists assimilation to the totality of the historical here and now'. While this is true, and as a maxim may be borne out in several of the chapters in this book, I also maintain that there is, in the case of *Ulysses* as with other texts and productions, a meaningful and mutually constitutive relationship between literature and the 'historical here and now', beyond the expedience or coincidence of publication. It seems to me at least of symbolic significance that what Joyce called his 'epic of two races' was published in Paris just five days after the Irish Race Congress, billed as 'the first Aonac na nGaedeal held in 700 years', had concluded in the Hotel Continental of that city.[9] The aims of the Irish Race Congress were to gather representatives of the race together to celebrate its achievements, and to determine the course of its future. Its outcomes were somewhat more mundane, as we shall see, but what it shares with *Ulysses*, among a broad range of literary and political representations in the long 1922, is its preoccupation with, and investment in, the forms and expressive possibilities of racial subjectivity.

As David Goldberg argues, 'literary and cultural production is particularly well-placed to mold, circumscribe, and stamp racialized identity, since racial significations are deeply implicit in the signs employed and employable'.[10] The key to understanding the constitutive role of literature in the production of racial knowledge is this sense of currency rather than causality. The gestation period of any work of literature, or for that matter, political event, is much longer than can be analysed within the confines of a year. Yet, to focus on the circulation of racial meanings within a year, especially what we may take to be the foundational year of Irish political and cultural modernity, is not merely a matter of reconstructing the immediate 'horizon of expectations' available to people in 1922. The risk of annualised historical study is to make all the events and texts of that year appear synchronic, arbitrary and, paradoxically, ahistorical. As Michael North argues, however, to study the cultural production of a year 'can be used to stage the seemingly inevitable opposition of the synchronic and the diachronic', and thus 'a kind of compromise between history and structure'.[11] In the case of *Ulysses* and the emergence of the Irish Free State, this staging is somewhat inevitable, for we are drawn to the novel which struggled into publication with a print run of 1,000 copies in Paris in February 1922, and to the formation in January 1922 of a provisional government which might have been cast back into oblivion by the end of the year, not simply for what meanings they generated then, but for what they became. In reading how *Ulysses* and the Irish state represented race and racism in 1922, we cannot pretend not to know about the history of dialogue between the state and Ireland's most famous novel since then. Most notoriously, on 11 June 2004, just five days prior to the 100th anniversary of 'Bloomsday' which was marked by a series of celebratory events sponsored by the Irish government, the same government won a referendum vote, proposing to amend the constitution to prevent children born in Ireland from automatic rights of citizenship, an amendment which Ronit Lentin argues was based upon 'crisis racism'.[12] The amendment complicates how we now read Bloom's seemingly confident assertion of his nationality, when he is confronted by the racism of the 'citizen': 'Ireland, says Bloom. I was born here. Ireland'.[13]

Lentin observes that the Irish state's response to the 'crisis' of immigration since the mid-1990s, culminating in the citizenship referendum in 2004, has been characterised by a sense of obligation 'towards the integrity of racist immigration and citizenship policies in Britain and the EU'.[14] The result of the referendum means that 'for the first time in eighty-three years, . . . *blood* [is] the cornerstone of Irish citizenship', for third-generation Irish migrants who need never have set foot in Ireland may claim Irish citizenship, while a child born in Dublin to

Nigerian parents has no such entitlement. In ways which are strikingly resonant with the 'Golden Blush' advertisement, the Irish state used the legislative occlusion of racialised migrants, and the imagery of a modernising, rational society, to align itself with the interests and ideologies of white, western modernity. What I am suggesting by this resonance is not continuity. The racial meanings and racist practices of Ireland in the twenty-first century are not the same as those of 1922, nor are they even necessarily the legacy of the 'foundations' I am tracing in 1922. Yet the conditions, forms and objects of racial and racist expression in Irish culture and politics in 1922 resolutely refute the myth that 'race' and 'racism' arrived in the 1990s, as if on a flight from Lagos or Vilnius. The 'micro-history' of race in 1922 offered in this chapter is, at best, akin to Foucault's notion of history as a 'history of the present', in which the challenge is to grasp 'when a cultural phenomenon of a determinate scale constitutes within the history of thought a decisive moment that is still significant for our modern mode of being subjects'.[15]

For contemporary political and social scientists, the relationship between the emergence of the Irish Free State and the exclusionary practices and policies of twenty-first century Ireland centres on the extent to which one can define the emergent state as a 'racial state'. Lentin and McVeigh, in particular, have advocated the view that the Irish state since its inception can be defined as a 'racial state', no less so than other western states,[16] although Bryan Fanning criticises their work for oversimplifying the model of the racial state adopted from David Goldberg's study.[17] Fanning himself has done much to establish the argument that both the Irish Free State and more broadly Irish society in the 1920s and 1930s expressed themselves through racialised discourses which distinguished a supposedly homogeneous 'true' national identity from the claims of various minority groups, especially Protestant, Jewish and traveller groups.[18] On the other hand, both Tom Garvin and Jeffrey Prager, in separate studies of the democratic institutions successfully forged by the Free State, distinguish between the civic nationalism of the State and the ethnic nationalism of the anti-treaty rebels, thereby suggesting that ethnically framed ideologies had little influence on the pragmatic key agents of the new state.[19]

This chapter is less concerned with resolving this question of the extent to which the emerging state fits the model of what Goldberg has called 'the racial state' than with identifying and delineating the instrumentalisation of race in Irish culture and politics in 1922. The dominant approach to race and racism in Irish cultural studies, influenced by post-colonial perspectives, has been to understand these as the structural effects, or ideological legacies, of English colonialism. Thus, for example, the most significant study of race in the work of James Joyce to date, Vincent Cheng's *Joyce, Race and Empire*, largely conceives of racial and racist expressions in Irish culture as symptomatic of a process of 'internalizing and propagating the received values of an oppressive colonizer'.[20] While the process of identity-formation and the articulation of forms of racial and national belonging in a colonised society are undoubtedly shaped by, and should in part be considered responses to, the pressures of imperial discourses of racial otherness, my study of 1922 is an attempt to grasp the process of adoption and manipulation of race as a conceptual instrument by cultural and political agents in Ireland (or, in the case of Joyce, of Ireland). To focus on the cultural production of one year, therefore, especially what one boot-polish advertisement called 'Ireland's Year of Brightness', is to attend not to the replication of pre-existing colonial structures and discourses of race, but to the iteration and historicity of racial and racist expression in modern Irish culture.[21]

History, Modernity, and the Racial Imagination

One may turn to various examples to find evidence of the currency of a racial imaginary in the emergent discourses of nationhood, some sources more esoteric than others. George Russell's *The Interpreters*, for instance, stages through the unlikely form of a Socratic dialogue an essentially pseudo-Darwinian debate about the fitness of various political philosophies for an emergent revolutionary state, with one character advocating in particular the dream of a racial home, a dream which although disparaged in the 'novel' comes closest to the arguments Russell was articulating in his non-fictional prose at this time.[22] In the equally strange *Back to Methuselah: A Metabiological Pentateuch*, George Bernard Shaw envisioned the disappearance of the Irish race altogether, once granted independent statehood, as, bereft of the stimulating itch of national struggle, the Irish 'race' was seemingly doomed to entropy.[23] A more mundane source for speculation about the future coalescence of race and state, although impressive in itself as an anthology of diverse contributors, is William G. Fitz-Gerald's *The Voice of Ireland: A Survey of the Race and Nation from All Angles by the Foremost Leaders at Home and Abroad* (1923).[24] The subtitle insists upon a singularity of race and nation belied by the heterogeneous arguments and assumptions of its many, distinguished contributors, but although some contributors make the case for a multi-racial understanding of Ireland, others for abandoning race as a tool of nationhood altogether, there are many contributors for whom the new state promises a racial home, and in the legislation and prescriptions which brought about 'compulsory Gaelic' in its schools, the ban on foreign games for GAA members, the censorship of foreign and immoral publications in the 1929 Act, we can see how such presumptions of homogeneity lead directly to material actions to enforce it, against the fact of heterogeneity. To examine this tension between a civic polity, evidently heterogeneous, and the ideology of racial homogeneity, however, we need to go further than establishing simply the currency of racial discourses and conceptions, but to explore how they were instrumentalised in Irish cultural and political texts in this transitional moment.

It is impossible, of course, to separate the meanings of race in 1922 from those of the Irish revival period which preceded it, and the work of W. B. Yeats is an especially revealing source for the examination of how revival notions of racial memory and racial consciousness inform the cultural nationalist project. In *The Trembling of the Veil*, completed in May 1922, W. B. Yeats chronicled the inspirations and efforts of he and his friends in bringing the cultural revival to fruition, especially through the 1890s, but his narrative assumes that 'recent events', namely the war of independence and the establishment of the provisional government, are the indirect consequences of the cultural work of he and his friends. He concludes with a tribute to Lady Gregory, for example, so 'that young men, to whom recent events are often more obscure than those long past, may learn what debts they owe and to what creditor'.[25] Whatever the political developments of 1922 symbolise for Yeats, they are the accumulations or dividends of the cultural investments set in place twenty or thirty years prior.[26] Yeats understands that work as broadly involved 'in a deepened perception of all those things that strengthen race', by which he means the race-consciousness and racial memory of the Irish.[27] The task he set himself, then, was to confine himself 'to some inherited subject-matter known to the whole people', or later he says 'an image, or bundle of related images' which unify 'nations, races, and individual men', which when expressed in artistic form recall and rejuvenate racial memory.[28] 'Have not all races had their first unity from a mythology that marries them to rock and hill?' Yeats asks, and later explains the contribution he and Lady Gregory made in reviving that mythology.[29]

The Trembling of the Veil also records Yeats's interest in forms and levels of consciousness, particularly as they relate to the racial imagination. He describes, for example, how his friends believed that the subconscious 'had an incalculable power, . . . even over events', and that this belief evolved a technique for accessing and manipulating the subconscious: 'for the most part one repeated certain names and drew or imagined certain symbolic forms which had acquired a precise meaning, and not only to the dark portion of one's own mind, but to the mind of the race'.[30] Yeats's claim that he and others can access the mind of the race is the subject of several passages of reflection in *The Trembling of the Veil*, in which Yeats frequently poses this potential as a question:

> Is there nation-wide multiform reverie, every mind passing through a stream of suggestion, and all streams acting and reacting upon one another, no matter how distant the minds, how dumb the lips? . . . Was not a nation, as distinguished from a crowd of chance comers, bound together by this inter-change among streams or shadows; that Unity of Image, which I sought in national literature, being but an originating symbol?[31]

It is typical of Yeats's inclination towards supernatural explanations, of course, that the 'imagined community' of nation or race is bound not by the print technologies of book and newspaper, as Benedict Anderson described, but by a psychic telepathy of 'streams or shadows', a 'Unity of Image' inherited by each generation from the last but which needs to be sought out by the artist-medium. Yeats depicts his work throughout the 1890s and beyond as a struggle to discover the means to tap the resources of this race-consciousness, to revive the ancient literature and culture in modern forms, and so awaken the 'Unity of Being' that is the nation or race. Yeats recognises, however, his naivety in pursuing a Unity of Being that is hardly 'possible without a Unity of Culture in class or people that is no longer possible at all'.[32] Here lies the principal object of division among nationalist intellectuals of the revival period, for precisely what forms this cultural work which might awaken a supposedly dormant nation should entail was a matter of rivalry and discord. Yeats credited the Abbey theatre, Lady Gregory's *Cuchulain of Muirthemne*, and Synge's *The Playboy of the Western World* for 'strengthening' the race, for example, while D. P. Moran, the author of *The Philosophy of Irish Ireland*, dismissed as 'mongrel' any attempt to bring Irish literature to life in the English language, and argued that 'The foundation of Ireland is the Gael, and the Gael must be the element which absorbs'.[33] As P. J. Mathews argues, Moran's 'essentialist views circumscribed Irish identity within the narrow con-fines of Gaelic Catholic experience and left no room for any expression of a Protestant Irishness', an essentialism which leads Mathews to label Moran a 'racial nationalist'.[34] It is clear from *The Trembling of the Veil* that Yeats too saw himself in some senses as a 'racial nationalist', although it is undoubtedly not a sense of 'race' that Moran would share nor even recognise. Yeats uses the terms 'we', 'our' and even 'our race' throughout *The Trembling of the Veil*, but these terms of belonging and ancestry are never defined or explained, and they remain therefore capacious, even as they are employed to make a case for racial distinctiveness and exclusivity.

As Roy Foster argues, *The Trembling of the Veil* is a more accurate reflection of Yeats's preoccupations in 1921 and 1922 than the time it takes as its subject matter.[35] It may be that as the new state was poised to come into existence Yeats felt the need to represent his own artistic life as inseparable from, and committed to, the racial imagination of the nation. 1922 was a watershed year in many respects for Yeats as much as it defined the parameters of the Irish Free State. In the Spring, Yeats and his family moved from England to Merrion Square in Dublin, and then to their new home, Thoor Ballylee, in which *The Trembling of the Veil* was completed. The move symbolised that Yeats saw his place as part of the new state, yet paradoxically, as Foster points out, the house in Merrion Square and, perhaps even more obviously, the medieval Anglo-Norman tower in Ballylee signify that Yeats 'had settled, at least in residential terms, into the traditions of his caste – at just the point when those traditions were dispersing and disappearing'.[36] By December of 1922, Yeats had been invited to become a Senator in the newly established upper house of the Free State parliament, a position he happily and eagerly accepted, and soon after became involved in trying to broker an end to the civil war. If his position in the Senate was a consequence of the cultural efforts he explains and celebrates in *The Trembling of the Veil*, however, he had by then almost completed a new work which took his racial imagination in a different direction, one that became more and more evident in his late poems and plays.

Meditations in Time of Civil War was written mainly in the summer of 1922, first during a stay in Lady Gregory's house in Coole Park, and then in Yeats's tower, and, as Foster writes, 'its contents are . . . intimately linked to the dislocations of 1922, and the collision of personal and national histories'.[37] A sequence of seven poems, diverse in form and tone, *Meditations* explores the relationship between the poet, the violence of the civil war, and the ancestral homes of the Protestant ascendancy, which were frequently the targets of Republican violence.[38] In the second poem, 'My House', Yeats describes Thoor Ballylee, and identifies a shared sense of isolation between his lonely writings in the tower and the 'man-at-arms' who

> Gathered a score of horse and spent his days
> In this tumultuous spot,
> Where through long wars and sudden night alarms

> His dwindling score and he seemed castaways
> Forgetting and forgot.[39]

He foresees the same fate of alienation from the warring local population for his 'bodily heirs', for whom he anticipates that his writings may
serve as 'Befitting emblems of adversity'.[40] In contrast to the public poet
Yeats was becoming, and the active cultural worker he depicts in *The
Trembling of the Veil*, the poet of *Meditations* is chastened into passive
submission by the civil war, and shrinks away from the triumphal identification with Irish independence, preferring instead to identify with
the alienation and impending ruin of the Anglo-Irish ascendancy tradition. *Meditations* abounds with images of empty houses, the deserted
or destroyed homes of the ascendancy class, and more pertinently with
images of a 'dwindling' inheritance and legacy. The fourth poem, 'My
Descendants', reflects on the fear of degeneration and ruin, that the
tower filled with love and friendship may, within a generation, become
a 'roofless ruin', and yet the poet finds some comfort for his friends and
family, it seems, to know that 'whatever flourish or decline/ These stones
remain their monument and mine'.[41] The immediate threat comes, of
course, from the Republican dissidents in the civil war, who did indeed
blow up the bridge that adjoined Thoor Ballylee, but the more persistent threat to the Anglo-Irish is degeneration within the 'race' itself. The
tower will become a 'roofless ruin', the poet considers, should

> my descendants lose the flower
> Through natural declension of the soul,
> Through too much business with the passing hour,
> Through too much play, or marriage with a fool?

The opening poem of the sequence, 'Ancestral Houses', recalls that the
great houses built by his racial ancestors were founded upon violence
and bitterness, but that these houses brought 'sweetness' and 'gentle-
ness', and thus the vitality which brought the houses into existence
might be lost in the leisured life afforded by them: 'What if those things
the greatest of mankind/ Consider most to magnify, or to bless,/ But
take our greatness with our bitterness?'[42]

Yeats's own solution to this fear of degeneration is to recast the
notion of racial inheritance, so that inheritance is figured not as the
absorption of given wealth, glory, or status, but as the struggle, reiterated in each generation, to match the original vitality of ancestral tradition with one's own labour and legacy, thus 'My Descendants' begins:

> Having inherited a vigorous mind
> From my old fathers, I must nourish dreams
> And leave a woman and a man behind
> As vigorous of mind.[43]

As Marjorie Howes argues, *Meditations* dramatises tension between the individual and his racial ancestry, and expresses profound ambivalence about ancestral inheritance, an ambivalence not simply about a civilisation founded upon violence, but about the very nature of foundations.[44] The crisis of violence and will which brought the Anglo-Normans into power in Ireland, and established the tower in which Yeats was writing, is doubly reiterated in the poem by the poet's struggle to initiate his own legacy, and the violence 'somewhere' in the surrounding countryside through which the new state, and a new political elite, is coming to power. In this sense, of course, it is a meditation upon the theories of foundation and tradition Yeats was working out in *A Vision* (1925). But it is also a meditation upon the fate of what he now figures as his racial kin, the Protestant landowners and ascendancy, within the new dispensation of the nationalist state he has helped to fashion. Gazing from the top of his tower in the final poem of the sequence, Yeats is reduced to acknowledging the paralysis induced by the violence around him, and visions of beauty must 'give place to an indifferent multitude, give place to brazen hawks'. The role of the poet henceforth, it seems in the final lines, is to suffice with the 'abstract joy,/ The half-read wisdom of daemonic images', having turned away 'and shut the door' on the bloodshed and burning beyond his tower.[45]

For all that *Meditations in Time of Civil War* is a poem about fears of racial degeneration, of violence and bloodshed, and of the fate of his descendants in the new Ireland, it is also about continuity, tradition, and shared experiences, even if those experiences are shared feelings of anxiety and isolation. The war provokes in Yeats a sense of race kinship with the 'man-at-arms' who felt just as besieged in the tower, and the medium through which he can feel this bond is the physical presence of the tower itself, which, even if it no longer houses his family in the threatening times ahead, will remain as monument. The tower thus serves to link the generations, and to figure therefore genealogy and tradition, just as the Japanese sword, 'Sato's gift', in 'My Table', symbolises the 'changeless work of art' born of violence, and passed 'From father unto son'.[46] The sense of telepathy with his racial ancestor is born out of crisis, a point which Yeats also makes (about a different sense of race kinship) in *The Trembling of the Veil*.[47] However, while *The Trembling of the Veil* charts the forging of a racial consciousness into a determined political will that gives rise to the nation-state, a process in which the poet is figured as receptacle and artificer, *Meditations* depicts a racial consciousness which is pitted against the public sphere, which takes refuge in individual isolation (the titles of five of the seven poems use the first person possessive, 'unique in Yeats's work', as Howes observes),[48] and which finds racial kinship in the adversities of the distant past, and in the precarious near future of his 'bodily heirs'. There were just a few weeks between the completion of *The Trembling of the Veil* and the drafting of most of *Meditations in Times of Civil War*, but between the two lies a profound change in Yeats's conception of his racial ancestry and calling, or at least a profound change in Yeats's deployment of a sense of racial belonging. What both texts share, however, is an understanding of race as the abolition of distance, historical or geographical. The poet's identification with the man-at-arms in his medieval tower finds proximity and resemblance based upon ancestral lines and a shared sense of alienation from the surrounding Gael. In *The Trembling of the Veil*, Yeats ponders the appearance of ghosts from another age in terms of racial memory:

> Were they really people of the past, revisiting, perhaps, the places where they lived, or must I explain them, as I explained that vision of Eden as a mountain garden, by some memory of the race, as distinct from living memory?[49]

In *Meditations*, as in *Trembling*, then, there is this underlying notion of a race as a 'Unity of Being', as having a collective memory, or collective bank of originary symbols, images, or myths, which constantly reiterate its sense of fixity and destiny. Yeats's rapid reconfiguration of his racial imagination, however, would suggest that race is not about descent but assent, that, as David Goldberg suggests, it is really about 'the meaning and nature of political constitution and community' in modern societies.[50]

The idea of the racial community promises to circumvent the potential anomie of modern social relations by collapsing historical distance. Yeats was not alone in deploying a conception of race as a historical concertina, folding ancestral connections together across time. Michael Collins used a similar image of the joining of the race across time to defend the legitimacy of the new state in his essay, 'Clearing the Road: An Essay in Practical Politics', when he wrote that the new government was 'as completely Irish in race and aims and policy as was the Government of our "Ard Ri," or High King, Brian Borumha – the last wholly Irish Government that ruled the entire nation'.[51] This is one clear instance of the way in which the attempt to legitimate a political community by appealing to an idea of racial history depends upon racist exclusion. Yeats, for example, may have had fond regard for the parliament which met in Dublin in the eighteenth century, and others may have marked the Tudor conquest of Ireland as the definitive political break between a degree of Irish sovereignty and colonial subjugation. But Collins makes clear that only a government 'completely Irish in race' commands the legitimacy and sovereignty of the Irish people, and by implication, the 'completely Irish' are hereby defined as Gaelic and Catholic. In 'Distinctive Culture', first published in 1922, Collins elaborates upon these implications. The difference between Ireland and England for Collins is one of racial purity. England is a mongrel nation, 'in which each new invasion [of foreigners] altered the social polity of the people', and 'English civilization to-day is the reflection of such changes'.[52] However, in the Gaelic civilisation which preceded English colonisation, Collins maintains:

> We had a native culture. We had a social system of our own. We had an economic organisation. We had a code of laws which fitted us. These were such in their beauty, their honesty, their recognition of right and justice, and in their strength, that foreigners coming to our island brought with them nothing of like attractiveness to replace them. These foreigners accepted Irish civilization, forgot their own, and eagerly became absorbed into the Irish race.[53]

Here we have an echo of D. P. Moran's argument that the Gael must be the element to absorb. Although Collins sees English colonisation as the destruction of Gaelic civilisation, he is keen to emphasise that the 'Gaelic soul of the Irish people still lives', especially in the remote and poor regions of the south and west. This 'soul' is the key, obviously, to the resurrection of a Gaelic nation based upon the principle that only a government 'completely Irish in race' can mould a social, cultural and economic system which 'fits' the Irish people. An important element in Collins's argument is this notion that English culture and English styles of governance do not 'fit' the Irish people, with the result that the attempts to foster English ideas in Ireland produce 'hideous medleys'.[54] Thus, Collins argues, as Patrick Pearse did before him, that freedom from English government is not enough: 'The extent to which we become free in fact and secure our freedom will be the extent to which we become Gaels again'.[55] The significance of race in understanding the politics of Michael Collins is not simply that he draws upon ideas of the racial composition of ancient Irish civilisation as a source of legitimacy for the establishment of the Irish Free State, but that he argues that racial purity will be a determining factor in the continued legitimacy of that state. According to this logic, the forms and styles of governance adopted by the Irish Free State were not the expressions of an emergent modern European nation, but the recovery of the mores and principles of an ancient, distinctively Gaelic civilisation. The justification for the independent existence of the state will only come from the degree to which it succeeds in folding time back on itself, and reconstituting itself as coterminous and synonymous with the race.

Yet this is not quite the Michael Collins familiar from historical and political studies. Collins was primarily responsible for drafting the *Constitution of the Irish Free State* (1922), for example, which nowhere refers to racial identity, and which gives expression to cultural distinctiveness only in providing equal official recognition for the Irish and English languages, and in attempting to define a notion of citizenship free from the language of subjecthood.[56] Both Garvin and Prager see Collins as essentially a civic nationalist, as distinct from the ethnic nationalism of the Republican idealists. Both detect some ambivalence about, or what Garvin calls sentimentality for, the views of the anti-Treaty faction, but as Prager writes, when it came to the treaty and the establishment of a provisional government, Collins 'came to espouse the values of the Irish-Enlightenment tradition'.[57] Collins's biographer, Tim Pat Coogan, sees his role in the making of the 1922 Constitution specifically as testimony to 'the nobler aspects of Collins's vision, the constructive thought for the future of a man who hoped it would be one of independence, democracy and peace'.[58] Collins consulted the constitutions and constitutional experts of several modern democratic states in drafting the Free State constitution, and these are the influences upon its defining sense of civic and political values, not the annalistic records of Brehon Law, nor the bardic traces of ancestral custom.

The disparity between the racial rhetoric of Collins's writings and his acknowledged role in stewarding into existence a state which espoused the language of democracy, equality, and (to some extent) pluralism raises a number of significant questions about the meanings of race in Irish political and cultural life in 1922. It is unlikely that the constitution was a sop to the demands of the international community, masking the 'real' racial agenda of the new political class in Ireland, given that the exemplars of democracy among modern nations were often themselves sources of racist practices and expressions, but if there was such a racial agenda as seems the case from Collins's writings, why was this absent from expression in the constitution? Were racial ambitions or prohibitions deemed to be outside the scope of, or undesirable in, legal discourse? If so, what models of the constitutionally or legally enshrined racial state were Collins and his constitutional committee reacting against? Alternatively, if the constitution should be taken as the 'true' expression of Collins's ideals, what function did the racial rhetoric of his writings serve? What constituency were these writings aiming to inspire or persuade? And why appeal to notions of racial purity, and the possibility of resurrecting the supposed racial characteristics of a civilisation which had not existed independently for 700 years, if Collins understood that the polity which would vote on the treaty and the government consisted of a heterogeneous, hybrid population which required a constitution guaranteeing equality, freedom of expression, freedom from religious discrimination, and so on? Democratic ideals do not necessarily clash with the idea of a racial community, however. In fact, Collins argues that as ancient Irish civilisation was democratic, democracy is a core value of the race.[59] Our third option here is to understand that Collins may uphold and espouse the racial ideals evident in his writings, the dream of a homogeneous state which reincarnates the virtues of an ancient race, at the same time as he does all in his power to effect the constitutional establishment of a modern, democratic, egalitarian state, if all the while the latter is understood to be the best vehicle through which the state can tolerate difference while working towards the absorption of difference. This comes closest to how David Goldberg characterises the racial dynamics of modern states as 'heterogeneity in denial, or more deeply yet as the recognition of heterogeneity at once repressed', which is to say that modern states give expression to tolerance of the heterogeneity which is the inevitable consequence of centuries of migration, transnational commerce, and imperial expansion, while legitimating the cohesion and identity of the nation by presuming and reinforcing ideas of homogeneity.[60] Thus, the racial discourses prevalent among Irish nationalist politicians (whether 'civic' or 'ethnic') might be theorised not just as instruments deployed in the interests of demanding independence and gaining political legitimacy for the nation-state, but as part of a broader anxiety about the globalising and anonymising processes of modernity.

This would in part explain the reasons why race appeals not just to a sense of historical continuity, but to a sense of transhistorical reincarnation, to the idea that the nation might be capable of reaching back beyond the centuries of cultural mixing, miscegenation, and global commerce to the supposed purity and insularity of premodernity. Central to this appeal throughout the Irish revival is the narrative of an uninterrupted, or at least a potentially re-sutured racial community. The meeting of ancient and modern members of the Irish race is illustrated on the cover design of Seumas MacManus's popular history, *The Story of the Irish Race* (first published in October 1921 and still in print today). The cover was designed by Thomas O'Shaughnessy, responsible for some of the best examples of stained-glass Celtic art in the revival period, and it shows an Iron Age Celtic warrior hand-in-hand with a modern scholar, both wearing cloaks and looking, one has to say, rather enamoured of each other. Behind them the sun rises over a megalithic dolmen, and the whole scene is framed by a Celtic interlace design with crosses and a harp, inspired by the illuminations of the

Book of Kells. The cover design makes visible the central assumption and assertion of the book, that what unites the dolmen, the warrior and the scholar across time is the continuity of 'race', while it also neatly symbolises three distinctive aspects of this race: the mysticism of the dolmen, the military prowess of the warrior, and the learning and lore of the scholar. MacManus's book is a compendium of contributions from various scholars, but mostly written by himself, which attempts to sketch 'the high spots in the story of our race', so as to counter the 'woeful lack of knowledge on the subject which [the author] found in the four corners of America'.[61] MacManus aims partly to enlist understanding and support for the Irish 'cause' among Americans, to whom 'Ireland's past [is] as obscure as the past of Borneo', while at the same time wishes the book to fill 'the minds and hearts of his people' with 'the history of the country that endowed them with the rare riches, spiritual and mental, that characterises the far-wandered children, and children's children, of the Gael'. To win American support, it seems, Ireland needs to be lifted out of the melting pot of global imperialism, and distinguished from places such as Borneo, which, it is implied, have not the saving grace of racial history to which MacManus lays claim for Ireland in his book. A race is nothing without a history, and the claim to racial distinction must therefore be based on historical longevity and historical achievements.

The Story of the Irish Race is a story of the origins, glories, suppression, and resurgence of a singular and continuous race. MacManus begins by acknowledging that the Irish race of ancient times was in fact comprised of three races, the Milesians, the Firbolg, and the Tuatha De Danaan, but quickly resolves this multiplicity into a single racial narrative: 'All three of these races, however, were different tribes of the great Celtic family, who, long ages before, had separated from the main stem, and in the course of later centuries blended again into one tribe of Gaels'.[62] As in the case of Michael Collins's view of racial history, MacManus explains the successive waves of migration and invasion of ancient and medieval Ireland as a process of absorption by the dominant Gaelic race, until the arrival of English colonists. In a chapter entitled 'Suppressing the Race', MacManus summarises the English colonisation of Ireland from the twelfth century onwards: 'Through these many dread centuries England's energies were concentrated upon an effort, seemingly, to annihilate the Irish race'. Colonisation is understood not as a contest over the right to rule, or the merits of one system of government and administration over another, or of one culture over another, but as a contest between race survival and race death. English colonisation is about the extinction of

Figure 1.2   Cover image from the 1921 edition of Seumas MacManus's *The Story of the Irish Race*

the Irish race, to which end 'The laws imposed upon Ireland from the Norman's first coming, down till to-day or yesterday, far surpassed in ferocity any of the repressive systems temporarily imposed upon any other of the sorest suffering conquered ones of the world'.[63] Even in sharing a history of colonial oppression with other 'races' around the globe, the Irish race must be seen to be distinctive, singular in the ferocity of the oppression suffered, and thus a narrative of subjugation by another 'race' or power can become a narrative of Irish racial strength and survival.

The happy ending demanded by such a teleological history of racial endurance comes as MacManus considers the work of the Gaelic League, the Gaelic Athletic Association and Sinn Féin at the beginning of the twentieth century. With the efforts of these organisations, MacManus writes,

> The centre of gravity in national life changed from the anglicised towns to the rural population, sturdy, unspoilt, patriotic, virile, the offspring and living representatives of the traditional Gael. Hence Irish politics began forthwith to reflect the mind of the real Irish race.[64]

In MacManus's history, the emphasis on seeking out and resurrecting the 'authentic' mind and morality of the Gael is explicitly cast in terms of a regime of racial truth, in which colonisation is seen as a perversion or corruption of a singular 'stream'. We might recall more broadly, however, how this same emphasis on authenticity, which we find in everything from Douglas Hyde's 'On the Necessity for De-Anglicizing Ireland' (1892) to Eamon de Valera's often quoted St Patrick's Day speech from 1943, draws implicitly upon an assumed continuity and homogeneity of racial identity, and how this has shaped the character of Irish politics since the emergence of the modern nationalist movements in the late nineteenth century. In this context, MacManus's racial history cannot simply be explained as the exaggerated product of the exilic imagination, or as a comforting narrative of transhistorical belonging for Irish-Americans who may never have set foot in Ireland, for its narrative of the Irish race accords with the principal assumptions and tenets of many of the leading works of Irish revival literature and history. In drawing upon the work of Douglas Hyde, Aodh de Blacam, 'Sean-Ghall', and MacManus's late wife, Ethna Carbery, MacManus was building his edifice of the Irish race on the foundations of literary and historical writings which were already popular in Ireland. And, in common with much of the revival work from which it drew, *The Story of the Irish Race* is not just a classic text of nationalist hagiography, but more perniciously, in the singular racial strain which it deems as origin and future of Irish identity, it is also part of what Paul Gilroy calls 'the historiography of ethnic absolutism'.[65]

MacManus's book looks forward to the establishment of a state suited to the needs and aspirations of 'the real Irish race', a state which conceives of itself as racially homogeneous, and which therefore sets out to order its population as a singular entity. As Goldberg argues, 'such homogeneity is achieved and reproduced . . . only through repression, through occlusion and erasure, restriction and denial, delimitation and domination'.[66] The civil war was only the beginning of that process, and was not about the defeat of ethnic nationalism, but a settlement of the parameters and institutions of the state which could then serve to manage the politics of racial and cultural homogeneity. The fact that the Irish state would be home to a heterogeneous population, whose residents considered themselves of many different racial identities, not to mention the variety of meanings which the word 'race' signified to them, did not get in the way of a good story. We can, with Tom Garvin, celebrate the achievement of democratic institutions and processes in the Irish Free State in 1922, when the pressure of internal political violence, and a climate of authoritarian rule in many countries in Europe and beyond, may have militated against such an achievement.[67] But when a state is formed in the belief that it is the organic expression of a homogeneous race or culture, it is no less susceptible to racial ideologies and no less likely to order its people according to racial distinctions for being democratic. Racial distinctions may be, as Goldberg writes, 'cemented silently into the fabric of state definition and pursuits'.[68] Racist effects need not be explicitly pursued, but will be 'sustained by their routinization in social and state practice, and by state silence and omission'. In the Irish Free State, and its successor, the Republic of Ireland, that 'routinization' took the form of a Catholic bias in education, health, social and cultural policy, anti-semitic and anti-traveller practices and rhetoric, immigration- and refugee-management practices which discriminated in favour of 'sameness' of religious identity, and censorship which left Gaelic literature unaffected, but which banned almost every notable Irish and foreign publication in the English language. Race remained the 'constituting power' lurking behind the 'constituted power' of the state, then, to use Giorgio Agamben's terms,[69] the apparently ontological source of sovereignty from which the democratically-conceived state derives its ultimate legitimacy and founds its practices of social and cultural organisation.[70]

'Beyond All Telling': The Irish Race Congress

The apotheosis of this process of imagining and shaping the future of the Irish as a 'race' ought to have been the Irish Race Congress which took place in January 1922 in Paris. If the Irish Race Congress has a reputation, however, it is for the ridiculous hyperbole of its conception, and the pathetic political squabbles which characterised its execution. It has merited meagre attention from historians, the subject of just three articles and a pamphlet to date, all of which see the Congress as an inglorious failure, its aims wrecked by the growing split over the Anglo-Irish treaty, and a widening gulf between the interests of the Irish in the newly emergent state and those of the Irish abroad.[71] In the most substantial treatment of the Congress, Richard Davis even suggests that it 'can almost be classified as a complete fiasco, unworthy of the attention of serious historians', the only significance of which is what it tells us about the role and ideals of the Irish communities abroad, specifically the Self-Determination for Ireland movement.[72] Davis indeed begins his pamphlet with the anecdote that even before they embarked for the Paris Congress, the delegates from Dáil Éireann were mistaken by an angry mob in Dublin for departing Black and Tans, and almost lynched, an 'inauspicious incident' which 'presaged the failure of the ambitious Convention'.[73] As a result of the split over the treaty, there was not one official delegation from Ireland but two, nominated separately by Arthur Griffith and Eamon de Valera, funded separately, and, even though some travelled to Paris in the same ships and trains, they apparently remained separate from each other on their journey. Eoin MacNeill, one of the appointed delegates of the provisional government, recorded in his notes a week of petty squabbles and recriminations, the proceedings of the Congress characterised by 'Numerous interruptions, much resentment'.[74] MacNeill's preliminary report to Griffith on the events of the week in Paris stated that 'De Valera's adherents carried on a constant campaign of partisan manoeuvring and misrepresentation of every kind and at every point'.[75] Michael Hayes, another government delegate, was outraged from the outset of the Congress when the Irish envoy in Paris, Sean T. O'Kelly, arranged a reception for de Valera's delegation but none for that of the government, and hosted a dinner, funded by the Dáil, at which no government minister was acknowledged or asked to speak.[76] The government ministers were not the only ones to complain: a delegate from Australia, Maurice J. O'Reilly, wrote to the provisional government to protest at the intrusion of domestic politics on the business of the Congress, asserting that it was made evident from the opening dinner, in which there was an argument over de Valera's toast to the third anniversary of the Irish Republic, that partisan politics would get in the way of the ambitious, unifying, 'racial' ideals of the Congress.[77] To date, however, the Irish Race Congress has been considered by historians as an incidental event in the history either of the civil war, or Irish nationalist organisations abroad. It has not been remembered for the racial ideals it was organised to express, nor has it been considered as a cultural event in its own right.

The idea to hold a World Congress of the Irish Race began in South Africa in February 1921, when the Irish Republican Association proposed a conference which would bring together delegates from the Irish communities around the globe in a bid to unite them in the struggle for freedom for 'their motherland'.[78] As an editorial in the South African-Irish periodical, *The Republic*, explained, the conference itself would be a platform for launching an organisation which would mobilise the resources of, and serve as a rallying point for the diaspora:

It is not the Ireland of four millions that we are thinking of now, nor even merely the potential Ireland of ten or fifteen millions. We are thinking also of the Greater Ireland, the *Magna Hibernia* across the seas, the millions of Irish people throughout the world.[79]

The aims of such an organisation would be far-reaching, and extend beyond immediate support for the military and political war against the British, to the formation of an international institution serving the needs of the race, 'with a permanent secretariat at the Hague or Geneva'.[80] If we have seen earlier in the chapter how the emergent state was the subject of speculation about how racial identity and racial ideals could be embodied in and expressed through the form of the state, it is worth stressing that the aims of the Irish Race Congress envisaged giving institutional expression not just to the teeming population which would inevitably flow from independence, but to the seemingly boundless fecundity of 'Magna Hibernia'.

Benjamin Farrington, the editor of *The Republic*, and, it seems, the most influential figure in the initiation of the idea for the Congress, recognised however that a world conference on such a scale could not be organised from South Africa, and so Art O'Brien, head of Sinn Féin in Britain, was asked to take on responsibility. O'Brien was close to de Valera, who himself had sought to orchestrate such an international organisation of Irish communities for some time, having sent his secretary Katherine Hughes to work secretly in various countries around the globe towards the formation of 'Self-Determination for Ireland Leagues'. Hughes played an important part in garnering support for the Congress, especially in Canada, Newfoundland, Australia, and New Zealand, and was its organising secretary. The Congress was not in itself wholly new as an idea. There had been an Irish Race Convention in Dublin in 1896 to enlist support for home rule. In the three years prior to the 1922 Irish Race Congress, there had been local conferences bearing the name of 'Irish Race Convention' in Philadelphia (March 1919), Melbourne (November 1919), and Ottawa (October 1920). The Philadelphia conference even lobbied the international Peace Conference in Paris to press for Irish admission and presumably therefore international recognition. But the Paris conference would be a World Congress, designed to reflect and express the will of the Irish race as an international entity.

Once in the hands of de Valera, O'Brien, and Hughes, the organisation of the Congress acquired practical momentum: the venue and dates were chosen, and invitations were issued from the office of President de Valera in late August. De Valera's involvement was crucial, yet it also proved disastrous for the Congress, as in the wake of the treaty split, it came to be understood, particularly by powerful Irish-American figures, that the Congress and the intended world organisation to emerge from it, would be no more than instruments in de Valera's attempts to oppose the treaty. But the dates were set for the conference before the treaty negotiations even began, and de Valera could hardly have foreseen that by the time it opened in Paris on 21 January, he would by then have resigned as President over the Dáil's ratification of the treaty, and been succeeded by Arthur Griffith. That partisan politics wrecked the aims of the Congress is in no doubt, but it is important to pay attention to what the Congress was intended to achieve before it fell foul of the first political manoeuvrings of civil war.

The Irish Race Congress took place from 21 to 28 January in the Hotel Continental, Paris. The event could not have been planned to take place in Ireland, as until the ratification of the treaty just two weeks before the opening of the Congress no one could have been certain that Ireland was a safe venue. As it happened, British troops began to evacuate their military bases in Ireland just days prior to the Congress. Nor was it thought desirable to hold the event in a city or country with a large Irish population, as presumably this would give the host community too much weight in what was meant to be a world meeting of the race. Paris was chosen as a neutral venue, an international city to rival London, which could provide the amenities and transport infrastructure necessary to host a large meeting of members drawn from around the globe, while also adding a symbolic dimension. The symbolism of Paris lay not just in its revolutionary, democratic legacy, nor in its status as capital of a global empire, but in its reputation as a centre of cultural modernity. Paris was, in the words of the Honorary Secretary of the Irish Race Congress, Thomas Hughes Kelly, 'the intellectual centre of the world', and therefore the 'most suitable meeting place'.[81] The aesthetic elegance of much of the regal and imperial architecture in the centre of Paris, combined with the modern reputation it had acquired for its art, architecture and literature, gave the city the aura of a spiritual and intellectual hub. The press notices released prior to the Congress played on this notion of Paris as a suitable venue to host what was 'the first Aonac na nGaedeal held in 700 years': 'Paris has for the moment become the Mecca of the Gael'.[82] The Hotel Continental which hosted the Congress was itself renowned for the magnificence of its interior decorations (something of which can be seen in the background to the official photograph of the Congress delegates), and the pioneering technologies used in its design and construction in 1878, including its ventilation system and electric lighting. It also boasted spectacular views over the city centre,

Figure 1.3 Photograph of the delegates at the Irish Race Congress, Paris, January 1922, reproduced from the Tierney/MacNeill photograph collection [LA30/PH/394] by kind permission of UCD Archives

overlooking the Tuileries Gardens, the Place de la Concorde, and the Eiffel Tower. Yet the history and modernity of Paris was, in a sense, a canvas against which, it was depicted, an ancient race was preparing to assume its own rightful position in the world. One press notice for the Congress recalled the tens of millions of Irish descendants around the world, before boasting that 'while Paris has seen more notable assemblies in the past ten years, none were more universal in scope than this Congress'. In this light the delegates were represented as heroic, 'like a new order of Crusaders, eager to help in the revival of Irish commerce, Gaelic arts and language, and to aid in the renaissance of Irish culture in every department of life'.[83] To consider what these press notices might mean in depicting the Irish in Paris as akin to Crusaders in Mecca is perhaps to speculate too far on a metaphor which obviously was intended merely to highlight the heroic ideals and symbolic significance of the Congress. The location of the Congress in Paris, however, was clearly designed to signal to the world its international scope and ambition, not just towards national self-determination, but towards some kind of institutional articulation of a transnational race. As such, Paris was emblematic of the 'first world' modernity to which the Congress sought access for the Irish 'race'.

There was no clear modern model for what the Congress was

intended to achieve, which could not be categorised as an empire since it involved people of Irish descent who could be loyal and patriotic citizens in their adopted countries, nor merely as a state, which as it evolved as the Irish Free State would be home to just 4 million of a race estimated to be 30 million or more. By referring to it as an 'Aonac' in press releases, invitations and programmes, the Congress was conceived, or at least represented, as a resurrection of the ancient festival of Aonac, and a single page document entitled 'Reviving Ancient Festival' explains what this might constitute:

> If the World Conference of the Irish Race becomes triennial, as desired by the President of Ireland, as it doubtless will, this generation will see a restoration of the ancient Aonac of Erin in all its old time splendour . . . . Those Ard Aonac of all Ireland were great national assemblies held every year at Tailtean, near the Court of the High King at Tara. These were reproductions on a more splendid scale of the Aonac held annually at the Courts of the Provincial Kings. Like these it was a Parliament of law-making, accompanied by formal banquets and dancing, chariot-racing, a tourney of knightly games and contests in bardic lore, music and the art of the Seanchie.[84]

The Paris Congress was to be the first modern incarnation of this ancient event, this time staging on an international level the 'Ard Aonac' which the document claims was a national celebration of the feats and traditions of the race. However, it was clear from the invitations and plans for the Congress that it had to be much more limited in scope than the Aonac Tailteann. Later in 1922, T. H. Nally published his study of the Tailteann games, stressing that ancient Ireland was no less accomplished in the physical sports than in the intellectual arts for which scholars had claimed its distinction, and arguing that the Aonac were 'physical, intellectual and manufacturing contests; as well as sports of every kind, poetry and singing recitals, contests for the manufacture of armour, weapons, and articles of home-manufacture'.[85] The Irish Race Congress was half-heartedly modelled on these lines, with an art exhibition, theatre performances, musical recitals, and a banquet, alongside the 'business' of the conference, although the athletics programme had to be cancelled.[86] The Congress was a much more mundane affair than the 'Aonac' notion perpetuated in the press releases would have us believe. It was essentially a series of lectures and discussions, which certainly prompted debate about culture, science, sports, economics, and politics, but staged no contests and made no laws. To represent the Congress as an Aonac, however, was to provide it with an air of legitimacy drawn from racial history, and perhaps also, controversially, to claim that the Congress was a higher authority than the newly constituted provisional government.

The racial conception of the Congress is evident in the choice of Honorary Vice-President, the Duc de Tetuan, a Spanish descendant of Red Hugh O'Donnell and head of the O'Donnell clan, who made the opening and closing speeches of the Congress. In both speeches, the Duc praised the 'vitality of the Irish Race', of which the Congress was held to be proof, and looked forward to the 'brilliant destiny' which lay before the Irish nation.[87] In newspaper reports of the Congress, the Duc attracted considerable interest as the blood-descendant of the 'Princes of Tirconaill', or 'a scion of the princely house of O'Donnell'.[88] He is reported at the opening ceremony to have been seated 'under a large shield of the O'Donnell's wreathed in the French and Irish Tricolour'.[89] There were numerous figures present who might have made for relatively neutral opening speakers, and to serve as symbolic presidents, such as Douglas Hyde, W. B. Yeats, or Archbishop Mannix. That the Duc was invited and chosen as 'figure-head' for the Congress indicated that the organisers sought to emphasise the purity of racial blood-lines and the nobility of Irish ancestry, a continuity between the Gaelic aristocracy of old, and the achievements of their descendants in their adopted lands. The sense of continuity between the dispersed Irish and their racial kindred in Ireland was advertised by the Duc himself, who, to loud cheers, told the delegates that 'since the beginning of the 17th century' his family and the other 'exiles of Erin' 'had never forgotten that Irish blood flowed in their veins. They had always preserved the memory of the Ireland they adored'.[90]

This theme was evident too in the greetings and messages of goodwill sent to the Congress from those unable to attend. The 'United Irish Societies of the Isthmus of Panama', for example, hailed 'the most august race in the world', and sent a prayer for the success of the Congress:

> May the memories of our great race, which has won its triumphs on the fields of sorrow and sacrifice, inspire you to guard the most glorious racial inheritance in history, and to transmit it, freshened by your devotion and enriched by your love, to posterity.[91]

The hyperbole of such sentiments might be explained as the consequence of distance or homesickness. Race gives the illusion of proximity, across time and space, in the notion of common blood or common memories, and therefore is understandably of greatest comfort to those who see themselves as separated from their homelands or kin. The messages of politicians from Ireland, however, were no less bound up with the sentimentality of race. The Minister for Foreign Affairs of Dáil Éireann, George Gavan Duffy, sent a telegram to the Congress on behalf of the government, which read:

> The government . . . expresses the ardent hope that this very historic reunion of the Gaels will cement yet more strongly the bonds linking to the Fatherland its children who throughout the whole world have done so much to spread its reunion.[92]

Sean T. O'Kelly, the Irish envoy in Paris, who read Gavan Duffy's telegram aloud to the Congress, proceeded to declare that 'The foundations are being laid here today of something that will grow and expand the world over, and the influence of the race through it will be felt the world over'.[93] The rhetoric of racial destiny, and racial cohesion across the globe, is pervasive throughout the discussions of the Congress, and often takes this form of reconfiguring the diaspora not as a sign of historical trauma and colonial subjugation, but as a sign of the vitality and potency of a race that could make its influence felt around the world.

The lectures too take the form of racial histories, and tie the cultural work of the revival, in varying degrees, to the task of reconnecting the present with its racial ancestry. W. B. Yeats was applauded loudly when he closed his lecture on 'The Lyrical and Dramatic Poetry of Modern Ireland' with a recital of Patrick Pearse's 'The Wayfarer', a poem which he argued was an instance of the way in which modern writers had found 'truth' by tapping the springs of ancient Gaelic literature, although Foster discerns that Yeats was playing politics in identifying the Abbey with Pearse, and allying himself with the new provisional government.[94] If so, the cultural programme of the Congress would bolster Yeats's claim, as the two plays chosen to represent the dramatic gifts of the Irish race were Synge's *Riders to the Sea* and Gregory's *The Rising of the Moon*.[95] Eoin MacNeill in his lecture finds legitimacy for the work of the Irish Race Congress in two lines from ancient Gaelic which Pearse had learned from MacNeill, and which form the motto of both the Congress and the organisation it spawned, Fine Gaedeal: 'Ba mó epirt in cach ré/ Airle De fhí hÉirinn n-uill' ['Beyond all telling is the destiny God has in mind for Ireland the peerless'].[96] Douglas Hyde's lecture is by far the most substantial engagement with the idea of racial history, and with explaining the work of the revival, specifically the Gaelic league, in the terms of a racial struggle:

> If throughout two-thirds of Ireland the population had been negroes or castaways planted there in the last century, they could scarcely have been more absolutely ignorant of their own past than were the Irish. And yet the Irish are neither negroes nor mongrels nor castaways, nor are they a people without a past. On the contrary, they boast almost the proudest race-heritage in Europe. They are the descendants of a stock to which almost every country in Western Europe owes, and frankly acknowledges that it owes, a debt of lasting gratitude.[97]

The task of the Gaelic league in this context, argues Hyde, was to educate the Irish people about their own racial inheritance, and to instil in them the pride that they should have in the achievements of the Irish race. That task is principally motivated, in Hyde's articulation of it, not by a drive for national self-determination, so much as a fear that the colonial education system depicted the Irish as 'a race of colourless mongrels', 'sprung from a race of nobodies or slaves'. It is motivated, in other words, by an anxiety about racial differentiation and distinction, that the Irish are emphatically not the same as 'negroes', 'mongrels', or 'castaways'. There is a moment in Hyde's lecture when the possibility of empathy, or solidarity, with other colonised peoples is glimpsed: 'When an aboriginal race comes in contact with a white race it has often been remarked that they lose their good characteristics, and in addition to their own bad ones adopt the bad ones of the whites. This is what was happening to us'. But it is clear from Hyde's eagerness to distinguish the Irish as white, western Europeans that he is not making an analogy here for the sake of solidarity, but to emphasise the absurdity of the Irish being seen as anything other than white Europeans, deserving of the status afforded white Europeans over and above the rights of the various racial others Hyde mentions in his lecture. What Hyde calls for in his conclusion is nothing less than the resurrection of the race responsible for the artistic and intellectual salvation of Europe. The idea that the Irish might embody the salvation of Europe was not peculiar to Hyde, either. In his opening remarks to the Congress, the Honorary Secretary, Thomas Hughes Kelly, was applauded when he envisioned that Ireland could be 'once more a beacon-light of spiritual and intellectual force in a world so long distracted by materialism and debased moral standards'.[98] Far from being preoccupied with the growing internecine divisions over the treaty and the fledgling state, then, the rhetoric of many of the speakers and organisers at the Irish Race Congress reveals loftier ambitions regarding the spiritual destiny of the race, and the potential forms which Irish racial expression could take across a global diaspora.

The rhetoric does run ahead of what would be practically possible, or even conceivable, however. The word 'empire' is never used to describe this transnational corporation of influence and power which the Irish racial diaspora is meant to embody, but the imagery of a fatherland and its children, or the beacon-light of civilisation and spiritual enlightenment shining across the world, is akin to the rhetoric of imperial possession and control. Davis argues that, with the exception of the Irish in Britain, however, the emigrant Irish communities around the world were unlikely to attach much significance to the idea of 'a vast Irish empire almost strong enough to offset the British'.[99] In South Africa, Australia, Canada, New Zealand and the United States, those of Irish birth or descent were more likely to see themselves as 'nationals of the lands they go to happening to be of Irish blood'.[100] Here lies the difficulty with advancing the aims of the Congress to establish an international institution, with a permanent secretariat, to encapsulate and represent the interests of the race. As David Goldberg argues, the notion of race as belonging is 'too vague alone to furnish a mode of discriminate differentiation and exclusion. If the sense of belonging is to have any force, it must either be manifest in or be predicated upon establishment of an authority (institutional or personal) in the body or person(s) of whom group members at least partially recognize themselves'.[101] The racial state, as an abstract conception, may be able to provide the diaspora with a compass point of identification and belonging, perhaps even a sense of cultural and spiritual values, but the form which Irish racial difference would take across the globe would evidently vary according to local political and cultural contests, unless Irish racial difference could manifest itself in an international authority. As it happened, the state that came into existence in 1922 was too hotly disputed by the Irish in Ireland to be a beacon of anything to the diaspora, and the possibility of an international authority for the Irish race was simply beyond imagination.

There were practical measures related to racial politics discussed at the Irish Race Congress. On Thursday 26 January, in discussions concerning the industrial and economic regeneration of Ireland, it was mooted that with increased prosperity the state may be able to make preparations for what the *Irish Independent* sub-heading called the 'return of [the] race', and some organisations abroad, notably the Irish Self-Determination League in Britain 'had decided to take an occupation census of its members' with this possibility in mind.[102] Behind this motion lay the idea that the Irish abroad could be regarded as a kind of migrant surplus labour force, ready to be recruited back into the Irish workforce as and when needed by industrial and economic developments. In the same discussion, the Irish organisations abroad were encouraged to promote knowledge of Irish imports and exports, so that, again, the Irish abroad might be simply overseas consumers of what Mary MacSwiney envisioned as an 'economic commonwealth'.[103] That the racial diaspora could be mobilised into transnational labour and consumer resources in the service of the state was perhaps a logical extension of the work the leagues for self-determination had been doing in garnering financial and moral support for political and military struggle in previous years, or of the custom of emigrants' remittances which were vital sources of income for many deprived regions of Ireland. That this process could be organised by, or into, the institutional form of a racially defined commonwealth, however, was also unlikely, given that members of the Irish communities in countries such as Canada and Australia were already economic and political citizens of a well-established empire, which would increasingly be defined as a common-wealth. De Valera was apparently very forthcoming with suggestions concerning possible forms of cooperation on a cultural level between the various constituent communities of the Irish diaspora, involving games, dances, music, and the Irish language, although MacNeill interpreted these proposals as attempts to cover up the political fights which were breaking out between the pro- and anti-treaty parties.[104] One sugges-tion which was added late as an amendment, and therefore outside the manoeuvring of Congress discussions, was 'That a register of the men and women of the race who had made worthy contributions to human achievement be kept at several national secretariats and at the central secretariat from which a contemporary "who is who" of the race and a concise Dictionary of Biography might be compiled'.[105] There is no record that this suggestion was acted upon, but it indicated some of the practical measures which were considered as means to consolidate an international conception of the Irish race and its achievements.[106]

The most important outcome of the World Congress of the Irish Race, as it was sometimes styled, was the establishment of the organi-sation called Fine Gaedeal, or 'Family of the Gael'. It was formally constituted in the proceedings of the Congress, and an election held to appoint its officials. De Valera was elected President, a controversial decision which made it hard for the provisional government or its sup-porters in Ireland or abroad to believe that the organisation would be, as it professed in its aims, 'politically non-partisan'. MacNeill was elected Vice-President, in a bid to ensure a balance between pro- and anti-treaty factions, but he appears never to have attended a meeting of the executive council, presumably believing that an election victory which styled de Valera effectively 'President of the Irish Race' was designed to trump the legitimacy of the provisional government, which could only claim authority over the Irish state. In any case, even the aims of the organisation proved a cantankerous matter for the Congress, with much time and energy devoted to contesting one word which de Valera had insisted on inserting into the primary aim of Fine Gaedeal: 'To assist the people of Ireland in their efforts to attain to the full their national ideals, political, cultural and economic, and to secure for Ireland her rightful place among the free nations of the earth'. The word 'full' was interpreted by the government delegation as an unequivocal rebuke of the achievements of the treaty, and an attempt to make the organisation implicitly partisan. A manifesto advertising the aims and rationale of the organisation was circulated not long after the Congress, and in reflection of some of the sentiments and ideas expressed during the Congress, it also makes interesting claims upon the racial loyalties of citizens abroad. '[Ireland] has done much for the world in the past', the manifesto reads, 'but many of the great achievements of her children in the various arts of peace and war have been ascribed to other lands, and Ireland has lost so much of her credit'.[107] It is hard to imagine quite what such a record of Irish achievements might constitute. Perhaps the victories won by descendants of the O'Neills and O'Donnells who served as officers in the French and Spanish armies should be accredited as Irish victories. Perhaps, for that matter, Wellington's victory at the Battle of Waterloo might be regarded an Irish victory. Perhaps the huge scale of Irish labour used in the construction of roads, railways, and canals in Britain, the United States, and various other parts of the globe means that much of the world's transport infrastructure might be considered the consequence of Irish ingenuity and determination. What the manifesto was proposing was nothing less than re-interpreting the recorded history of western achievement and civilisation along racial rather than national lines, and attributing achievement according to the blood lines of racial descent of those persons involved, rather than the authorising power of the empire or nation to which credit had been given. The hyperbole of racial vision pervaded the Fine Gaedeal manifesto:

> In the glorious future, growing ever younger and stronger, and deriving from her children everywhere much strength that has hitherto been dissipated, she will help to illumine the world with a spark of that noble spirit which has kept her true to her splendid ideals, in spite of the strangle-hold of an alien domination and an alien civilisation.

The aims of the Irish Race Congress and the organisation it brought into existence, Fine Gaedeal, are precisely where we can trace the perhaps inevitable slide of the racial expressions of difference and separatism (which were shaped by, and in turn informed, the cultural and political movement for national independence) into racist claims of superiority and greater 'enlightenment'.

That Ireland might 'illumine the world' was the ultimate race-fantasy of those who had made the spiritual and moral righteousness of an oppressed nation the lynchpin of the political struggle for independence. But it was a dream foundering on the spent and divided forces which had fought that struggle. The Irish Race Congress was itself testimony to those failing energies and aspirations. A mere 100 delegates turned up for a Congress meant to showcase the vitality of the race. In the case of the United States alone, six delegates were present out of an anticipated sixty, while, as Roy Foster observes, 'carpetbagging "spokesmen" turned up from the exiguous Irish communities of Bolivia and Java, and recently returned missionaries were wheeled on to represent the Irish of China'.[108] The surviving records of the Fine Gaedeal executive council likewise make for a pathetic story. In the executive meetings in June and September of 1922, only two members of the council managed to attend, and records of meetings cease after 1924. Even by October 1922, de Valera had written to Ernie O'Malley of the IRA to ask for funds to keep Fine Gaedeal going, but O'Malley replied with regret that he had no funds to spare. The final document in de Valera's files concerning Fine Gaedeal is a note from the Munster and Leinster Bank in 1930 requesting that he settle the overdraft on the Fine Gaedeal account.[109] The 'family of the Gael' had outspent its meagre budget long before, and its bid for a triennial 'Aonac' festival of racial pride, and a world organisation of the Irish race with permanent representation in The Hague or Geneva, was already a distant memory, a vague if ambitious scheme which had failed probably by the time the delegates left Paris in January 1922.

It is tempting to contrast the failure of the Irish Race Congress in 1922 with the spectacular success of the International Eucharistic Congress in Dublin in 1932, and to speculate that race proved comparatively less significant than religion as an agent of social cohesion in the Irish Free State. To do so, however, would be a misreading of the significance of racial ideologies for the new state. The Irish Race Congress failed not because of a lack of conviction among Irish politicians and intellectuals in its racial ideals, as we have seen, but as a result of the emerging and widening split over the outcome of the treaty negotiations. Conversely, the Eucharistic Congress succeeded ten years later arguably because it managed to articulate racial ideals through public spectacles of religious devotion. John Turpin argues this case, that the

> vast public religious assemblies in Ireland in 1929 [Catholic Emancipation Centenary Celebrations] and 1932 [31st International Eucharistic Congress] responded to that hunger for mass spectacle and solidarity of believers. It was an Irish parallel to the well-organised and colourful political rallies of continental Europe and to the traditional displays by European monarchies.[110]

Both of these celebrations enveloped the racial triumphalism of the new state (which could not find expression in national independence celebrations as a result of the disputed legitimacy of the state) within the less contentious spectacles and rallies of Catholic triumphalism. Ironically, the civil war may have been responsible for deflecting on to Catholicism the more visible ideological onus of social cohesion in the new state, whereas, as the aims and ideals of the Irish Race Congress make clear, there might otherwise have been a more overt and powerful role played by racial ideologies. However thwarted by the exigencies of the partisan politics of the time, the Irish Race Congress sought to give expression to the racial ambitions of Irish cultural and political nationalisms, and to formulate the institutional and intellectual bases of a global Irish race anchored in a newly formed racial state.

Ulysses: 'The Secret of the Race'

Across the Seine and a few streets to the south of the Hotel Continental, at 9 Rue de l'Université, James Joyce was working furiously to finish correcting the final proofs of *Ulysses* in time for it to be published on his fortieth birthday, on 2 February. It was a short walk from his rooms to the Hotel Continental, but there is no evidence that he attended any part of the Irish Race Congress, despite the fact that some of its events extended an open invitation to any Irish visitors to attend. He was, however, aware of its proceedings, and observed the coincidence that he had mentioned the Duc de Tetuan of Spain in *Ulysses*, and that the Duc was himself present at the Congress.[111] The coincidence, or confluence, of *Ulysses* and the Irish Race Congress, runs much deeper than this serendipitous mention of the Duc de Tetuan, as we shall see, for *Ulysses* is as much an exercise in imagining the future relationship between race and state as the Irish Race Congress had attempted to be. Ellmann records the significance which Joyce attributed to publishing works on his birthday, or the birthdays of his friends and family, but the urgency with which *Ulysses* was completed was also, I would contend, partly energised by the 'birthday' of the new Irish state.[112]

'[Ulysses] is the epic of two races (Israel-Ireland)', wrote Joyce, and in the crucial years of its composition, both 'races' were nearing the political settlements which would define and establish the parameters of formal statehood.[113] The 'Balfour Declaration' of 1917 gave formal British recognition to the aspiration of Jewish people to create a 'national home' in Palestine, an important precursor to the eventual formation of the state of Israel. The Sinn Féin electoral victory of 1918, followed by the war of independence of 1919–21, made it increasingly likely that an Irish state of some form would emerge from the combination of democratic mandate and insurrectionary violence. While

Joyce thanked T. S. Eliot for his celebration in the *Dial* of the 'continuous parallel between contemporaneity and antiquity' manipulated in
Ulysses, and encouraged him to make more of the idea that the novel
worked on a 'two-plane' method (the famous 'mythic method' which
came to define high modernism through the work of both Joyce and
Eliot),[114] there is another 'two-plane' method at work in the manipulation of a parallel between the nascent national and racial consciousness
of 1904 and the development of political nationalism in later years,
which would eventually result in the Irish Free State in 1922. *Ulysses*
can be seen to play with this parallel in various episodes. Councillor
Nanetti, for example, with whom Bloom discusses advertising logos in
'Aeolus', would have been known to Joyce's Dublin readers as having
become nationalist Lord Mayor of Dublin in 1906.[115] Bloom is also
reputed for having given Arthur Griffith 'the idea for Sinn Féin', which,
while it existed as a nationalist slogan in 1904, was only formed into a
political party in 1905, and by the time *Ulysses* was published, had led
the nationalist movement through electoral victory and political negotiations with the British government to the formation of the state.[116]
Most comically, perhaps, Molly recalls Bloom pointing out Griffith to
her as 'the coming man', upon which Molly thinks 'well he doesnt look
it thats all I can say', whereas, of course, by the time the novel was published, Griffith had not only led the delegation to London to negotiate
the treaty but had in fact been installed as the first President of the Irish
Free State just weeks previously.[117] Ellmann argues that Joyce may well
have included this tribute to Griffith as 'the coming man' in 'Penelope'
in his final revisions, when he would have known that Griffith had
become President.[118] *Ulysses* constantly plays upon this foreknowledge
of what is, in 1904, still to come, and mobilises our understanding of
what has taken place in between the time of its setting and the time
of its publication. From the opening parodic invocation, '*Introibo ad
altare Dei*', from the psalmist's prayer for delivery from oppression, to
Molly's closing recollection of her promise to Bloom, 'yes I will Yes',
the novel calls our attention to the future anteriority of what it presents,
and more particularly to the messianic time of nationalist and racial discourse.[119] In doing so, it hails before us, sometimes vividly in 'Cyclops'
and 'Circe', for example, a vision of the state to come, and situates
its depiction of Bloom's struggle with questions about his own racial
identity within the context of the formation of a state premised upon
an imagined racial home. Ellmann recognised the importance of this
relationship between *Ulysses* and the Irish state some time ago when he
wrote that '*Ulysses* creates new Irishmen to live in Arthur Griffith's new
state', yet its full significance remains relatively unexplored.[120]

Since Ellmann's time, and partly in response to Ellmann's renowned reading of Joyce as a liberal European modernist, much attention has been devoted to the study of Joyce in relation to Irish literary and political contexts, including groundbreaking and thorough analyses by Seamus Deane, Declan Kiberd, Enda Duffy, and Emer Nolan.[121] There has also been a substantial amount of critical work on the representation of Jewish identity and culture in *Ulysses* in recent years, by Ira Nadel, Neil Davison, and Marilyn Reizbaum.[122] The historical evidence concerning the lives and experiences of Jews in Ireland has also been substantially brought to light by two eminent Irish historians, Dermot Keogh and Cormac Ó Gráda, substantially showing that Joyce's knowledge of Irish Jewry was limited at best.[123] At the same time, Vincent Cheng and Len Platt have devoted studies to the significance of 'race' conceptually and historically in the work of Joyce, examining the sources and debates upon which Joyce's representations of racial identity and racist abuse were founded.[124] Through this and other critical and historical work in Joyce studies, it has become evident that both Joyce and his writings are both profoundly enmeshed in the racial politics of the early twentieth century, and at the same time deeply ambivalent about the very idea of 'race'. If it is possible to see in Joyce's depiction of Bloom a detailed critique of the racist underpinnings of the emergent nationalist state, it is also possible to see, as Len Platt observes, that 'Joyce was not entirely immune from the temptations of race discourse'.[125]

To make the same point, specifically regarding Joyce's treatment of 'the Jew', Ira Nadel quotes the passage from Joyce's 1899 'Ecce Homo' essay in which the student Joyce describes in derisory terms a rich Jewish man, with 'that horrible cast of countenance, so common among the sweaters of modern Israel'.[126] There are traces of such an acceptance of anti-semitic characterisations of Jews in *Stephen Hero*, *A Portrait of the Artist as a Young Man*, and, one might also argue, in some of the characteristics attributed to Bloom in *Ulysses*. More broadly, however, *Ulysses* marks a new departure in Joyce's depictions of race in that it insistently questions racial identifications and conceptions, whereas *Portrait* largely assumes the fact of race, for example, in the eleven instances in which the word 'race' appears.[127] Stephen's avowed desire in the famous closing lines of *Portrait*, 'to forge in the smithy of my soul the uncreated conscience of my race',[128] accepts unproblematically that Stephen belongs to a 'race', which he has consistently identified as Irish through the novel, while casting the role of the artist as forging the 'conscience' of the race. Pericles Lewis argues that the word 'uncreated' here may not mean that Stephen is inventing this 'conscience', but rather, following the theological meaning of 'uncreated' as something which is eternal and self-existent, that this 'racial conscience . . . is itself the source of all experience, something permanent like God and unlike all mortal creatures'.[129] The artist's role is therefore merely to re-present, or forge within his own self, the unchanging 'racial conscience'. Lewis draws our attention to the etymological (and theological) meanings of the words in this often-quoted line, and likewise, the word 'conscience' which might strike readers now for its moral sense, is first explained by the *Oxford English Dictionary* as 'inward knowledge or conscious-ness', which took the place in Middle English of 'inwit'. Thus, the 'conscience of my race' comes closer here to meaning the inner wisdom or understanding possessed not individually but within the race, or in a phrase used in both *Portrait* and *Ulysses*, 'the secret of the race'.[130] It is more common in Joyce criticism to find Stephen's aspiration to forge 'the uncreated conscience of my race' read as an indication of Stephen's (and Joyce's) critical departure from the orthodoxies of the nationalist racial imagination, inventing a presumably liberal sense of moral values for a race badly in need of them. However, the fixity of notions of race in *Portrait* should alert us to the more likely meaning that Stephen's solution to the political and cultural problems of his age is to turn to race, and specifically to the idea that human beings exist in separate and distinctive racial groups, as the *a priori* of human experience and expression. Hence, it is only through discovering the knowledge of his race within himself that Stephen will become an artist (an argument echoed in only slightly different terms in Jack B. Yeats's lecture at the Irish Race Congress). This reading is further borne out if we recall an earlier scene in *Portrait*, in which Stephen tries to explain to Lynch why different races 'all admire a different type of female beauty', dismissing the eugenics argument that 'every physical quality admired by men in women is in direct connection with the manifold functions of women for the propagation of the species', and resolving instead that 'though the same object may not seem beautiful to all people, all people who admire a beautiful object find in it certain relations which satisfy and coincide with the stages themselves of all esthetic apprehension'.[131] Aesthetic apprehension, then, although it may be experienced by all humanity, can only occur through the medium of racial knowledge or 'conscience', and thus racial difference is the fact, the natural law, which shapes Stephen's destiny before and beyond the callings of 'nationality, language, religion'.[132]

Stephen's quest to divine the 'inwit' of his race, much closer in spirit to the racial politics of many of Joyce's revival contemporaries, may have been one reason why Joyce lost interest in Stephen in *Ulysses* as a character with 'a shape that can't be changed'.[133] Both Bloom and

Molly are notably more protean in their racial identifications and composition than Stephen, who remains to some extent morbidly fixated on the notion of racial ancestry, particularly paternity, throughout the novel. The differences between Stephen and Bloom are brought home, as it were, in the 'Nostos' part of *Ulysses*. In 'Eumaeus', while Stephen and Bloom exchange meaningful, doubtful glances in response to the ignorant racial myths which pepper the conversation of Skin-the-Goat and the sailor, Bloom's attempt to build on this shared antipathy later founders, inexplicably to Bloom, over the question of belonging. In telling Stephen of the anti-semitic abuse he suffers at the hands of the Citizen earlier in the day, Bloom goes on to explain that Jews have a proud history in Europe, and have benefited every country to which they have migrated. He proceeds to share with Stephen his vision of how Ireland might be organised along equitable lines in terms of labour and income, but when Stephen mutters the remark 'Count me out', Bloom, assuming that Stephen feels left out of this vision, moves to reassure him: 'You have every bit as much right to live by your pen in pursuit of your philosophy as the peasant has. What? You both belong to Ireland, the brain and the brawn'.[134] But Stephen rebukes Bloom for the notion that Stephen must be important because he belongs to Ireland, and says instead 'I suspect . . . that Ireland must be important because it belongs to me'. Again, as with the line from *Portrait*, it is customary to read Stephen's retort here as a stubborn declaration of the higher role of the artist above the demands of mere patriotism. But in the retort lies a slyly delineated border between Stephen's sense of belonging, and Bloom's. Bloom reasserts to Stephen the declaration he made in the company of the Citizen – 'I'm . . . as good an Irishman as that rude person' – but Stephen distinguishes between Bloom's sense that he belongs to Ireland, a notion of affiliation or attachment, and his own sense that Ireland belongs to him, which is closer to the idea of immanence and inheritance. Bloom is struck by the rebuke, and feigns that he hasn't heard Stephen properly, to which Stephen, cross-tempered, tells Bloom 'We can't change the country. Let us change the subject'. As Marilyn Reizbaum argues, 'Stephen's sentiments overall reflect a prevalent paradoxical attitude towards Jews, with a peculiarly Irish inflection'.[135] On the one hand, Stephen and others in the novel repeatedly invoke analogies between Jewish and Irish histories, and express solidarity with the oppressed plight of the Jews, but this does not translate into a comfortable sense of common belonging or even accommodation. Stephen, for example, perceives Bloom in visceral, repugnant terms as 'a strange kind of flesh of a different man', when Bloom leads him by the arm.[136] As much as the analogies with Jewish people may serve as instruments in the armoury of Irish nationalist rhetoric, there is an obvious disjuncture between the Jew as analogous figure and the Jew who lives next door, and this has evident implications for the social and cultural possibilities inherent in any 'Nova Hibernia'.

For much of the day that is represented in *Ulysses*, Stephen remains troubled by his early encounter with Mr Deasy and his rabid anti-semitism, but as he sits drinking cocoa in Bloom's kitchen, Stephen's relations with Bloom continue to be marked by similar racial and racist discourses to those expressed more violently by Deasy. When Deasy explains to Stephen that England is dying because it is 'in the hands of the jews', Stephen offers counter-arguments, rational debate, but he has no answer except the beginning of a smile, when Deasy runs after him, and pathetically out of breath, alternately coughing and laughing, tells him that 'Ireland . . . never persecuted the jews . . . [because] she never let them in'.[137] 'Nestor' ends with this scene, providing no response from Stephen, but none is needed. Deasy has been firmly undermined, by his undignified rush to catch Stephen in order to impart an inane racist joke, and by his obvious yet incredible ignorance. The novel proceeds to show or imply the existence of many Jewish Dubliners, and if the year 1904 is remarkable for any reason in Irish history it is for the occurrence in January of that year of the Limerick pogrom against the Jewish community, the single most significant instance of anti-semitic persecution in Ireland. What marks Deasy's anti-semitism, then, is its self-parodic excess, that the man who sees Jews as degenerate is himself shown to be physically unfit, that a man whom the narrative describes as having 'wise shoulders' as he walks away from Stephen is still gesticulating his pleasure at his own racist jibe. This is an early indication in the novel that anti-semitism is the refuge of the pathetic and the ignorant. Yet Stephen seems unable to immune himself from its logic, from its allure, even as he is sharing cocoa with Bloom and swapping titbits of information about Irish and Hebrew culture.[138] When Bloom sings the opening lines of 'Hatikvah' (The Hope), which expresses the aspiration towards a national home in Israel for the Jewish people, Stephen reciprocates, bizarrely, with an anti-semitic ballad, 'Harry Hughes', which tells of a boy who broke the windows of a Jewish neighbour and then was beheaded with a penknife by 'the jew's daughter'.[139]

The contrast between Stephen and Bloom could not be more stark than in this scene. Bloom sings a song of freedom from oppression, of new beginnings, but cannot remember beyond its opening lines. Stephen replies with a song of hatred, revenge, and ritualised murder, a modern version of a thirteenth-century English anti-semitic song, 'Sir Hugh, or The Jew's Daughter', which, as Neil Davison argues, perpetuates a myth of the Jew as blood-thirsty and vampiric.[140] Joyce reinforces the vivacity of the song by providing not just its words but its musical score also.[141] What should we glean from the fact that Stephen recalls this song so vividly, and also elects to sing it to Bloom at this moment, when Bloom has simply encouraged Stephen to respond to his Hebrew song of a coming homeland? Stephen ought to respond with a song expressing Irish national aspirations, or perhaps a song from the Irish diaspora looking towards the hope of a free Ireland, according to the logic of their exchange up to this point. Instead, his song bears within it the traces of a history of racial and religious persecution of the Jews at least 600 years old. Perhaps Stephen is providing a context for understanding 'the hope' expressed in 'Hatikvah', the necessity of the Jewish people finding a homeland in which they will no longer be persecuted. Perhaps he is reiterating, in refracted form through this song, his reply to Deasy's anti-semitism that 'History . . . is a nightmare from which I am trying to awake'.[142] Davison argues that despite 'its inescapable anti-Jewishness, Stephen's "ballad" may have represented to him his own victimization as a son, an outcast, and an Irishman', and that, although this allows Stephen to make a parallel with Bloom's experiences, it 'refuses to accept the specifics of Bloom's life and history as a Jew'.[143] Stephen's song ultimately makes Bloom uncomfortable, not by the thought of the Jew's broken windows (he is relieved, looking at his own unbroken window, that he has not suffered such abuse), but by the thought of what the song implies for the future of his daughter, 'a jew's daughter, all dressed in green'.[144] Such thoughts should not be separated from the fact that Bloom has carried in his pocket for most of the day an advertisement inviting investment in 'Agendath Netaim', a company selling plantations in Palestine for prospective Jewish settlers, which symbolises the choice which faces Bloom of remaining in Ireland or emigrating to a potential Jewish state of Israel.[145]

Stephen's explanation of the song resembles the comparative methodology of Frazer's *The Golden Bough* in extrapolating from the specifics of one story of ritualised murder to an account of 'the victim predestined' who is immolated, unresisting, in a 'secret infidel apartment'.[146] The song is abstracted into a universal rite, adaptable to, and discernible in, the myths and legends of any culture, but also, of course, denuded of its historical and cultural specificity. That Stephen may see himself as 'the victim predestined', and thereby construct a disturbing analogy anticipating his own immolation at the unlikely hands of Bloom as 'secret infidel', goes further to illustrate what is puzzling and troubling about this scene, Stephen's seeming entrapment in anti-semitic discourse, his inability to fly by this particular net. The narrative questions which follow, however, identify Bloom, the 'host', as both 'victim predestined' and 'secret infidel'. Bloom is made aware, as he has been made aware on several occasions in the course of this one day, of the narrow scope within which his Jewishness is a subject of accepted caricature in Irish society. The 'hope' of 'Hatikvah', or indeed the 'hope' of 'Agendath Netaim', seem painfully far-fetched, perhaps, in the light of this awareness, which casts a shadow not simply over his own wearisome struggle to assert his right to be and identify himself as Irish, but also over the future of his daughter.

'Ithaca' raises through a number of notoriously difficult sentences the problem of epistemological authority in relation to racial representations. Although we are told that neither Stephen nor Bloom 'openly allude to their racial difference', it is clear that racial difference is the subtext of their conversation, and to some degree, in condescending ways. Bloom speaks, and is expected to speak, as an authority on all matters Hebrew and Jewish, while Stephen speaks, and is expected to speak, as an authority on all matters Gaelic and Irish. The unspoken racial division between them clearly forces both into adopting positions of cultural authority on what is assumed to be the inner understanding of their respective races. The basis upon which both Bloom and Stephen rest their assumptions about racial difference and the authority to speak is questioned, however, at several points in the chapter:

> What, reduced to their simplest reciprocal form, were Bloom's thoughts about Stephen's thoughts about Bloom [and Bloom's thoughts] about Stephen's thoughts about Bloom's thoughts about Stephen?
>
> He thought that he thought that he was a jew whereas he knew that he knew that he knew that he was not.[147]

The reply only makes full sense when read against the pronouns of the question, in which case it reads: Bloom thought that Stephen thought that Bloom was a jew whereas Bloom knew that Stephen knew that Bloom knew that Stephen was not.[148] This makes Stephen's identity neutral, the unexamined or unproblematic norm, in contrast to Bloom who is, definitively, markedly, 'a jew'. The difference between 'thought' and 'knew', of course, also highlights that being 'a jew' is a matter of suspicion and speculation, hence the many euphemisms and insinuations of Jewishness which appear throughout *Ulysses*. That racial difference is a source of anxiety, or specifically that Bloom's Jewishness is a source of anxiety for both of them, is clear in the way in which the 'fact' of Bloom's Jewishness is filtered through these layers of conjecture.

A similarly difficult grammatical structure is evident in the sentence used to explain why Bloom is sad after Stephen has sung 'Little Harry Hughes': 'He wished that a tale of a deed should be told of a deed not by him should by him not be told'.[149] In trying to make sense of this sentence, it is tempting to add some punctuation, but without it part of the difficulty is recognising which person the pronouns refer to.[150] Bloom is clearly the subject of the first pronoun, and since Stephen has been singing the ballad, we can assume that the last pronoun (indicating the teller of the tale) is most likely Stephen. But does Bloom wish that Stephen would not tell this story of a deed not done by Stephen, or does Bloom wish that Stephen would not tell this story of a deed not done by Bloom? But notice that even here, to make sense of the sentence, the difference between the name and the name of one's race is elided, because it should surely read: '[Bloom] wished that a tale of a deed should be told of a deed not by [his race] should by [Stephen] not be told'. In other words, either Stephen shouldn't tell stories of a deed which was not done by the Irish (that is, it was done by the Jews), or, Stephen shouldn't tell stories of a deed which was not done by the Jews (that is, it was not done at all, but invented to disgrace the Jews). Either Stephen is out of turn for speaking about matters outside his own race, or he is out of turn for perpetuating lies about the deeds of another race. At this point, we might also suspect that Bloom has cause to reflect back with further dismay on Stephen's 'cross-tempered' rebuke about 'belonging' after Bloom had been praising the achievements of Jewish people.

Bloom's wish, however convoluted its expression in the catechistical formula of 'Ithaca', begs the question about the agency involved in Stephen's anti-semitic song, about what forms of authority make it possible or desirable for Stephen to sing this song to Bloom, in Bloom's house, about Bloom's supposed or assumed race. Bloom barely remembers 'Hatikvah', revealing that he is an unlikely spokesman for the aspirations of a race, and in any case we know too much about his own mixed ancestry, multiple baptisms and divided loyalties, his questioning of his religious and racial identities, to find him wholly credible in this role. Stephen, on the other hand, offers words, music, and cultural commentary on 'Little Harry Hughes'. He abounds with authority, taking hold of the representation of other races with consummate ease, yet what seems to trouble Bloom is the source of such authority, the source of this culturally sanctioned power to designate and tell stories about 'the Jew', and, more worryingly for Bloom, 'the jew's daughter'. Even if we understand Stephen's motives as liberal and benign – Davison argues that he is not an anti-semite, for example, just a committed nihilist[151] – his most significant exchanges with Bloom, in 'Eumaeus' and 'Ithaca', find him repeatedly rebuking and rebuffing Bloom's attempts to define himself as both Irish and Jewish, and, as surely as does the Citizen in

'Cyclops', forces Bloom to play the role of outsider, of the homeless Jew for whom Ireland is merely an attachment.

Although Stephen is commonly understood in Joyce criticism to symbolise the hope that Bloom may find a surrogate for his dead son, Rudy, the accumulated meanings and tensions of racial difference in the 'Nostos' part of *Ulysses* seem to militate against this hope, or at least make it more difficult to find credible. Stephen's struggle with racist stereotypes is shown to be in continuity with the slurs and antagonisms which Bloom has suffered and surmounted throughout the day. In Stephen's mind there are echoes and traces of racial fears of 'the Jew' as stranger, as secretive, and as the 'cuckoo'. It is an obvious point to make that *Ulysses* shows the pervasiveness of anti-semitism in Ireland in 1904, even and perhaps especially when Irish experiences are con-ceived as analogous to Jewish experiences, and Stephen is not immune from this. *Ulysses* also shows this anti-semitism to be inseparable from an equally pervasive discourse of racial expression and racist exclusion. Bloom himself is full of thoughts and stereotypes of racial difference, and schemes for racial improvement in physical, social, cultural, and economic terms. Even the physical exercises he learns from Eugen Sandow's book, to fight against the deteriorations of middle age, are intimately linked to discourses of racial improvement, as Vike Plock argues, and specifically to Zionism.[152] His anxieties about physical fitness are also inseparable from his anxieties about endemic, hereditary illness and weaknesses, thoughts of which immediately beset his mind after Stephen has sung his anti-semitic song. His mind abounds with the imagery of Orientalism, fantasies of miscegenation, and dreams of racial salvation, both Irish and Jewish.

The culmination of Bloom's racial imagination comes in the 'Circe' chapter, of course, in the pantomimic fantasy of his elevation to politi-cal glory, and his immediate fall from grace. Whether Bloom is exalted or castigated in this fantasy, holding court or on trial, his successes or failures are attributed to racial causes. J. J. O'Molloy defends Bloom as 'the whitest man I know', for example, and excuses his imagined crimes as merely 'due to a momentary aberration of heredity'.[153] Bloom's admirers when he is appointed Lord Mayor laud his 'classic face', and 'forehead of a thinker', indexing the physiognomic pseudo-science of racial characterisation.[154] So too, when he is persecuted, the accusa-tions against him – 'moral rottenness', 'arch conspirator', 'odious pest', 'bisexually abnormal', or 'womanly man', to take a few examples – either echo familiar anti-semitic tropes, or are explicitly traced to perceived racial and hereditary defects. But 'Circe' is also the chapter of racial cameos and masquerades. Bloom's father appears to him early in the chapter, 'A stooped bearded figure . . . garbed in the long caftan of an elder in Zion and a smoking cap with magenta tassels', and proceeds to speak to Bloom in a caricatured pidgin English: 'Second halfcrown waste money today. I told you not go with drunken goy ever. So. You catch no money'.[155] Later, when accused of misdemeanours, Bloom affects a music-hall parody of a Chinaman – 'Him makee velly muchee fine night'[156] – and Elijah appears in blackface, and addresses God in minstrel dialect: 'Big Brother up there, Mr President, you hear what I done just been saying to you'.[157] These racial masquerades serve to counter the epistemological foundations of the racism behind Bloom's accusers and defenders, revealing through parodic excess that race is all construction and performance. As Len Platt argues, 'black and Oriental identities, in both *Ulysses* . . . and the *Wake*, are specifically and emphatically removed from any pretence of the authentic or "organic" by being placed almost without exception in the world of play-acting and make-believe'.[158] In *Ulysses*, 'Circe' is the chapter that does this most forcefully, condemning the racial stereotypes and slurs which have been suffered by Bloom throughout the day as the figments of some grotesquely pantomimic cultural imagination. Yet Bloom suffers too from this hyperbolic racial imagination, and his dream-vision of 'the new Bloomusalem in the Nova Hibernia of the future', of 'Mixed races and mixed marriage', and the 'Union of all, jew, moslem and gentile', is the point at which his admiring audience begins to turn against him, with a priest, Father Farley, leading the denunciations of Bloom as 'an anythingarian seeking to overthrow our holy faith'.[159] The dissolution of race through inter-racial breeding is Bloom's reformist solution to the problems of a society beset by racist exclusion and discrimination, his solution for a new 'free lay state', but it proves to be the undoing of the brief consensus which greets his imagined rise to power. Even in the realm of fantasy, then, race is shown to be the glue of social cohesion, and there is little hope for those deemed to be racial others that they will be regarded as anything more than tolerated minorities.

The problem with Bloom's vision as a blueprint for a harmonious free Irish state is that for many Irish nationalists there would already be clear resemblances between what Bloom described as a happy future and what they saw as the insufferable present. For example, Professor Eoin MacNeill, the first Minister for Education in the Irish Free State, whose presence at the Irish Race Congress is discussed above, had written in a draft paper on Irish education as early as 1899 or 1900:

> We are not the national brothers and sisters of mild Hindoos, Digger Indians, Cape half-breeds, Maoris, Malays, or any of the other packages in the Imperial White Man's Burden. With such, we can have but a forced and

1922   59

artificial community, of no true benefit to either party. Our greater family can only be Irish – we must be either Irish or outcasts.[160]

Arthur Griffith, the first President of the Irish Free State, whom Joyce greatly admired, according to Ellmann, had railed against doctrines of racial equality, and was notoriously anti-semitic in his editorials in his newspaper, the *United Irishman*.[161] Joyce objected to the anti-semitism, dismayed that Griffith was 'educating the people of Ireland on the old pap of racial hatred', while lauding Griffith's 'Sinn Féin' ideas.[162] MacNeill's solution to what he saw as the dilution of the Irish race inherent in its colonial status was an education system which taught 'Our youth . . . to *feel* their position in the nation, the greater family, to feel that the interests of the greater family are their own interests also'.[163] Deasy impresses the same point about racial belonging upon Stephen when he condenses the meaning of Englishness into the phrase, 'I paid my way': 'Can you feel that? *I owe nothing*. Can you?'[164] Stephen confesses that he cannot, which proves Deasy's point about racial intuition, but as we saw earlier, Stephen later impresses upon Bloom a similar sense of the 'inwit' of racial belonging. That Bloom, already deemed an unwanted outsider, a parasite or cuckoo in the sacred homeland of the Irish race, should express a vision of a cosmopolitan, racially mixed Ireland, then, would merely confirm his exclusion from the 'inner understanding' of the race.

In *Ulysses*, race is repeatedly figured as a secret. If you don't know the secret, or you don't *feel* the secret, then you are not of the race. When Stephen says in *Portrait* that he desires to forge this knowledge in his soul, or when MacNeill says that Irish youth must be taught to feel it, they do not mean that the secret can be told or learned *ab initio*: they mean that the secret can be remembered, or rekindled, as if it is lying dormant awaiting the spark of racial consciousness. What condemns Bloom, and condemns him specifically as an Irish Jew, is that his life and his history are precisely concerned with the sharing of secrets, that is with secrets which are no longer secret. From his family's change of name, to his wife's affair with Blazes Boylan, Bloom's secrets are no longer secret: even his sexual secrets are paraded and scrutinised in the fantasy scenes in 'Circe'. Bloom symbolises, in other words, the erasure of secrecy. If he succeeds as an Irish Jew, as an 'anythingarian' or 'half and half', he will give the lie to the secrecy of race, to the idea of race as an inner understanding beyond the ken of anyone not enclosed within its skin. This is why, in his many racially defined encounters through the day, he is expected to uphold the myth of secrecy, to embody secrecy, conspiracy, and forbidden knowledge, as a presumed Jew and a suspected Mason.[165] In the famous episode in which Lyons mistakenly believes Bloom has given him a betting tip for the horse, 'Throwaway', for example, the misunderstanding arises because, somehow, Lyons expects Bloom to be secretive, covert, when Bloom is anything but. Lyons borrows Bloom's newspaper to view the list of horses in the Ascot Gold Cup, but Bloom tells him to keep it:

> – I was just going to throw it away, Mr Bloom said.
> Bantam Lyons raised his eyes suddenly and leered weakly.
> – What's that? his sharp voice said.
> – I say you can keep it, Mr Bloom answered. I was going to throw it away
> that moment.
> Bantam Lyons doubted an instant, leering: then thrust the outspread sheets
> back on Mr Bloom's arms.
> – I'll risk it, he said. Here, thanks.[166]

The mistaken idea that Bloom has tipped the horse to win the cup, which it duly does, precipitates the Citizen's violent attack on Bloom in 'Cyclops' for his supposed secrecy about the money he is assumed to have won, a supposition which reinforces the Citizen's stereotype of Jewish pecuniary meanness. What is puzzling about this scene, however, is why Lyons assumes that if Bloom had a betting tip to give him, he would do it so furtively. We can blame the unlikely coincidence of Bloom's phrase 'throw it away' coming at the same time as Lyons spots the horse's name, 'Throwaway', in the paper for this misunderstanding and its consequences, but it is not the only culpable source. Lyons expects Bloom as a Jewish Mason to harbour secrets, to possess secret knowledge, and if generous enough to share it, to communicate it secretively. Thus, 'I'll risk it' denotes a leap of inter-racial faith, trusting that Jewish intuition might be worth a bet. Lyons, of course, doesn't follow through, fails to make the bet, and when the horse wins, he damns Bloom twice over, for possessing this suspect racial intuition in the first place, and then concealing the fact of his winnings. Bloom, meanwhile, has no secret to hide on either count.

This too comes to light in 'Ithaca', when Bloom becomes aware of the Gold Cup result, and reflects on the coincidental premonition of this win in his encounter with Lyons. What strikes Bloom as an amazing instance of serendipity has merely confirmed Lyons and the Citizen in their implacable devotion to racial determinism. In the retrospective account in 'Ithaca' of his meeting with Lyons, Bloom is described as 'bearing in his arms the secret of the race, graven in the language of prediction'.[167] It is a deliberately ambivalent phrase which refers to the newspaper in Bloom's arms either, through Lyon's eyes, as the bearer of Jewish racial intuition, or, as the newspaper in question is the *Freeman's Journal and National Press*, perhaps the reference is a faintly ironic allusion to the newspaper as bearing 'the secret of the race'. The ambivalence about which race is at issue, and the dismissal of racial conspiracies of Jewish secrecy and intuition, clearly exposes the lie of racial conscience for what it is, an artificial instrument of social cohesion which serves ultimately to exclude and misrepresent the thoroughly amenable Bloom.

Andrew Gibson argues that a recurrent problem in Joyce criticism is 'its reluctance to think Jews and Irish together', and rightly insists that '[Joyce's] Jew is a historically specific Irishman'.[168] Gibson refocuses the debate about Joyce's Jewish theme on the immediate political contexts in 1904 in which the Irish-Jewish analogy was a controversial and urgent source of disagreement between nationalist and unionist intellectuals. In presenting *Ulysses* as an intervention in such debates, however, Gibson undervalues the historical specificity of when *Ulysses* was written and published. As the novel itself makes clear, most notably in Molly's allusion to Griffith, the political debates which preoccupied Ireland in 1904 had altered radically by the time Joyce was preparing the final drafts of *Ulysses*. *Ulysses*, I would argue, does not direct our attention repeatedly to the bygone issues of whether nationalists or unionists were more likely to be anti-semitic. Instead, it is already anticipating the instrumentalisation of racial difference within the political and cultural institutions of the new Irish state. Joyce constantly brings us back to the future, to the state-to-come, as a horizon of constraint upon the hope and possibility which Bloom undoubtedly symbolises.

'For Joyce the creation of the Irish Free State was the culmination of his hopes', wrote Richard Ellmann.[169] The coincidence of the creation of the Free State and the publication of *Ulysses* was also observed at the time: Valery Larbaud's famous lecture on *Ulysses* in December 1921 made the point that 'Joyce has given young Ireland "an artistic physiognomy, an intellectual identity"'.[170] Yet, when *Ulysses* was published, Joyce urged his publisher Sylvia Beach to send copies of the book and notices of its publication to Ireland as soon as possible, 'as with a new Irish postmaster general and a vigilance committee in clerical hands you never know from one day to the next what may occur'.[171] It is the latter note of wariness concerning the prescriptive racial forms a state defined by Gaelic Catholic nationalism would take which characterises much of *Ulysses*, and circumscribes the dormant potential for openness and plurality which Bloom represents. In 'Ithaca', as Stephen is about to take his leave from Bloom, Bloom considers the 'irreparability of the past', and they both find common ground in silently contemplating the stars, which may be interpreted either as a gesture towards the insignificance of human differences when compared with celestial constellations, or as a dismal resignation to the fact that they have failed to find common ground in terrestrial matters.[172] But their silence, and their awkward regard of 'the reciprocal flesh of theirhisnothis fellowfaces', as they prepare to part are clear signs of the difficulty of any future relationship.[173] Enda Duffy argues that *Ulysses* presents us with an image of 'a single community', and 'works to present this community in the way in which the new nation will envision it', but if this is the case, the vision of the new nation is far from a hopeful one for Bloom.[174] What 'Ithaca' makes clear is that Bloom and Stephen are divided, seemingly irreparably, by race and racism. Stephen's inability to move beyond the constraints of racial discourse does not augur well for the possibility of thinking 'Jews and Irish together'. Stephen even appears to play the 'Jew's Harp' as he walks away from Bloom's house, which as Duffy suggests, is difficult to interpret as anything other than a taunt.[175] But after Stephen leaves, Bloom returns to his kitchen, and there, in an elaborate ritual fashion, he burns the 'Agendath Netaim' prospectus, thus symbolising his refusal to relinquish his rightful claim to be both Irish and Jewish, his resilient defiance of the hardening logic of the racial state-to-come. Bloom's 'homecoming' is not complete, however, until Molly, herself an exemplar of the mixture of races which Bloom eulogises in 'Circe', reaffirms her desire for Bloom.[176] She does so while recalling memories of when 'he asked me to say yes', that 'I was thinking of so many things he didn't know of', the streets of her remembered childhood in Gibraltar filled with 'the Greeks and the jews and the Arabs and the devil knows who else from all ends of Europe'.[177] It is under this sign of the post-racial community, of the romance of hybridity, that Molly and Bloom together exemplify the affirmation of hope and resilience.

Coda: The Irish Jew

'We are still learning to be James Joyce's contemporaries', wrote Richard Ellmann at the beginning of his biography, and never more so, I would aver, than when it comes to reading Joyce's work in relation to its historical contexts, especially reading *Ulysses* in relation to the moment of its production in 1922.[178] Cormac Ó Gráda's work on the Jewish community during Joyce's time has shown that Bloom bears little relation to the historical specificities of that community, and concludes that 'Joyce knew less of Jewish Dublin before he left in 1904 than his many interpreters suppose'.[179] As an Irish Jew of Hungarian parentage, Bloom would have been an outsider to the Dublin Jewish community, most of whom had come from a small number of villages in north-western Lithuania, stayed close together in what came to be known as 'Little Jerusalem' in southside Dublin, and would have found it difficult to accept Bloom for his mixed-faith parentage, for his atheism, and for 'marrying out' to a non-Jew. Ó Gráda even wonders if Bloom and the Lithuanian Jews would have been able to communicate in the 'nocturnal conversations' Joyce imagines, since Bloom appears to have just a smattering of Yiddish, and the new immigrants in 'Little Jerusalem' may only have had sufficient English to get by.[180] Joyce had no known communication with anyone from the Lithuanian Jewish community in Dublin, and gleaned most of his information regarding Dublin Jewry from *Thom's Directory*. Ó Gráda finds that whereas *Ulysses* is 'a rich source for the historian of Ireland and its capital city . . . . The same cannot be said for [Joyce's] account of Irish Jewry'.[181] One has to conclude from this that Joyce was less interested in the socio-economic and cultural specificities of life for the Dublin Jewish community than he was in the relative position this community occupied as the racial scapegoat of the emergent discourses of institutional nationalism.

As such, then, *Ulysses* is more revealing about anti-semitism, and the particular agencies and discourses which give expression and legitimacy to anti-semitism, than it is about the social practices and histories of Irish Jewry. Stephen's racial taunts and anxieties are there not just to indicate that Bloom commands the greater empathy of his author, but to advertise the degree to which Bloom is already heavily pre-figured in Irish culture. However mixed his racial ancestry, however wavering his national loyalties, however loose his religious observances and beliefs, he is marked and figured as a Jew, with all the apparently fixed historical, religious and cultural associations this figuration has in Ireland and further afield in the early twentieth century. Joyce's inaccuracies in presenting a Dublin Jew of 1904 also reveal, I would suggest, that he was more attuned to the strategic situation of Jewish people in Ireland as the momentum towards a national state gathered pace. Ó Gráda records that most Irish Jews in 1904 were likely to be loyalist, for example: Bloom's 'Sinn Féin' sympathies represent an acknowledgement of the later, post-1916 hegemony of the national independence movement, with Griffith (ironically known for his anti-semitism as much as his nationalism) described by Bloom as 'the coming man'. Had Bloom been depicted as a loyalist, devoted to King and Empire, perhaps the Citizen's reaction to him would be fully explicable (if not excusable) in terms of anti-colonial politics. Instead, Bloom's acceptance of the nationalist cause, and his declaration of Irish nationality, allow us to see anti-semitism and racism as constitutive factors in the discourses of Irish cultural nationalism, and constitutive factors in the formation of the Irish Free State. The 'leave us alone' dictum of the Sinn Féin philosophy is shown to be addressed not just to the British Empire, but to anyone not circumscribed as 'us'. For Joyce, the Irish Jew was the paradigmatic figure in 1922 of that process of exclusion, and Bloom may be, to borrow Yeats's phrase, one of those 'befitting emblems of adversity' in the new state.

Joyce was not alone in representing the Irish Jew in figurative terms. Just six weeks prior to the publication of *Ulysses* in Paris, John MacDonagh's comedy, *The Irish Jew*, opened at the Empire theatre in Dublin, on 12 December 1921. The review of the following day in the *Irish Independent* records its popularity with the audience,[182] and it continued to perform through much of 1922, billed as 'Easily the most successful comedy presented on the Irish Stage during the present generation',[183] was revived in 1923 at the Queen's Theatre, billed simply as 'Ireland's greatest comedy', and revived again at the Olympia (the new name for the Empire) in 1926.[184] The American actor and producer, Morris Waxman, bought the US rights to the play and starred in the central role when the play was performed in Detroit in September 1923. It may also have been performed in New York at some point in the early to mid-1920s.[185] No copy of the play has been found, and it was never published (unlike some of MacDonagh's subsequent plays which were published in the *Dublin Magazine*), so the account given of the play below is based solely upon newspaper reviews and programme notes.[186]

The titular central character of *The Irish Jew* is Abraham Golder, a Jewish Lord Mayor of Dublin, who is a devoted nationalist. He replaces a portrait of Disraeli with one of Robert Emmet in the reception room of the Mansion House, and learns to recite Emmet's 'Speech from the Dock' for his inaugural Mayoral banquet, at which he intends to wear a copy of Emmet's uniform.[187] The plot concerns a swindle prior to 1916 by some of the councillors of the Dublin Corporation to sell a site for a National Picture Gallery – as it happens a site owned as a cinema house by the Mayor – but they are 'defeated by the honesty of the Lord Mayor, the Jew of the title, a Hebrew without blemish, who defies and studies the guile of Christian corporators'.[188] The Mayor's devotion to Irish nationalism is unwelcome, perhaps like Bloom's in *Ulysses*, for it seems that 'by following in the footsteps of the great Irish martyrs, [he] has incurred the hostility of the "Nationalists" in the council, whose agents burn down the picture palace and plot to drive him out of the chair'.[189] 'He is pressed on the one hand by party intriguers using various popular cries, and on the other by the offer of a title, to follow different courses, but resists all influences and shows a strength of mind which the audience might not be inclined to suspect on its first experience of him'.[190] Much of the action is farcical, showing the Mayor's determined efforts to outwit his opponents, and in the fourth and final act, 'his victory over trickery is complete, though it might be remarked that the finale is a little beyond what might be expected from even the most extravagant humorous critic'.[191]

The reviews lavished high praise on the play, without exception, both for its entertainment value as a popular farce, and for the quality of its acting. The cast for the first Dublin production included Paul Farrell as Abraham Golder, Harry O'Donovan as the villain Alderman Barry, Jimmy O'Dea as Councillor Woods, and Frank Fay as Alderman Sir Alfred Peel. It was a strong cast which drew widespread applause and acclaim, and its revivals in Ireland, and press interviews with the author, reveal that it remained high in public esteem.[192] MacDonagh himself was a pioneer to some extent, especially in film-making and radio productions, but when he died in 1961, he received a short obituary in *The Irish Times* which barely mentions his successes as a playwright.[193] The fact that both Joyce and MacDonagh were working on literary representations of an Irish Jew, that both entertain the fiction of a Jewish Lord Mayor of Dublin (albeit Bloom does so in the fantasy world of 'Circe'), and that both characters are victims of nationalist violence and abuse despite their own nationalist sympathies who nevertheless triumph with resilience by the end, should alert us to the wider significance of the Irish Jew in the cultural contexts of Ireland in the long 1922. Bloom and Golder would obviously have to agree to disagree on the iconography of Robert Emmet, for whom Bloom, it should be recalled, has his own irreverent gesture, but the fact that Emmet figures largely in both texts is significant, especially given the Messianic lines for which Emmet's speech is most noted: 'When my country takes her place among the nations of the earth, then, and not till then, let my epitaph be written. I have done'.[194]

MacDonagh's own explanations for why he created the character of Golder, the Irish Jew, are worth noting in reflecting on the significance of the racial figuration of Irish Jewry on the eve of Irish independence. In an interview published in advance of the Dublin production, MacDonagh said 'I hope *The Irish Jew* will please all and offend none – especially our Jewish friends. As a matter of fact, I anticipated a perceptible expansion of Jewish chests, because the Jew I drew is more Irish than at least some of the Irish themselves'.[195] In Detroit, where MacDonagh attended the opening performance, he also said in interview, 'If this theme can make one Irishman ashamed to have an Irish

Jew accomplish what the Irishman should have done, then the play has achieved its purpose'.[196] In this complicated distinction between degrees of Irishness, in which the Jew can be more Irish than the Irish, but still not yet an Irishman, the figure of the Irish Jew clearly served as a means of co-opting the racial other into the galvanisation of national belonging. The specificities of Golder's Jewishness matter little, other than for the comic stereotypes of Jewishness meant to keep the audience laughing. Instead, any racial other will do, just as Andrew Gibson reminds us of Joyce's reply to Jacques Mercanton as to why Bloom was Jewish: 'Yes because only a foreigner would do. The Jews were foreigners at that time in Dublin'.[197] The opening scene of *The Irish Jew*, in which Golder replaces the portrait of Disraeli with one of Emmet, speaks volumes about the cultural politics of the play. Golder, it seems, has necessarily to renounce his identification with Jewishness (Disraeli was the first person of Jewish parentage to become Prime Minister of Great Britain, although he had been baptised an Anglican when he was thirteen), in order to affirm his allegiance to Ireland through the figure of Emmet. As Disraeli was also the political rival of Gladstone and the Liberal Party, which had attempted to legislate for Home Rule in Ireland, the symbolism of this switch of portraits is doubly marked with racial and national significance. Moreover, the fact that Golder will inaugurate his own Mayoral persona in the copied uniform of Emmet, and speaking Emmet's words, suggest in this context that Golder can only show his Irishness through an elaborate, and farcical, masquerade.

While Joyce and MacDonagh were working with strategic figurations of Jewishness in relation to nationalist discourses, there were also important writings produced by Jewish intellectuals, which tell their own stories about the relationship between Jewish citizens and the emergent state. The Chief Rabbi of Dublin, later Chief Rabbi of the Irish Free State, Isaac Herzog, whose son, Chaim Herzog, would become President of Israel, wrote a brief account of the 'origin and citizen aims' of the Jewish community in Ireland in Fitz-Gerald's *The Voice of Ireland*. As well as recalling the proud history of the small Jewish communities in Ireland since the seventeenth century, and the high offices attained by Irish Jews, Herzog also used his short essay to assert both the rights and responsibilities of Jews in Ireland:

> Jews have proved themselves throughout history, wherever they have been accorded the rights of man, devoted and patriotic citizens of their adopted country, contributing to progress along all lines. And the Jews of Ireland will, in common with their Christian fellow citizens – with whom they are on the friendliest of terms – do everything in their power for the regeneration of the land which they cherish and love.[198]

Herzog was articulating the complex negotiation of identities and loyalties in a multi-racial state for a Jewish community proud to identify itself as racially distinct, deserving of equal rights within the law, and proud to pledge its allegiance as a community to the civic body of the Irish state. At the same time as Herzog was voicing the dedication of Irish Jews to the new state, Hannah Berman was writing fictional stories about the Lithuanian Jewish communities from which her family had come to Ireland. She had already published her much regarded novel, *Melutovna*, in 1913.[199] In the first issue of the *Dublin Magazine*, in August 1923, Berman published a short story, 'The Charity Box', about the desperate struggle to survive famine, war, and eviction in the poor villages of Lithuania. The story opens with a horribly prescient and implacably historical scene of Jewish refugees, driven out of their villages and on to a huddled train, the air 'thick with the stench of hundreds of people lying on top of one another – sighing, groaning, wailing, cursing, and praying', and the people 'no longer horrified by the dead bodies which we had not the strength to throw out of the windows'.[200] The narrator is both misogynist and anti-semitic, and shows himself to be callously indifferent to the suffering relayed to him by an old Jew on the train, who has attempted to rob a charity box in order to feed his wife and children. By the end of the story, the old man is sobbing, wanting to return home to his wife and children, and to repent to his community for his attempted crime, if only he can escape from the train. 'I turned away in disgust from the strange jew, who was, after all, only a tearful old woman', concludes the narrator, who has addressed the old man as 'Mr Jew' throughout their conversation.[201] The illustration to the story provided by the Irish-Jewish artist, Harry Kernoff, shows emaciated, skeletal bodies huddled, miserable, in a dark space which could be a train, or a workhouse. 'The Charity Box' juxtaposes a familiar story and image of the survivors of famine and oppression, then, with a narrator who although he shares the same murderous train journey, and presumably similar circumstances, as those around him, shows cruel disregard for the suffering of others. It makes available in a fledgling Irish magazine a story of suffering analogous to Irish histories of famine and oppression, while showing the bitter irony of a shared history which is not shared, an analogy which seems only to work in one direction. It offers, then, a vital corrective to the discourses of Irish nationalism which were content to raise analogies with the histories of other peoples which strengthened the causes of Irish independence, but which spectacularly failed to achieve a mutual understanding of what it meant to have shared histories, much less a shared future.

Notes

1. Interestingly, a black Virginian man is represented in the advertisement of another Dublin cigarette manufacturer, Goodbodys, which appeared on the front page of the *Freeman's Journal*, 2 May 1922. He is depicted holding a cigarette, under the caption: 'A Genuine Virginian, Made in Dublin'. This further develops the story as told in the *Golden Blush* advertisement of Irish manufacturing industries taking foreign raw materials (produced by black labour), and here selling their products back to 'genuine Virginians'.
2. Robert Emmet, 'Speech from the Dock', *Field Day Anthology of Irish Writing, Vol.1*, ed. Seamus Deane, pp. 933–9.
3. Steve Garner, *Racism in the Irish Experience*, p. 138.
4. Tom Garvin, *1922*, p. 2.
5. Robert Welch (ed.), *The Oxford Companion to Irish Literature*, p. 313.
6. Two studies to date have taken 1922 as a key year in which literature and culture were redefined by intellectual 'masterworks' – Michael North's *Reading 1922* and Marc Manganaro's *Culture, 1922*.
7. Terence Brown, 'Ireland, Modernism and the 1930s', in Patricia Coughlan and Alex Davis, eds, *Modernism and Ireland*, p. 24.
8. Fredric Jameson, *Marxism and Form*, p. 313.
9. 'Press Notice: Irish Race Congress, January 19th', Eamon de Valera Papers, UCD Archives, P150/1603.
10. David Theo Goldberg, *Racist Culture*, p. 149.
11. Michael North, 'Virtual Histories', p. 408.
12. Ronit Lentin, 'Ireland: Racial State and Crisis Racism', pp. 610–27.
13. James Joyce, *Ulysses: The 1922 Text*, ed. Jeri Johnson, p. 317. I am using this edition of *Ulysses*, which reprints in facsimile copy no. 785 of the first edition of the novel, first to observe the primary principles of an historical approach to the text. Johnson's facsimile edition obviously presents the text as its few readers in 1922 would have had available to them. Second, as several textual critics have shown, the 1922 text, although it contains an estimated 2,000 errors, is no less reliable than subsequent editions, which have either introduced more errors than they corrected, or have been controversial in their choice of corrections. Gabler's edition, for example, which is widely used, returned to pre-1922 extant manuscript sources and autographed corrections as a 'continuous copy-text', a practice which is by no means common among textual scholars.
14. Lentin, 'Ireland: Racial State and Crisis Racism', p. 620.
15. Michel Foucault, *The Hermeneutics of the Subject*, p. 9.
16. See Lentin and McVeigh, *After Optimism?*
17. Bryan Fanning, 'Book Reviews', pp. 943–4. See Goldberg, *The Racial State*.
18. Bryan Fanning, *Racism and Social Change in the Republic of Ireland*, especially chapters 3 and 4, pp. 30–86.
19. Garvin, *1922*, pp. 151–2; Jeffrey Prager, *Building Democracy in Ireland*, p. 31.
20. Vincent J. Cheng, *Joyce, Race and Empire*, p. 291.

21. 'Themax Boot Polish: 1922 – Ireland's Year of Brightness', *Irish Independent*, 2 January 1922, p. 1: 'Emerging from the blackness and gloom of a long night of agony and despair Ireland stands to-day on the threshold of a bright and glorious future – a future in which all her sons and daughters may share with pride and hope. The makers of Themax polishes have pleasure in announcing, at this juncture, that at last after many experiments they have produced a boot polish which is absolutely perfect'.

22. George Russell (Æ), *The Interpreters*. For the non-fictional prose in which Russell articulates similar views to the character of Lavelle in *The Interpreters*, see George Russell (Æ), *The Inner and the Outer Ireland* and 'Ireland: Past and Future', in *The Voice of Ireland*, ed. W. G. Fitz-Gerald, pp. 86–92.

23. Bernard Shaw, *Back to Methuselah*, passim.

24. *The Voice of Ireland*, ed. Fitz-Gerald, passim.

25. W. B. Yeats, *Autobiographies*, p. 381.

26. Lady Gregory uses this metaphor indeed in a letter to Yeats dated 7 September 1921: 'Some how all the work you & I & Hugh & Hyde & others have done seems to be worth so much more now that independence is in sight – it is a sort of deposit account to the credit of the country'. Quoted in Roy Foster, *W.B. Yeats: A Life, II: The Arch-Poet*, p. 204.

27. Yeats, *Autobiographies*, pp. 299–300.

28. Ibid., pp. 190, 194.

29. Ibid., p. 194. Later, for example, he praises Lady Gregory's two volumes of Irish heroic tales: 'They contain our ancient literature, are something better than our *Mabinogion*, and almost our *Morte d'Arthur*' (pp. 380–1).

30. Ibid., p. 372.

31. Ibid., p. 263. Yeats switches between the terms 'race' and 'nation', but the terms seem interchangeable for Yeats, as for other Irish writers at the time.

32. Ibid., p. 355.

33. D. P. Moran, *The Philosophy of Irish Ireland*, pp. 43, 34.

34. P. J. Mathews, *Revival*, p. 98.

35. Foster, *W.B. Yeats: A Life, II*, p. 201.

36. Ibid., p. 210.

37. Ibid., p. 223.

38. 'Meditations' was first published as seven poems, rather than seven sections of one poem, in *The Dial*, 74.1 (January 1923), pp. 50–6.

39. W. B. Yeats, *Yeats's Poems*, p. 309.

40. Ibid., p. 310.

41. Ibid., p. 311.

42. Ibid., p. 309.

43. Ibid., p. 311.

44. Marjorie Howes, *Yeats's Nations*, pp. 120–30.

45. Yeats, *Yeats's Poems*, p. 314.

46. Ibid., p. 310.

47. Yeats, *Autobiographies*, p. 363.

48. Howes, *Yeats's Nations*, p. 121.
49. Yeats, *Autobiographies*, p. 267.
50. Goldberg, *Racist Culture*, p. 83.
51. Michael Collins, 'Clearing the Road: An Essay in Practical Politics', in *The Voice of Ireland*, ed. Fitz-Gerald, p. 43.
52. Michael Collins, *The Path to Freedom*, p. 98.
53. Ibid., p. 97.
54. Ibid., p. 101.
55. Ibid., p. 103.
56. See *Constitution of the Irish Free State (Saorstát Eireann) Act, 1922, Acts of the Oireachtas*, 1 (1922). This is not to say that the debates surrounding notions of Irish citizenship were free from racial connotations. Mary Daly cites an example from ongoing negotiations between the Free State and the British governments in December 1923 in which the Irish Minister for External Affairs, Desmond FitzGerald, argued against what the Anglo-Irish Treaty referred to as the 'common citizenship' of the British Commonwealth, objecting to the capaciousness of the term 'British Subject' which 'included everyone from Mr Baldwin [the British Prime Minister] to an undiscovered savage in British Guiana'. The struggle of the Irish government throughout the 1920s to gain permission to have passports which made particular reference to the bearer being an Irish citizen and not just a British subject may be seen partially, therefore, not just as a consequence of nationalist arguments about independent citizenship, but as a consequence of Irish anxieties about being indistinguishable constitutionally and politically from every 'undiscovered savage' in the British empire. See Mary Daly, 'Irish Nationality and Citizenship Since 1922', p. 380.
57. See Garvin, *1922*, p. 133, and Prager, *Building Democracy in Ireland*, p. 59.
58. Tim Pat Coogan, *Michael Collins*, p. 312.
59. Collins's own ambiguous commitment to democracy is discussed at some length in John M. Regan's important study, *The Irish Counter-Revolution, 1921–1936*. Regan's book examines the anti-democratic tendencies within the conservative consolidation of the new state.
60. Goldberg, *The Racial State*, p. 16.
61. Seumas MacManus, *The Story of the Irish Race*, p. xi.
62. Ibid., p. 1.
63. Ibid., p. 399.
64. Ibid., p. 685.
65. Paul Gilroy, *Small Acts*, p. 72.
66. Goldberg, *The Racial State*, p. 33.
67. See Garvin, *1922*, passim.
68. Goldberg, *The Racial State*, p. 161.
69. Giorgio Agamben, *Homo Sacer*, pp. 39–48.
70. Collins's constitution was forced to acknowledge the King as the 'constituting power' as part of the treaty, despite all attempts to avoid this, but a presumed and mythologised sense of racial sovereignty underpinned the coming-to-being of the new state, and it is only in the 1937 constitution, the preamble of which declares that 'We, the people of Éire . . . give to

ourselves this constitution', that the paradoxical relationship between constituting power and constituted power can be seen.

71. See Gerard Keown, 'The Irish Race Conference, 1922, Reconsidered', pp. 365–76; Dermot Keogh, 'The Treaty Split and the Paris Irish Race Convention, 1922', pp. 165–70; T. K. Daniel, 'The Scholars and the Saboteurs: The Wrecking of a South African Irish Scheme, Paris 1922', pp. 162–75; and Richard Davis, *The Self-Determination of Ireland Leagues and the Irish Race Convention in Paris, 1921–1922*.

72. Davis, *The Self-Determination of Ireland Leagues*, p. 100.

73. Ibid., p. 88.

74. Eoin MacNeill Papers, UCD Archives, LA1/F/235.

75. Michael Hayes Papers, UCD Archives, P53/143. This document can also be found in the National Archives of Ireland as NAI DFA ES Box 11, File 77, and is reprinted in Ronan Fanning et al., eds, *Documents on Irish Foreign Policy, Vol.1: 1919–1922*, pp. 387–90.

76. Michael Hayes Papers, UCD Archives, P53/145.

77. Michael Hayes Papers, UCD Archives, P53/151.

78. That the idea originated in South Africa seems in itself significant, as a number of recent commentators have identified strong associations between Irish nationalists and South Africa, not just during the Boer War, but in the years immediately preceding independence in 1922. These associations are particularly problematic for those who wish to see Irish independence as the precursor to black and Indian liberation movements later in the twentieth century. See Piaras MacÉinrí, '"A Slice of Africa"', pp. 257–74.

79. *The Republic*, 12 March 1921. Quoted in Keown, 'The Irish Race Conference, 1922, Reconsidered', p. 365.

80. Davis, *The Self-Determination of Ireland Leagues*, p. 95.

81. Minutes of the Irish Race Congress, Eamon de Valera Papers, UCD Archives, P150/1603.

82. 'Press Notice: Irish Race Congress, January 19th', Eamon de Valera Papers, UCD Archives, P150/1603.

83. 'Press Notice: Irish Race Congress, January 2_', Eamon de Valera Papers, UCD Archives, P150/1603. It is unclear from the incomplete date given on the notice whether this was issued on 2 January, prior to the Congress, or sometime from 20 to 29 January, during or after the Congress.

84. 'Reviving Ancient Festival', Eamon de Valera Papers, UCD Archives, P150/1603. This document is undated, but it refers to replies to invitations to the Irish Race Congress, although the Congress has evidently not yet taken place, which would suggest sometime in late 1921, or the early weeks of January 1922.

85. T. H. Nally, *The Aonac Tailteann and the Tailteann Games*, p. 21.

86. 'Irish Race Congress' [Interview with Kathleen Hughes], *Freeman's Journal*, 12 January 1922, p. 6.

87. Minutes of the Irish Race Congress, Eamon de Valera Papers, UCD Archives, P150/1603.

88. 'Irish Race Congress', *Irish Independent*, 21 January 1922, p. 5; 'Irish Race Congress', *Meath Chronicle*, 28 January 1922, p. 6.

89. 'Irish Race Congress', *Southern Star*, 28 January 1922 [no page number].

90. Ibid.
91. Minutes of the Irish Race Congress, Eamon de Valera Papers, UCD Archives, P150/1603.
92. Ibid.
93. Ibid.
94. The notes of Yeats's lecture are contained in Minutes of the Irish Race Congress, Eamon de Valera Papers, UCD Archives, P150/1603. See Foster, *W.B. Yeats: A Life, II*, pp. 206–7.
95. Both plays were performed by the Dramatic Section of the Irish Club in Paris at the Salle Hoche on Friday 27 January.
96. MacNeill's lecture is summarised in Minutes of the Irish Race Congress, Eamon de Valera Papers, UCD Archives, P150/1603. The translation quoted here is that adopted by the Irish Race Congress and Fine Gaedeal. MacNeill's own translation is slightly different: 'Greater than can be told in every age has been God's design for "this grand Ireland"'.
97. Hyde's lecture is recorded in Minutes of the Irish Race Congress, Eamon de Valera Papers, UCD Archives, P150/1603.
98. Minutes of the Irish Race Congress, Eamon de Valera Papers, UCD Archives, P150/1603.
99. Davis, *The Self-Determination of Ireland Leagues*, p. 101.
100. Ibid., p. 99.
101. Goldberg, *Racist Culture*, p. 53.
102. 'Industrial Future in Ireland', *Irish Independent*, 27 January 1922, p. 5.
103. Ibid., p. 5.
104. Eoin MacNeill Papers, UCD Archives, LA1/F/235.
105. Eamon de Valera Papers, UCD Archives, P150/1603.
106. It is not certain if there was any relation between these practical suggestions and the appearance in January 1922 of the first and apparently only issue of a journal entitled, *Erin, and Greater Ireland: The Journal of the Irish Race*, which aimed to collect a register 'of the Race of Erin'. The editorial expressed pride in the possibility that the '50,000,000 people of the race of Erin now alive can exercise great power and influence'. The journal was edited by Diarmait MacConroi, and published in London.
107. 'Fine Gaedeal: The Irish Race' manifesto, 1922. Mary MacSwiney Papers, UCD Archives, P48a/356.
108. Foster, *W.B. Yeats: A Life, II*, p. 207.
109. Eamon de Valera Papers, UCD Archives, P150/1605.
110. John Turpin, 'Visual Culture and Catholicism in the Irish Free State, 1922–1949', p. 73.
111. Richard Ellmann, *James Joyce*, p. 525. For the reference to the Duc de Tetuan, see *Ulysses*, p. 316.
112. Ellmann, *James Joyce*, p. 523.
113. James Joyce, *Selected Letters of James Joyce*, p. 271.
114. Ellmann, *James Joyce*, p. 527.
115. Joyce also noted this Italian Lord Mayor of Dublin 'merely as a curiosity' for his Triestine audience in his lecture, 'Ireland, Island of Saints and Sages', given in April 1907, and collected in James Joyce, *The Critical Writings of James Joyce*, p. 163.
116. Joyce, *Ulysses*, p. 321.

117. Ibid., p. 700.

118. Richard Ellmann, *The Consciousness of Joyce*, p. 88.

119. Ibid., pp. 3, 732. This reading of *Ulysses* as inhabiting a future anterior space, as looking forward to the 'state-to-come', overlaps thematically with Paul K. Saint-Amour's brilliant reading of the novel's 'proleptic orientation' towards nuclear catastrophe: see 'Bombing and the Symptom', pp. 59–82.

120. Ellmann, *The Consciousness of Joyce*, p. 89.

121. See Seamus Deane, *Celtic Revivals*, Declan Kiberd, *Inventing Ireland*, Enda Duffy, *The Subaltern Ulysses*, and Emer Nolan, *James Joyce and Nationalism*.

122. See Ira B. Nadel, *Joyce and the Jews*, Neil R. Davison, *James Joyce, Ulysses, and the Construction of Jewish Identity*, and Marilyn Reizbaum, *James Joyce's Judaic Other*.

123. See Dermot Keogh, *Jews in Twentieth-Century Ireland*, Dermot Keogh and Andrew McCarthy, *Limerick Boycott 1904*, Cormac Ó Gráda, *Jewish Ireland in the Age of Joyce*, and Cormac Ó Gráda, 'Lost in Little Jerusalem', pp. 17–26.

124. See Vincent J. Cheng, *Joyce, Race, and Empire* and Len Platt, *Joyce, Race and Finnegans Wake*.

125. Platt, *Joyce, Race and Finnegans Wake*, p. 7.

126. Nadel, *Joyce and the Jews*, p. 56. Nadel is quoting from 'Royal Hibernian Academy "Ecce Homo"', collected in Joyce, *The Critical Writings*, p. 34.

127. James Joyce, *A Portrait of the Artist as a Young Man*, p. 35 (three times), p. 166, p. 176, p. 184, p. 199, p. 215 (twice), p. 225, p. 228. These are the same eleven references to the word 'race' which Cheng identifies (Cheng, *Joyce, Race and Empire*, p. 17), but there are allusions to race also in phrases such as 'another of his kind' (p. 91) and 'one of us' (p. 183).

128. Ibid., p. 228.

129. Pericles Lewis, 'The Conscience of the Race', *Joyce Through the Ages*, p. 88.

130. In *Portrait*, the phrase is 'the secret of her race', p. 199, while in *Ulysses*, 'the secret of the race' is what Bloom bears in his arms while he proceeds towards the Turkish baths, p. 629.

131. Joyce, *Portrait*, p. 189.

132. Ibid., p. 184.

133. Ellmann, *James Joyce*, p. 459.

134. Joyce, *Ulysses*, p. 599.

135. Reizbaum, *James Joyce's Judaic Other*, p. 45.

136. Joyce, *Ulysses*, p. 614.

137. Ibid., p. 33, p. 36.

138. Michael Groden records that in the early draft of 'Cyclops' contained in a notebook in the University of Buffalo (Poetry Collection, MS V.A.8) Stephen Dedalus 'appears in two scenes and hears and participates in the anti-semitic taunting of Bloom by the men in Barney Kiernan's pub'. Groden surmises that Stephen's behaviour in 'Ithaca' 'is probably related to the aspect of Stephen's character that Joyce removed from "Cyclops"'. See 'Joyce at Work on "Cyclops"', pp. 219–20.

139. Joyce, *Ulysses*, pp. 641–4.
140. Eighteen variations of this song are listed in Francis James Child, ed. *The English and Scottish Popular Ballads*. Vol. III, pp. 240–3. See Davison, *James Joyce, Ulysses and the Construction of Jewish Identity*, p. 19. In the *Irish Times* review of Hannah Berman's novel, *Melutovna*, cited below, the reviewer made reference to the 'Beiless' ritual murder trial in Kiev, in which a Jew was accused and found not guilty of the ritual murder of a boy whose body was found 'bled white' from over forty wounds. The case highlighted that the belief in Jewish blood-sacrifice of Christian children continued to exist in certain places. 'Those who are desirous of understanding the conditions which make a Beiless case possible should read *Melutovna*' writes the reviewer. See 'Melutovna', *Irish Times*, 14 March 1914, p. 20.
141. Gifford notes that Joyce recalled the song from memory, although it may be based on a late variant of 'Sir Hugh, or the Jew's Daughter' which had removed the anti-semitic references and been revised as 'Little Harry Hughes and the Duke's Daughter'. See Don Gifford, *Ulysses Annotated*, p. 579. Ellmann records that Joyce asked a young composer who was working with him on translating sections of *Ulysses*, Jacques Benoît-Méchin, to write out the musical notations for the song. See Ellmann, *James Joyce*, p. 521n.
142. Joyce, *Ulysses*, p. 34.
143. Davison, *James Joyce, Ulysses and the Construction of Jewish Identity*, p. 234.
144. Joyce, *Ulysses*, pp. 643–4.
145. Nadel notes that the name of the company was 'Agudath Netaim', and was not established until 1905. See Nadel, *Joyce and the Jews*, p. 100.
146. Joyce, *Ulysses*, p. 645.
147. Ibid., p. 634. The words inside square brackets were added as corrections in the 'Errata' list issued with the second impression of *Ulysses* printed on 12 October 1922, and obviously make sense of the question.
148. It is also possible to read this sentence to focus more fully on the uncertainty of Bloom's Jewishness, however, if we followed the correspondence of pronouns between the reply and the question up to the last pronoun, so it would read: Bloom thought that Stephen thought that Bloom was a jew whereas Bloom knew that Stephen knew that Bloom knew that Bloom was not.
149. Ibid., p. 645.
150. Gerald Gould cites this sentence as one among many examples of Joyce's fault in 'putting everything in', like a 'waste-paper basket', and mocks the sentence by following it with an example of nonsense from Carroll's *Alice in Wonderland*. See *The English Novel To-Day*, p. 22.
151. Davison, *James Joyce, Ulysses and the Construction of Jewish Identity*, p. 234.
152. Vike Martina Plock, 'A Feat of Strength in "Ithaca"', pp. 129–39. Plock argues that Sandow's exercises were intended to be of universal benefit, and therefore could be seen as a counter-narrative to the racial exclusivity of eugenics movements, but that physical culture became an important strand in the campaigns of many racially defined organisations, including the Zionist movement.

153. Joyce, *Ulysses*, p. 439. For an interesting analysis of Bloom's attempts to secure an unambiguously white ethnicity, see Suzanna Chan, '"I Treated You White": *Ulysses*, Gender and the Visual Culture of "Race"', in Faragó and Sullivan, eds, *Facing the Other*, pp. 19–31.
154. Ibid., p. 455.
155. Ibid., p. 416.
156. Ibid., p. 439.
157. Ibid., p. 478.
158. Platt, *Joyce. Race and Finnegans Wake*, p. 121.
159. Joyce, *Ulysses*, p. 457, pp. 462–3.
160. Eoin MacNeill Papers, UCD Archives, LA1/J/82.
161. On this point, see Richard Davis, *Arthur Griffith and Non-Violent Sinn Fein*, pp. 106–7, and Emer Nolan, *James Joyce and Nationalism*, pp. 21–2.
162. Ellmann, *James Joyce*, pp. 237–9.
163. Eoin MacNeill Papers, UCD Archives, LA1/J/82.
164. Joyce, *Ulysses*, p. 31.
165. Arguably Bloom's Jewish and Masonic reputations are indistinguishable in this instance, since both Jews and Masons were widely suspected of conspiratorial behaviour. Catholics were prohibited from involvement in Freemasonry by Pope Leo XIII's *Ab Apostolici* of 1890, and prohibition was made Canon Law in 1917.
166. Joyce, *Ulysses*, p. 82.
167. Ibid., p. 629.
168. Andrew Gibson, *Joyce's Revenge*, pp. 42–3.
169. Ellmann, *The Consciousness of Joyce*, p. 89.
170. 'Comment', *The Dial*, 72 (June 1922), p. 663.
171. 'Letter to Sylvia Beach, 11th February 1922', *James Joyce's Letters to Sylvia Beach*, p. 11.
172. Joyce, *Ulysses*, pp. 649–53.
173. Ibid., p. 655.
174. Duffy, *The Subaltern Ulysses*, p. 190.
175. See Joyce, *Ulysses*, p. 657, and Duffy, *The Subaltern Ulysses*, p. 178.
176. For a discussion of Molly's indeterminate and complex ancestry, see Jonathan Quick, 'Molly Bloom's Mother', pp. 223–40.
177. Joyce, *Ulysses*, pp. 731–2.
178. Ellmann, *James Joyce*, p. 3.
179. Ó Gráda, 'Lost in Little Jerusalem', p. 24.
180. Ibid., p. 23.
181. Ibid., p. 22.
182. 'A First Night: "The Irish Jew" at Empire', *Irish Independent*, 13 December 1921, p. 4.
183. *Irish Independent*, 4 August 1922, p. 4.
184. *Freeman's Journal*, 10 February 1923, p. 4.
185. The play was also reputed to have been produced in Broadway in New York, and revived many times, but no evidence has been found of a Broadway performance, although newspapers in New York reported that either a New York or Philadelphia run was planned by Waxman. The 'Broadway' reputation is suggested by Séamas Ó Maitiú in *W&R*

Jacob, in his account of the occupation of the Jacob's Biscuit factory in the Easter Rising of 1916, in which John MacDonagh served as a volunteer under the command of his brother, Thomas, who was executed for his part in the Rising. The account is extracted on the website of the National Archives of Ireland: http://www.nationalarchives.ie/topics/1916/jacobschapter.html

The *Irish Times* also suggested a New York performance in a feature article in 1928 which reported that a theatrical manager, Al Wood, had told MacDonagh that *The Irish Jew* was 'a million dollar title for the booking office' in New York, although the article also observes that 'Full of fun, the Irish Jew was not quite the atmosphere for New York', which implies that it either did not run, or was a flop. See *The Irish Times*, 19 May 1928, p. 6.

Two New York newspapers reported Waxman's plans for a New York production of *The Irish Jew*: the *Daily News* on 22 April 1923, and the *Herald* on 29 April 1923. Press cuttings were provided for these reports by The Billy Rose Theatre Division from The New York Public Library for the Performing Arts from the clipping file for *The Irish Jew*.

186. Intrepid theatre historians, Robert Hogan and Richard Burnham, also record finding no copy of *The Irish Jew*, and have to resort to the same means in their brief account of the play of reconstructing plot and theme from newspaper reviews. See *The Years of O'Casey, 1921–1926*, pp. 46–8.

187. Helen C. Bower, 'The Irish Jew', *Detroit Free Press*, 24 September 1923. The press cutting was provided for this review by The Billy Rose Theatre Division from The New York Public Library for the Performing Arts from the clipping file for *The Irish Jew*. The replacement of a portrait of Disraeli with one of Emmet might have been particular to the American performance. The programme notes for the Detroit production, which was performed in the Detroit Opera House, commencing on 23 September 1923, indicates that the play was condensed from four acts into three, and without copies of the play script for either the Dublin or Detroit performances it is impossible to determine what other changes may have been made. Programme notes for the Detroit production also supplied by The Billy Rose Theatre Division from The New York Public Library for the Performing Arts.

188. '"The Irish Jew" at the Empire', *Freeman's Journal*, 13 December 1921, p. 3.

189. Ibid., p. 3.

190. 'A First Night', *Irish Independent*, 13 December 1921, p. 4.

191. Ibid., p. 4.

192. Jimmy O'Dea, who appeared in several MacDonagh plays and radio productions, records that MacDonagh planned to revive *The Irish Jew* in the late 1950s, when Robert Briscoe was Lord Mayor of Dublin. O'Dea was beginning as a comedy actor when he appeared in *The Irish Jew*, and later became one of Ireland's most popular comedians. See 'Talking to Jimmy O'Dea', *Irish Times*, 29 December 1962, p. 8. The National Library of Ireland holds some papers of John MacDonagh, among which is a note headed 'Idea for Show', which suggests a play with then Jewish

Lord Mayor of Dublin, Robert Briscoe, as a central character, with his 'chaplain Rabbi', and other characters, listed as '14 prods and a Jew', who receive an 'Irish enthusiast from NY'. While not a revival of *The Irish Jew*, MacDonagh was clearly interested in reviving the idea of a play with a Jewish Lord Mayor of Dublin as its central character to coincide with Briscoe's time as Mayor. The notes suggest that the comic element MacDonagh was interested in here was that the Irish-American character, enthusiastic for the land of his roots, would be received by characters who were 'all foreigners or new Irish'. John MacDonagh Papers, National Library of Ireland, NLI MS 20,648 (3) 'Notes for Plays, etc.'

193. 'Obituary: John MacDonagh', *Irish Times*, 3 July 1961, p. 7.
194. Robert Emmet, 'Speech from the Dock', *Field Day Anthology of Irish Writing, Vol.1*, ed. Seamus Deane, pp. 933–9.
195. Quoted in Hogan and Burnham, *The Years of O'Casey, 1921–1926*, p. 46.
196. Bower, 'The Irish Jew', *Detroit Free Press*, 24 September 1923.
197. Gibson's chapter is titled 'Only a Foreigner Would Do' in *Joyce's Revenge*, pp. 42–59 (see pp. 55–6). The quotation comes from Nadel, *Joyce and the Jews*, p. 139.
198. Isaac Herzog, 'The Jewish Community: Its Origin and Citizen Aims', in *The Voice of Ireland*, ed. William G. Fitz-Gerald, p. 288.
199. Hannah Berman's *Melutovna* was reprinted in New York in 1975 by Arno Press in a series on the 'Modern Jewish Experience'. Berman published a second novel, *Ant Hills* in 1926. She authored the factual account of the Zlotover family in *Zlotover Story: A Dublin Story with a Difference*, which was completed and published after her death (1955). She was also the translator of some of the best-known work of Yiddish writer, Sholem Aleichem, *Stempenyu* (London: Heinemann, 1913) and *Jewish Children*, an anthology of tales (London: Heinemann, 1920). Catherine Hezser includes a brief mention of Berman's work in '"Are you Protestant Jews or Catholic Jews?"', pp. 159–88. Ó Gráda uses Berman's work more broadly, including unpublished manuscripts, in *Jewish Ireland in the Age of Joyce*. Keogh refers briefly to the Berman family and to Berman's literary reputation in *Jews in Twentieth-Century Ireland*, 67, p. 241.
200. Hannah Berman, 'The Charity Box', p. 32.
201. Ibid., p. 38.

Chapter 2

Face Value: Racial Typology and Irish Modernism

And here's John Synge himself, that rooted man
'Forgetting human words,' a grave deep face.
You that would judge me, do not judge alone
This book or that, come to this hallowed place
Where my friends' portraits hang and look thereon;
Ireland's history in their lineaments trace;
Think where man's glory most begins and ends,
And say my glory was I had such friends.
                    W. B. Yeats, 'The Municipal Gallery Revisited', 1937

As Roy Foster comments in his biography, there is a hollow ring to the end of Yeats's late poem, 'The Municipal Gallery Revisited'.[1] It is a preposterous notion that Yeats might be judged not for his books, but 'in the roll-call of his acquaintance'.[2] The poem reflects upon the portraits and history paintings hung in the Dublin Municipal Gallery of Modern Art, a collection which celebrated the cultural and political history of the newly independent nation. Yeats alludes in passing to the portraits of Casement, Griffith, and Higgins, and paintings by Lavery, Keating, and Orpen, but it is finally 'we three alone' – Gregory, Synge, and himself – whose contributions to the making of the modern nation he comes to extol. The poem closes with what Foster describes as 'an implicit epitaph for himself, and his own assumption into the heroic frieze of portraits'. To look upon the portraits of Gregory and Synge, Yeats suggests, is also to look upon his own portrait. He anticipates, again preposterously, that he will live on, or that his reputation will endure, not through his books, or even his work with the Abbey theatre, but through the eyes of the visitors to this gallery, who will gaze upon his portrait and those of his friends, and judge. Perhaps the 'you' addressed in the poem will stop 'here', as he has done, and find 'John Synge himself . . . a grave, deep face'. The word 'himself' in this line is, as W. J. McCormack reads, superfluous, or a Hiberno-English

tinge which sits oddly with the rest of the poem,[3] but it serves to emphasise the fanciful notion that John Synge is here, embodied rather than
embalmed in his portrait. It exemplifies the double act of prosopopoeia
(from the ancient Greek for face, mask or person – *prosopon*, and make
– *poeia*) taking place in the poem. The portraits themselves are making
faces of the dead, breathing life once more into Gregory and Synge and
the others, but Yeats also brings the dead back to life by demanding our
attention to these faces.

It is upon Synge's 'grave deep face' that 'you', or at least, 'you that
would judge', are commanded in the next lines to 'look'. A series of
imperatives follow, as McCormack notes: 'do not judge alone', 'come',
'Look', 'trace', 'Think', and 'say'.[4] What we are commanded to do here,
however, is at once both clear and, on closer inspection, more perplex-
ing. Judge me not by reading my books, but by thinking of who my
friends were. This would be the simple paraphrase, but it would ignore
the specific action Yeats demands: 'Look thereon', upon these faces,
and 'judge'. How should we judge Yeats by looking upon the faces of
his friends? What are we looking for (or at) in the faces of Gregory and
Synge that would illuminate the reputation or character of Yeats? Is
Yeats really suggesting physiognomy by proxy here? The phrase 'Look
thereon' seems to recall Shelley's 'Ozymandias', in which, below the
shattered visage of the 'King of Kings', the inscription on the pedestal
similarly commands the reader to 'Look on my Works, ye mighty, and
despair!', but if so, aside from the self-mockery that this would imply
(by no means an unfruitful reading), the awed admiration prescribed by
Ozymandias's 'Look' sits oddly with Yeats's sense of looking as judge-
ment. For Yeats, looking upon the faces of his friends is both a passive
gaze of adulation and, paradoxically, an active, critical inspection, a
reading of the face, as if these faces are the true bearers of his inscrip-
tions, rather than his books. The face is understood, then, as both the
idealised surface, the spectacle basking in the gaze of others, and the
cryptic façade wherein lies the codes of our being (and, by Yeats's imagining, the codes of other kindred beings too).

The analogy with Shelley's poem may illuminate another facet of
Yeats's lines too, for in both cases the command to look is at once a
sign of supreme confidence and an indication of anxiety. If the faces
of Gregory and Synge convey their own importance, why the repeated
imperatives to 'look', 'think', 'say', and so on? Is there a danger that
we might not recognise these faces for what they are? Yeats, after all,
recounts his own fallacy in 'Easter 1916' in failing to recognise those
'vivid faces', coming from 'counter or desk', as the faces of men and
women who were capable of heroic action. The anxiety intimated in

both poems is about the failure to recognise what we should be able to recognise in a face. In short, as much as 'The Municipal Gallery Revisited' is about prosopopoeia, there lurks within it the fear of prosopagnosia, or face-blindness.

Yeats's bold claim for what we might read in the faces of Lady Gregory and John Synge is that we must trace 'Ireland's history in their lineaments'. Once more we could simplify this to mean that Gregory and Synge, and by extension Yeats, had their part to play in the momentous changes in recent Irish history, and that these portraits capture something of that history, but this is to ignore, again, the action demanded by Yeats. How might we trace a national history in the 'lineaments' or features of the face?[5] How should we begin to read a face as an index of the history of a nation? And yet, this connection between the face and national history is exactly the implication of any national portrait gallery (and the Municipal Gallery perhaps came closest to having a 'national portrait collection' in Ireland at the time).[6] To look upon the face of Griffith, who sat for Lavery in the midst of the treaty negotiations in 1921, or upon Lavery's oil sketch of Casement on trial, or Orpen's portrait of Michael Davitt, is by implication to gaze upon these faces as markers of moments in history, and so, of course, the faces of Synge and Gregory might also be read in this way, taking their places among all the other faces of Irish history. But what does it mean to trace in their 'lineaments' this history?

'Lineaments' appears with some frequency in Yeats's poems, and, of course, should be traced to Blake's influence.[7] In many of his poems, Yeats uses 'lineaments' to mean the outline or form of the body. This is the meaning suggested in 'Michael Robartes and the Dancer', for example, in the lines 'The lineaments that please their view/ When the long looking-glass is full', and in 'The Gift of Harun Al-Rashid', in the lines 'The soul's own youth and not the body's youth/ Shows through our lineaments'.[8] In the later poems, however, 'lineaments' is used to mean the distinctive features of the face, and, in each case, implies a connection with race. This is first discernible, perhaps, although somewhat ambivalently, in 'The Gyres', in which 'Old Rocky Face', a mythic figure symbolising time, is commanded to 'look forth', and see that 'beauty dies of beauty, worth of worth,/ And ancient lineaments are blotted out'.[9] 'Lineaments' here is capable of sustaining both the sense of a face, the features of which are blotted out by time (as indeed in an old rock face), and 'lines' of ancestral descent. The connection between face and race is more clearly articulated, however, and more closely related to 'The Municipal Gallery Revisited', in Yeats's use of the word 'lineaments' in 'The Statues':

We Irish, born into that ancient sect
But thrown upon this filthy modern tide
And by its formless spawning fury wrecked,
Climb to our proper dark, that we may trace
The lineaments of a plummet-measured face.[10]

In a poem which reflects upon Greek statues, and how their seemingly static, calculated forms transcended time, Yeats pits the permanence and beauty of these forms against the 'filthy modern tide', but at the same time claims that 'One image crossed the many-headed' through time, that these forms have their modern descendants. The 'plummet-measured face' has generally been read as an allusion to the Greek sculpture made possible and beautiful by Pythagorean mathematics. Richard Ellmann argues thus, and quotes from Yeats's prose that 'when the Doric studios sent out those broad-backed marble statues against the multiform, vague, expressive Asiatic sea, they gave to the sexual instinct of Europe its goal, its fixed type'.[11] It is important, however, to take Yeats's lines at face value, so to speak: the plummet measures just the vertical axis, determining the perpendicular, or 90-degree angle, and so 'a plummet-measured face' is one defined specifically by the vertical angle. Yeats appears to be referring in this poem not just to the art made possible by Pythagorean numbers, but also to the influential racial theories of Petrus Camper, who determined that the 90-degree facial angle of Greek statues was the ideal, from which human races and apes deviated in degrees ranging from the European at 80 degrees, to the Angolan African at 70 degrees, and to the Orangutan at 58 degrees.[12] The 'facial angle' theory, widely influential on nineteenth-century anthropology, where it evolved into the terms 'prognathism' (protruding jaw and mouth) and 'orthognathism' ('regular', vertical features), came to be associated with a link between cranial shape and intelligence quotient.[13] It is perhaps already familiar to an Irish studies readership through the simianised features of Irish faces depicted in *Punch* cartoons of the nineteenth century, where the jutting lower face signified low intelligence, and affinity with other 'inferior' races and species.[14]

In the last stanza, Yeats introduces the Irish, first through an allusion to Pearse summoning 'Cuchulain to his side', and then more fully as 'We Irish', as the descendants of the ideal beauty of the Greek statues, the racial profile which determined the distinction between civilisation and barbarism. According to F. A. C. Wilson's reading of the poem, Yeats proposes the Irish as the intellectual saviours of the modern world, destined to 'resuscitate the laws of intellectual beauty' as 'they preserve an unconscious knowledge of the great Indo-European archetype' through a kind of race-consciousness.[15] The 'lineaments of a plummet-measured face' are traced through time, through a racial history of the Irish which Wilson also suggests might contain a reference to Milesian ancestral origins in Egypt. In the final lines of the poem, at the darkest point in Yeats's historical 'gyres', the Irish are prophesied to climb to that height whereupon 'we' might trace these lineaments, presumably lineaments which will reflect the measure of 'our' faces, since 'we' are part of that same 'ancient sect'. Yeats's use of this 'plummet-measure' to determine Irish racial genealogy might be understood as an anti-colonial corrective to the racist caricatures of *Punch* fame, except that it obviously has more sinister racist connotations of its own.[16] The purpose of the apparently approving allusion to Camper's theory is not simply to stake a claim for racial equality, but to privilege a narrative of Irish (and European) racial destiny over those whose facial (and therefore racial) profiles don't measure up.

In these late poems, then, written at a time when Yeats was most obviously affiliated with various forms of fascist and racist politics, we find the recurrent figure of tracing racial history through the 'lineaments' of the face.[17] But again, we must ask, what does this mean? How are we to trace the lineaments of the face? As the scene takes place in an art gallery, we must presume that this is entirely a visual activity, although 'trace' also suggests touching, and intimates that to look upon these faces is not to do so as a detached observer, but to connect with them, face to face. And what measure of the face are we looking for? Is history encoded in the bone structure, the skin pigmentation, the eye and hair colour, the 'cephalic index'? Is Yeats really inviting us to undertake a kind of physical anthropology, and read faces as the biometric indices of racial history? In itself, this is not a novel or surprising discovery in relation to W. B. Yeats. Yeats's interest in eugenics, and specifically forms of scientific racism, as well as his flirtations with the racial philosophies and racist ideologies of fascism, is well documented.[18] The focus on the face as a figurative register of historical and racial identity was not the peculiar obsession of Yeats in his late dabble with racial ideologies, however, but, as I will argue, was a matter of wider currency and significance in cultural representations of the Irish in the first half of the twentieth century, particularly from the 1920s to the 1940s.

The argument of this chapter is that contradictory readings of the symbolic meanings and expressive capacities of the face run parallel to each other through a series of representations drawn from art, science and literature during this period. I aim here for a conjectural microhistory of the face as a contested figure, showing the processes at work in making the face a marker or cipher of racial identity, and equally the discombobulation of those processes through a progressive erasure of the philosophical grounds upon which we might read the face. The face is, inevitably, a significant trope in any field of human science or cultural study, since, as Emmanuel Levinas's work suggests, it defines and expresses human relations through the primary communicative, social moment of the face-to-face encounter. 'The proximity of the other is the face's meaning', writes Levinas.[19] The argument of this chapter takes its bearings from two qualifications of that idea, however. The first is Deleuze and Guattari's insistence that the face is not a universal, but has an entirely specific economy and valency in the era of modernity.[20] I further refine and narrow the boundaries of that historical understanding of the face in this chapter to fix upon this micro-history of the face in Ireland in the aftermath of partition and political independence, without losing sight (I hope) of the likelihood that this micro-history is but an exemplary iteration of the wider salience of the face as a racial figure in modern discourse.

The second qualification of Levinas's conception of the centrality of the face as a figure of human relations lies in the radical doubt which Wittgenstein places upon whether the face can be said to have 'meaning'. Our figures of speech about the face (take for instance, Wittgenstein's example, 'I can think of this face as courageous too') reveal a mistaken ascription of a mental character or state to the face.[21] It is as if, Wittgenstein writes, 'we are getting hold of a thing which is *in* the face and different from it . . . as though there existed a double of its expression, as though the double was the prototype of the expression and as though seeing the expression of the face was finding the prototype to which it corresponded'.[22] The number of times Wittgenstein relies upon fictional hypotheses ('as though') in this sentence recognises that our means of description of the face is highly figurative. In discussing Wittgenstein's rich analogy between understanding music and understanding facial expression, Roger Scruton deduces that Wittgenstein's tendency to understand the face as an intransitive expression implies that 'To understand an expression is to grasp a *Gestalt*, and to attribute to that *Gestalt* a social currency', but that Wittgenstein believes we are mistaken if we seek to 'look behind [expressions] to what they mean'.[23] Scruton disagrees that this is a viable model for understanding music, for there is a 'state of mind that lies behind the expression, and which is revealed in it'. It will become evident that much significance lies in the difference between these two understandings of reading the face, and it is Wittgenstein's insistence that 'the face impresses itself upon me . . . and I, as it were, cut a seal from the impression' which is borne out in the readings of the face which follow.[24]

How the Irish Became White, Again

'Ireland is a land of long faces'.[25] This was not the idle, witty observation of a social commentator on Ireland during the economic war, but a scientific conclusion reached by a group of physical anthropologists who surveyed 10,000 Irish men and almost 2,000 Irish women between 1934 and 1936. The Harvard Irish Study, as it became known, was conceived by Professor Earnest Hooton in the early 1930s when the Harvard Department of Anthropology was awarded a generous grant by the Rockefeller Foundation. The Rockefeller grant enabled Hooton and his colleagues to conceive of new and wide-ranging projects, and they decided to embark on a racial history and survey of Ireland. The project entailed three related endeavours. First, an archaeological expedition to Ireland was undertaken, which aimed to recover skeletal remains and cultural artefacts in order to shed light on the history of the Irish people. Second, a social anthropological mission was carried out in a specific locality in Ireland (County Clare), which aimed to study the social, economic, political and cultural structure of contemporary Irish life. Third, and most pertinent to this chapter, a physical anthropological mission was conducted, which aimed to survey the racial characteristics of the Irish population, by means of anthropometric measurements of an adequate sample of subjects across the country. This last phase was closest to Hooton's research interests, and although it appears he never visited Ireland throughout the duration of the survey, he took responsibility for tabulating the anthropometric data and writing up the published findings of the physical anthropology mission. As we will see, this element of the study constituted a science of racial typification which used the face as the primary site of racial identification.

There are complex reasons why Ireland was chosen as the subject of this study. Physical anthropology was still considered to be a fledgling discipline, and it had not yet been used and developed to its full potential. The Rockefeller grant enabled Hooton and his colleagues to undertake a more extensive project than had ever before been conceived within the discipline, namely the biological survey and scientific interpretation of a modern state, or large population group. In this sense, the Harvard study should be contextualised as an important moment in the evolution of the modernist state, in which social and physical sciences were understood to be strategic instruments vital to the bio-political ambitions of the state (what Foucault called bio-power).[26] There were certain practical criteria which made Ireland advantageous as the subject of such study. The Rockefeller grant covered a period of eight years, from 1931 to 1939, with the money tapering off in the last three years.[27] This gave Hooton a period of five years for intensive field work, and the final three years for publication. Ireland was felt to be small enough for teams of archaeologists and anthropologists to cover within a five-year field trip, especially as it was also sufficiently familiar in language, customs and culture to be accessible to the researchers available in Harvard. Indeed, the two anthropologists who made a preliminary trip to Ireland in 1932, Lloyd Warner and Hugh Hencken, were able to establish high-level contacts in the Irish Free State very quickly, so that by the time Hooton wrote up the research proposal for the project later that year he could report that they had enlisted the active support of Cardinal MacRory, Catholic Primate of all Ireland, Mr James MacNeill, the Governor-General, Professor George O'Brien (economist), Mr James Delargy (folklorist), Professor MacAlister (archaeologist), Professor Eoin MacNeill (historian), and Dr Adolf Mahr, keeper of antiquities at the National Museum.[28] Lloyd Warner, one of Harvard's social anthropologists, also had a meeting with the newly elected President of the Irish Free State, Eamon de Valera, who endorsed the Harvard study and sanctioned his ministers to provide whatever assistance was necessary to the project.[29] The assistance gained through this endorsement was invaluable to the success of the project. The Free State government provided annual grants to the archaeological expedition to pay for excavation workers, under the Board of Public Works scheme. Ministers also directed civil servants and Gardaí to help with physical anthropology measurements, including being measured themselves and garnering members of the public to be measured. The level of cooperation was extensive, and the published findings of the Harvard Irish Study record acknowledgements and debts of gratitude to various high-ranking members of the Irish Free State, and also the government of Northern Ireland, where ministers and police officers were equally cooperative.[30] This cooperation was rewarded, of course. The cultural artefacts of the archaeological excavations were to remain the property of the Irish museums, for example. It was also anticipated that the physical anthropological work would pay dividends, although to what ends for the Irish governments was never specified. In June 1936, the secretary to the Free State Minister for Education, Seósamh Ó Neill, wrote to Hooton to express the Minister's pleasure at the completion of the anthropometric measurements, and to note that he looked forward to this data being made available to Irish government and scientists.[31]

Ireland was chosen partly because cooperation was anticipated, although the extent of assistance from both governments could not have been expected. There were also very pragmatic reasons for choosing Ireland in terms of the political and financial possibilities of the study, and the science of anthropology more broadly, in the United States. Ireland was recognised as 'the country of origin of more than one-fifth of the population of the United States' in Hooton's research proposal, and the study came at a crucial time in the fortunes of the Irish in America. In the 1930s, while the study was being conducted, Hooton drew up lists of prominent and wealthy Irish-Americans – judges, politicians, businessmen, academics – and wrote to them soliciting their financial support. In the published findings of the physical anthropological study, *The Physical Anthropology of Ireland* (1955), Hooton discussed the Irish-American context in his prefatory acknowledgements, but in a slightly less pragmatic manner:

> Here in Massachusetts we live among Americans of recent Irish extraction; we work with them; we play with them; sometimes we dispute with them, and most of the time we are governed by them. The Irish-Americans are a people of great vigor, ability and charm; they are a friendly people unless deliberately antagonized; they never lack a most appealing sense of humor. In the Harvard Department of Anthropology, we felt that no more fitting place could be found for a thorough anthropological survey than this small island, the ancestral home and the shrine of the devotion of so many of our fellow citizens, friends, and Harvard associates, both in the faculty and among the alumni.[32]

The Irish-Americans were upwardly mobile, if not indeed firmly in the ascendancy, at the time when Hooton was conceiving, conducting and publishing the Harvard Irish study, and so it was politically advantageous to honour the 'ancestral home' of these potential benefactors with the fruits of modern scientific research. This was especially expedient given that the study would 'prove' that the Irish were resoundingly white, of ancient European lineage, and a healthy, civilised nation. Science, so applied, could conclusively remove the taint of nineteenth-century English colonial slurs on the Irish as negroid or simian, slurs which had also been commonly directed against Irish-Americans in the United States before the emergence of what Noel Ignatiev has called the 'white Republic'.[33] Moreover, Hooton had his sights on more extensive projects for physical anthropology than Ireland, namely a complete anthropometric survey of the population of the United States, and for this the gratitude and support of the Irish-American political and financial elite would be beneficial, to say the least.

The remaining reason why Ireland was chosen is of a more scientific nature in relation to testing theories of racial admixture, specifically in relation to 'the white race'. Hooton was acknowledged as among the leading experts in anthropology on theories and practices of race mixture. Ireland offered an interesting case for study of this phenomenon, geographically and historically. As an island, 'the last outpost of the civilization of western Europe', as Hooton put it,[34] the influx of various waves of migration was relatively simple to isolate and determine. The racial characteristics identified in the data collected through anthropometric measurements in Ireland, once divided into 'sub-racial types', could be correlated with known patterns of historical migration: the English and the Scots, the Anglo-Normans, the Vikings, the Celtic, and pre-Celtic Irish.[35] The earliest waves of migration were tracked in relation to recent historical and mythological studies in Ireland, and in particular confirmed the work of T. F. O'Rahilly in *Early Irish History and Mythology* (1946).[36] Hooton had already devised a scheme for categorising 'sub-racial' types within the 'white race' with his Harvard colleague, Carleton S. Coon, for a study of American criminals around 1930, and he applied this scheme to the Irish when tabulating the anthropometric data. 'The conventional primary criteria used for dividing up the white race are hair color, eye color, and head form (notably as expressed by the length-breadth or cephalic index). Sometimes stature and the nasal index are used as secondary criteria', Hooton wrote when explaining the sorting criteria used in the Irish study.[37]

The physical anthropology mission to Ireland was directed by Hooton, but conducted by his research student, C. Wesley Dupertuis, and also a National Research Council Fellow, Helen Dawson. Dupertuis began in 1934, but was joined in 1935 and 1936 by his wife, Helen Dupertuis, who was a trained statistician, and who helped to record the measurements. Dupertuis measured over 10,000 Irish men, in every county, while Helen Dawson measured just short of 2,000 Irish women, mostly in the west of Ireland. For each man or woman who agreed to be part of the study, 125 measurements and observations were recorded (see Figures 2.1 and 2.2). Although these included observations on health, age, educational standard, and occupation, the sociological data took second place to the preponderance of physical measurements and observations. Dupertuis began recording measurements in Moate, County Westmeath, on 16 February 1934, and completed thirty measurements in the first day. The last male sample, No. 10123, was recorded in Mountbellew Bridge, County Galway, on 9 April 1936.[38] The Gardaí, parish priests, and civil servants all played a role as 'drummers-up' and 'whippers-in', as Dupertuis called them, enlisting men to be measured, usually in the Garda barracks of villages or townlands.[39] It is indicative of the bias of the sample, however, that 'No special effort . . . was made to secure samples from the larger urban areas, since it was felt that the country people were perhaps more truly representative of Irish racial types and less likely to be mixed with recent foreign blood than would be the city dwellers'.[40] This obviously corrupts the sample, as an assumption about what constitutes a 'truly representative' Irish type was already determining the method of selection, but more interestingly perhaps, it shows contiguity with the rural bias of contemporary Irish social, economic, and cultural policies.

Both Dupertuis and Dawson used the techniques devised by Hooton, and illustrated in Hooton's book, *Up from the Ape* (1931), to measure their subjects (see Figure 2.3).[41] They were the standard techniques of anthropometric science during the period.[42] These measurements are concentrated mainly in and around the face, as can be seen from the recorded data in Figures 2.1 and 2.2.[43] They range from total face height and face breadth, to very particular details of eyebrow thickness, depth of nasion depression, the degree of prominence of the malars, the integumental thickness of the lips, the breadth of the nostrils, the degree of prognathism in the face, and the slope or angle of the forehead and nose (the significance of which we noted earlier in Yeats's poetry). Some of these measurements were deemed to be significant indicators of 'racial health' as well as racial type. For example, the tests of bite, loss and wear of the teeth were indications of the degree of degeneracy affecting the lower half of the face, signs of the functional atrophy produced as a consequence of the advanced evolutionary development of the 'white race', for which the need for strong masticatory apparatus had been nullified by modern techniques of food production.[44] Head circumference was also understood to be a measurement which indicated signs of evolutionary degeneration. From the measurements made by Dupertuis and Dawson, it was possible to subdivide Irish people into sub-racial types. The record cards indicate that Dupertuis was working on a very rough schema of sub-types (see column 76 on Figure 2.2), which was mainly associated with counties or regions (Sligo, Leitrim, Midland, etc.) or vaguely defined types (John Bull, Pred. Nordic, Red Head), but these were not found to be useful analytical categories.

Hooton re-organised this data into the schematic sub-racial types he had devised with Coon, and in Figure 2.4 these sub-racial types are listed in descending order of population size within the Irish sample. For each of these types, Hooton and Dupertuis provided a physical description, based upon the measurements collected, which could serve as a diagnostic tool for facial recognition of racial characteristics. The most numerous type, Nordic Mediterranean, for example, had mixed-colour eyes (81.3 per cent blue-brown), larger than ordinary brow ridges, pronounced depth in the nasion depression, a tendency toward sloping foreheads, pink skins, and low, waved hair.[45] The Keltic, the second

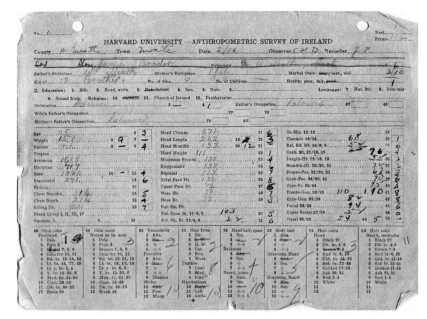

Figure 2.1 The first record card of anthropometric measurements taken by C. W. Dupertuis in Ireland in 1934 (front). Harvard Irish Study Records, unacc., Peabody Museum of Archaeology and Ethnology, Harvard University

most numerous type in Ireland, had smaller heads than average, narrow foreheads, but longer proportions in the upper face than any other type. They were light-skinned, with blue, or grey-blue eyes, with flat-brown to dark-brown hair.[46] In some cases, photographs were taken of the men for illustrative purposes (see Figures 2.5, 2.6 and 2.7).

The photographs were published in two sections in the second volume of *The Physical Anthropology of Ireland*. The first section organised the photographs according to the county or region of their birthplace. This section is perhaps a remnant of Dupertuis's earlier scheme which suggested a regionally differentiated 'look' to the Irish. The second section organised the photographs by Hooton's sub-racial types. The men's faces are shown from front and side perspectives, with their sub-racial type listed below. The racial tag under each page or row of photographs demands that we look at these photographs in a certain way, that we look to establish racial identification. The faces immediately are de-individuated, robbed of their presence in the here and now, and they tell a different story, a story of racial history, of migration, inter-breeding, and adaptation in some, or purity, overcoming, and succession in others. Every face remarks upon its ancestral white, European heritage, its stamp of racial memory linking back to

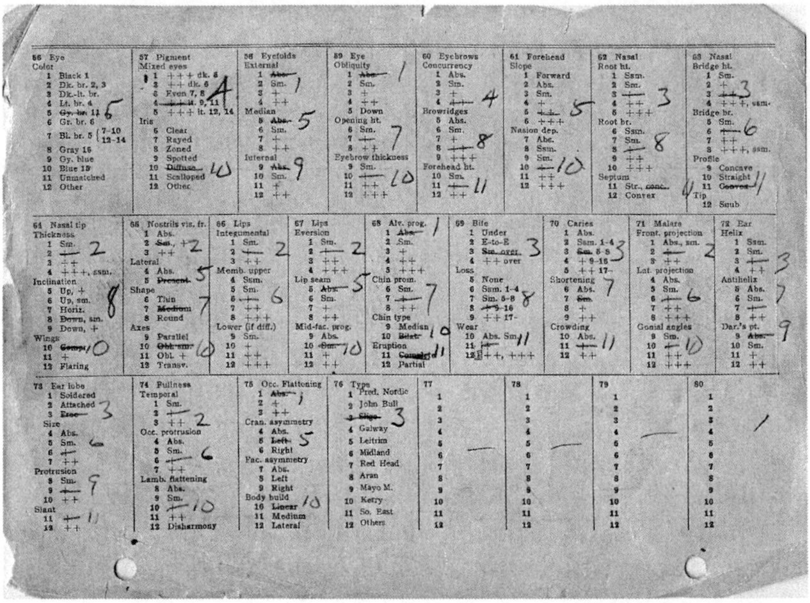

Figure 2.2   The first record card of anthropometric measurements taken by C. W. Dupertuis in Ireland in 1934 (back). Harvard Irish Study Records, unacc., Peabody Museum of Archaeology and Ethnology, Harvard University

the Baltic, say, or the Mediterranean. The photographs lift the reader out of the statistical divisions of races according to scales of eye colour pigmentation, or metrical lengths of nose, and insist on each whole face, the indefinable sum of all of its parts, as a racial icon. The statistical tables leave margins for error, and show fine, millimetre distinctions between racial types, but the photographs fix the image of a race. They give each race a face, and in doing so, accentuate race as a visual presence in Irish culture.

Maps were also provided to show the regional distribution of each type, and the data was consistently analysed in relation to county and geographical distribution, as well as religious divisions. Dawson was surprised to see the inclusion of substantial sections comparing Catholic and Protestant subjects, writing to Hooton 'I know how little "stock" you put in such a division. It is always a dangerous classification'.[47] Hooton seems to have been himself surprised by the way in which religious divisions manifested themselves in racial differences, noting as 'remarkable' the morphological variations between Catholic, Church of Ireland, and Presbyterian subjects.[48] When analysed according to general categories (skin, hair, eyes, eye slits, eyebrows, forehead, nose, lips, prognathism, teeth, malars, ears, and cranial shape),

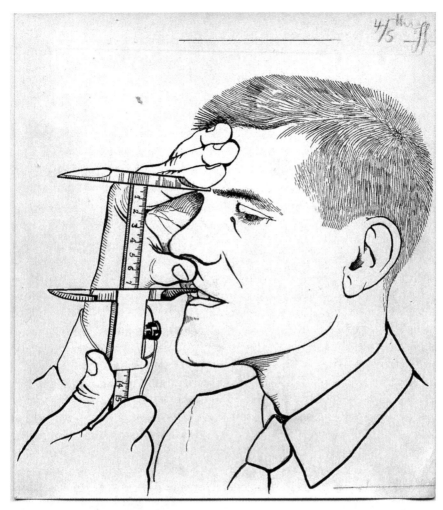

Figure 2.3   E. A. Hooton's illustration of facial measurement techniques as used in the physical anthropology expedition in Ireland. E. A. Hooton Papers, #995–1, Peabody Museum of Archaeology and Ethnology, Harvard University

Catholics and Anglicans differed significantly in ten of those thirteen categories, and because this exaggerates the degree of difference somewhat Hooton broke this down to indicate that Catholics and Anglicans differed in 44.5 per cent of the more detailed subcategories. Catholics and Presbyterians diverged to a greater extent, in 72.22 per cent of the subcategories. On the other hand, Anglicans and Presbyterians differed only in 12.7 per cent, although when arranged according to height, Presbyterians were tallest, followed by Catholics, and then Anglicans. Hooton's conclusion when comparing Catholics and Anglicans was

RANK	TYPE	% OF TOTAL SERIES
1	Nordic Mediterranean	28.9%
2	Keltic	25.3%
3	Dinaric	18.6%
4	Nordic Alpine	18.4%
5	Predominantly Nordic	6.8%
6	East Baltic	1.1%
7	Pure Nordic	0.6%
8	Pure Mediterranean	0.3%

Figure 2.4   Table of racial types categorised in the Harvard Irish Study. Earnest A. Hooton and C. Wesley Dupertuis, *The Physical Anthropology of Ireland*, Papers of the Peabody Museum of Archaeology and Ethnology, vol. 30, no. 1, 1955. Reprinted courtesy of the Peabody Museum of Archaeology and Ethnology, Harvard University

that 'these samples have been derived from distinct anthropological universes'.[49] They were racially different, in other words, although it should be noted that Hooton was comparing the total Catholic series with the Protestant series mainly confined to the Northern counties, and given that there were sometimes fairly wide divergences in terms of racial types between regions, this may skew the conclusions somewhat. A comparison of Catholic and Protestant morphological traits within the same region would have been more 'scientifically correct'. It should also be noted that when comparing the three groups according to metric differences alone, Catholics and Anglicans were more closely related to each other, than either group to Presbyterians. Nonetheless, the study offered scientific evidence, it seemed, for the view that there were racial differences at stake in the sectarian divisions which had exercised Irish politics for three centuries. Moreover, *The Physical Anthropology of Ireland* indexed the visible means of differentiating Catholics and Protestants racially. Anglicans, for example, had higher and steeper foreheads, larger brow ridges, somewhat thicker noses and lips, more protruding ears, flatter malars, and more narrowly elliptical heads. Presbyterians, when compared with Catholics, had more pronounced skin vascularity, higher and steeper foreheads, smaller brow ridges, more golden-brown hair, more convex nasal profiles, and less pronounced malars. Again, by reading the face, the racial history and racial divisions of Irish society could be identified.

It is important at this point to stress that the Harvard Irish Study should not be considered as the importation of American racial measurement techniques which had no currency in Ireland. Although there

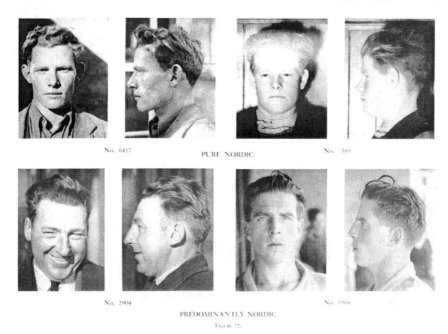

No. 6417　　　　PURE NORDIC　　　　No. 389

No. 2904　　　　　　　　　　　No. 3968

PREDOMINANTLY NORDIC

Figure 72.

Figure 2.5　C. W. Dupertuis's photographs of Irish men, categorised by
E. A. Hooton according to sub-racial type. Earnest A. Hooton and C. Wesley
Dupertuis, *The Physical Anthropology of Ireland*, Papers of the Peabody Museum
of Archaeology and Ethnology, vol. 30, no. 1, 1955. Reprinted courtesy of the
Peabody Museum of Archaeology and Ethnology, Harvard University

were no departments of physical anthropology in Irish universities, there were physical anthropologists, particularly in the department of anatomy in Queen's University Belfast. A group of physical anthropologists had gathered around the Chair of Anatomy, Professor Thomas Walmsley, a morphologist by training, and whose main contribution to physical anthropology was a series of essays published in the *Ulster Journal of Archaeology* with John M. Mogey and David P. Gamble during the years 1939–46 entitled 'The Peoples of Northern Ireland'.[50] Walmsley instructed and inspired Michael A. MacConaill, for example, who conducted a 'pilot' anthropometric and racial survey of demobilised members of the Irish Army in 1923.[51] He had already published the findings of research he had undertaken to survey the Nordic racial types of the men of Rathlin island.[52] In his masters thesis, presented to Queen's in 1928, MacConaill made a study of the correlation of measurements in forty crania of mixed racial type, and made recommendations concerning standard facial and cranial measurements, showing his commitment to developing the science of racial biometrics.[53] In the 1930s, he was publishing essays on the particular methodological

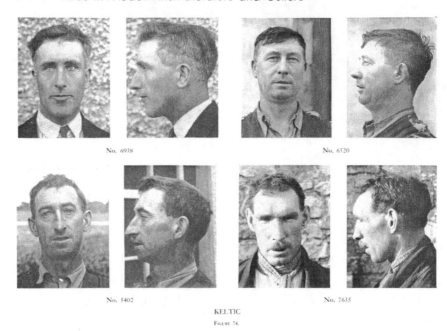

No. 6938   No. 6520

No. 5402   No. 7635

KELTIC
Figure 74.

Figure 2.6   C. W. Dupertuis's photographs of Irish men, categorised by
E. A. Hooton according to sub-racial type. Earnest A. Hooton and C. Wesley
Dupertuis, *The Physical Anthropology of Ireland*, Papers of the Peabody Museum
of Archaeology and Ethnology, vol. 30, no. 1, 1955. Reprinted courtesy of the
Peabody Museum of Archaeology and Ethnology, Harvard University

problems of racial anthropometry in leading journals, such as the *Annals
of Eugenics* and the *American Journal of Physical Anthropology*.[54] John
M. Mogey, another of Walmsley's students, made an anthropometric
survey of some 700 inhabitants of counties Antrim and Derry in the
1930s. David P. Gamble made a statistical analysis of Mogey's survey,
and added measurements of 100 mental hospital patients taken by
himself, in his essay, 'Physical Type and Mental Characters: Preliminary
Notes on the Study of the Correlation Between Racial Types and Types
of Psychotic Disorder, Based on a Sample of the Irish People'.[55] Gamble
provides similar detail in his racial typology of Irish people as Hooton
and Dupertuis, although his schema of types differs considerably.
Again, the face is the focus of the greatest number of measurements and
warrants the most detailed description. Gamble provides the means by
which we might recognise racial types by studying the face, and so, for
example, here is his description of the 'Beaker' type:

> A long, broad, squarish face, with prominent cheek bones, and a broad,
> deep jaw with well-defined gonial angles. The face is solid in appearance,
> but often fairly fleshy, with deep naso-labial furrows. The head is shorter

No. 6494   DINARIC   No. 5965

No. 6746   No. 5349

NORDIC MEDITERRANEAN

FIGURE 80.

Figure 2.7   C. W. Dupertuis's photographs of Irish men, categorised by E. A. Hooton according to sub-racial type. Earnest A. Hooton and C. Wesley Dupertuis, *The Physical Anthropology of Ireland*, Papers of the Peabody Museum of Archaeology and Ethnology, vol. 30, no. 1, 1955. Reprinted courtesy of the Peabody Museum of Archaeology and Ethnology, Harvard University

and broader than the average, and is usually fairly high. The parietal bones rise steeply, and are practically parallel for a considerable distance. The forehead is broad, slightly rounded and fairly high, with average to strong brow ridges, and little constriction. The eyebrows are usually thin. The nose is generally straight or wavy in profile, though concave noses are not uncommon, and a thickened upturned tip is characteristic. The nostrils are usually wide, and the nasion depression is deep. The hair is often deeply waved. The hand long and narrow, and not fleshy, and the medius is short in relation to the hand.[56]

Gamble's initial observations on the mental hospital patients were in order to establish the racial identity of the patients, cross-matched with the work undertaken by Mogey. Then, attempts were made to correlate the physical characteristics of the patients with their mental disorder (all the patients in the survey were either 'schizophrenic' or 'manic depressive'), but neither body measurements nor weight provided satisfactory indices of the mental health problems. The analysis of racial types in relation to mental disorders yielded the most fruitful results, according to Gamble, showing that race seemed to have a bearing on the likelihood of an individual reacting psychologically in one way or another. Mediterraneans, for example, were found to tend heavily towards schizophrenia. About other racial types, Gamble identifies racial traits taking on exaggerated or uncontrolled forms when affected by mental illness: the Beaker type is '"touchy" in temperament, often aggressively impulsive'; the 'Iron Age Group A' type is 'extremely talkative, with a continued flow of language and generally noisy, often abusive and sometimes with paranoid attitudes'; while the Palaeolithic type is 'slow and cautious, generally pleasant, and mild tempered, but may become talkative when once started'.[57] Gamble regretted that the findings were currently based on too small a sample, but were significant enough to warrant publication at this stage. There was apparently promising evidence that types of mental disorder could be attributed to the characteristics of particular racial types.

Hooton had been arguing throughout the 1930s that physical anthropologists needed to work on large amounts of measurement data, such as that made possible in the Irish study, because only in sufficient quantity could the larger patterns of racial history and racial admixture be identified. It was clear that the sub-racial types which comprised the Irish population were heavily intermingled, but that by charting patterns across regional variations, and linking those with known migration movements or historical influxes, distinctive sub-racial origins could be identified and coded. The findings of their research would frustrate anyone who wished to argue that there was a 'pure' Irish race, let alone confer any mark of superiority or inferiority on that race. However, on a more subtle level, it would argue that through the unique combination of sub-racial types and historical admixture, the Irish were a racially distinctive people.

To put this in relative terms, the Irish and the English peoples may be comprised of the same or very similar sub-racial types, but the difference between them lies in the proportion of these types, the extent and nature of their intermixture, and the differing degrees of dominance and persistence of each sub-type. The result could be very different peoples, metrically or morphologically, even though comprised of the same identifiable racial strains. In *The Races of Europe* (1939), an attempt to summarise the archaeological and anthropological evidence for the historical evolution and contemporary distribution of the 'white race' in Europe, Carleton Coon compared the results of Dupertuis's research on the Irish with various, less ample research on the British. He concluded that there were 'several important racial differences' between the British and the Irish:

In the first place, none of the regionally differentiated British groups shows as great a reëmergence of the northern Brünn race as that in Ireland. In the second, brunet Mediterraneans, difficult to isolate in Ireland, have survived or reëmerged in large numbers in Wales and in the manufacturing districts of the Midlands and of Scotland. In the third place, the numerically predominant racial element in the British population is Nordic, with the Keltic Iron Age variety more important than the Anglo-Saxon or Germanic form. Brachycephals of Bronze Age inspiration are not uncommon as individuals, but have no large modern area of concentration.[58]

The most extraordinary claim that Coon made, disputed for methodological reasons by Hooton, but supported by Gamble, was that in the Irish population one could see evidence of an ancient racial strain – the upper Palaeolithic Brünn race of Northwestern Europe – re-emerging, having absorbed many other sub-racial types through differential breeding. In fact, he described a composite picture of the living Irishman, taken from the mean of Dupertuis's measurements, and drew conclusions from this composite picture as to what upper Palaeolithic man might have looked like. Coon was arguing that in terms of racial history, the Irish were the modern re-incarnation of ancient European ancestors, or more precisely, that an older racial element within the Irish population was overcoming the newer racial strains. He too provided photographic illustrations of these racial types, supplied by Dupertuis. They are collected on one page, and headed 'Upper Palaeolithic Survivals in Ireland', suggesting that when we look upon the faces of these living Irish men, their upper Palaeolithic ancestors are brought back to visibility. Race is thus understood as revenance, as the ghostly return of racial ancestry, even racial memory, seeping through the bone structure and manifesting itself in the morphology of the face. Coon's interpretation of the data was putting a new spin on the argument made by an earlier anthropologist, William Z. Ripley, in a book of the same title as Coon's, that 'Ireland has always been a little behindhand'.[59] Ripley suggested that the 'emotional' temperament of the Irish (and the Welsh), derived from an early Mediterranean source, and that this had persisted in Ireland because of its insularity: 'Ethnic invasions, if they took place at all, came late and with spent energy'. It should not be surprising at this point in the discussion to note that physical anthropology was a science closely bound to raciology, and that many of the anthropologists involved in studying the Irish population were committed in various forms and to varying degrees to eugenicist viewpoints.

Ripley, Coon, and Hooton disagreed on various issues in their analysis of the Irish, although in the case of Coon and Hooton, contemporaries and colleagues, indeed sometimes collaborators, at Harvard, the disagreements were not hugely significant. What all three shared in their published studies on race was the conviction, amply demonstrated by the photographic plates used to illustrate their publications, that racial differences manifested themselves visually, and especially in the face. The face was a racial marker, and each face could be read as an indicator of racial type, or combination of racial types. Ripley, writing in 1899, cannot help but betray the physiognomic convictions of his generation, and read the metrical and morphological traits of each race as indicative of temperament. Hence, the Irish are emotional and loquacious, while the English are stoical and reserved. Neither Coon nor Hooton seems interested in this spurious art of ascribing emotional characteristics on the basis of physical features. They are not prone to make speculations on how quickly a man might rise to violence or fall into depression. Instead, they are concerned with the science of race in relation to observable or measurable forms of physical and social life. Anthropometry lent itself to military uses, for example, in determining the optimum physical characteristics for men performing specific military duties – fighter pilots, tank drivers, parachutists, or submariners – or, more controversially, as David H. Price has argued, in trying to identify the racial physical characteristics of enemies which would leave them susceptible to particular kinds of biological or chemical warfare.[60] So too, anthropometry can have beneficial uses in health service planning and health science research, although Hooton himself was sceptical about the development of the medical sciences, which he accused of 'nullifying the purging effect of natural selection'.[61] Hooton believed that the principal benefit of anthropometry was in identifying the physical and sociological health of a race, or a people with all of its constitutive sub-racial strains.

The anthropometric observations of the Irish people, once codified into sub-racial types, were then cross-referenced to a sociological profile of each sub-racial type. This was an account of how each of the constitutive Irish types fared in terms of educational attainments and employment status. The 'Keltic' type, for example, was described as follows:

> The Keltic type is by far the most poorly educated type in Ireland. It has the highest proportion of illiterates and the highest proportion of persons who know no Keltic [Gaelic]. It is slightly deficient in persons speaking Keltic and Keltic only, but its greatest deficiency comes in the group studying Irish at school (23.7 per cent). Occupationally, also, it is the most lowly type. It leads in hired laborers and tinkers; is second in navvies. It also leads in farmers and herdsmen and is high in factory workers. It is notably deficient

in the mercantile class, in clerks, professional men, soldiers and students. This type has the proportions of Catholics and Protestants which are approximately average for our entire Irish morphological series – 90.34 per cent of Catholics.[62]

In contrast, Pure Nordics (of which there was a very small percentage among the population sample) and East Baltics were found to be high achievers in education and, not surprisingly therefore, in occupational status too. Sociological profiles, if they are linked to county or regional areas, or social classes, might be useful tools for governments and scientists to identify root social causes – a county poorly served by schools, for example, or in which employment opportunities seemed to be especially low. When linked to racial types, however, sociological profiles suggest that the educational attainments and occupational rank of each sub-racial group are indicative of the capabilities of that group. There are some who are born and bred to be navvies, others who are born and bred to be teachers and clerks, yet others who are born and bred to be leaders, entrepreneurs, and inventors. The logic was inescapable. One could argue that the potential findings of Gamble's research on the relationship between Irish racial types and kinds of mental disorders were equally far-reaching in their implication that mental illness was racially determined.

The Physical Anthropology of Ireland offered no prescriptions about what one should do with such scientific findings, but Hooton's publications and lectures on other subjects leave us in little doubt as to the possible uses of the Irish material. For much of the 1930s and into the 1940s, Hooton was arguing in various papers and lectures for an extensive use of anthropometry in determining the racial characteristics, and corresponding biological and mental health of the population of the United States, and controversially, as a scientist committed to some aspects of eugenicist programmes of 'race hygiene', was arguing that 'if we can rid ourselves of the feeble-minded, the insane, the incurably diseased, the criminalistic, and the non-productive members of each race and nationality in our democracy, the remainder, however diverse in racial and natural origins, will work out its own salvation'.[63] This quotation perhaps exaggerates the malevolence of Hooton's beliefs. It is unlikely he meant the word 'rid' in the Nazi sense of programmatic extermination. He was more frequently and unequivocally an advocate of enforced sterilisation, of selective intermarriage and breeding, and of using anthropometry to identify and promote the relative talents and capabilities of each race. He did not identify any race with social inferiority or weakness, but instead argued that each race contained elements of inferiority and weakness which needed to be expunged from that race through eugenicist programmes of birth control, sterilisation, and 'rigorous medical examinations for persons intending marriage'. It was also imperative, he argued, that we understand racial differences fully, so that society could maximise the potential of each race:

> if it were ascertained that the Negro has transcendent gifts in music, it should be the national policy to encourage Negroes to enter this field and to afford them special opportunities. And if Nordics are especially good at war, they ought to be preferentially conscripted.[64]

In relation to the anti-semitism of the 1930s, for example, Hooton publicly professed his admiration for Jewish people, and argued that they displayed higher levels of intelligence and achievement than most other racial groups.[65] He concluded that it would be to the benefit of general levels of intelligence in American society were the Jews to intermarry more frequently with people of other races. This is, on the one hand, markedly different from contemporary racial slurs on Jewish people as inferior and weak, but it is also a sign of the way in which, for Hooton, Jewish people constituted a distinguishable race with markedly different social and biological characteristics to other races, the selective breeding of which characteristics could be of scientific benefit to wider society. Hooton tackled the Nazi ideology directly, in a paper entitled, 'A Scientist Looks at the Race of Supermen', but his argument concerning the causes of Nazism, and his solution to how it should be defeated gave some grounds for reservation about Hooton's politics. Nazism was not, Hooton asserted, the infection of an otherwise decent people by 'an unusually virulent disease carrier'. It was the product of

> one of the most complicated racial hashes which can be found anywhere in the world. . . . German militarism can be destroyed only by the dissolution of the German nation and the dispersal of the relatively harmless, or seemingly uninfected members of the German population among the more civilised and peaceable groups of the world.[66]

An elected member of the Massachusetts House of Representatives, Edmond J. Donlan, filed a resolution against Hooton as a result of this paper, seeking sanctions against his teaching at Harvard on the grounds that he had 'advocated the extermination of the whole German race, a characteristic Nazi device'.[67] Donlan wrote to Hooton, however, that his study of Irish people 'suggests a ray of hope for your salvation', a remarkable suggestion that one could cleanse the iniquities of one's racist views by currying favour with the Irish. Interestingly, another correspondent attacked Hooton's paper on the Jewish people as providing a 'blueprint for anti-semitism' by claiming that Jews have distinguishable facial characteristics easily recognised by anyone, and by embellishing the paper with 'a series of pictures of blown-up noses that are deliberately misleading to the layman'.[68]

As a scientist committed to the study of race, and committed to various eugenics projects, Hooton routinely commented on who and who should not be permitted to reproduce and survive, repeating, almost as a mantra, that the 'feeble-minded, the insane and the criminalistic' deserved extinction. He attacked humanitarianism, medical science, and the welfare society for going against the principles of natural selection, and for according equal rights to anyone who was not among the 'mentally and physically sound, the economically capable, and the socially minded'.[69] It is important to remember that Hooton was not voicing extreme or dangerous views in the context of his own times. As Diane Paul has argued, before the Second World War, eugenics provided 'satisfactory and reasonable' explanations of widely believed trends of physical and social degeneration, and posited national remedies, based upon the scientific thinking of the time.[70] Hooton conceived of the anthropometric survey of racial types in Ireland as a gift to an emergent nation, and de Valera, his government, and senior members of the religious and educational authorities received the Harvard researchers in this spirit.[71] In the United States, the influence of eugenicists on national programmes of biological engineering was well known. The Immigration Act of 1924, for example, which privileged immigration from Northern European countries, restricted immigration from many other regions, and barred entry from Asian countries, was largely influenced by Madison Grant's book, *The Passing of the Great Race* (1916), which celebrated the superiority of the Nordic race, and Lothrop Stoddard's *The Rising Tide of Color Against White Supremacy* (1920), which argued that immigration of non-white races would further erode the genetic supremacy of the whites. At the same time, the Eugenics Record Office in Cold Spring Harbor succeeded in advocating for legislation to enforce sterilisation of the 'mentally defective' in thirty states, stating that sterilization should be widely used as a tool to prevent the spread of 'socially inadequate classes', which included the

(1) Feeble-minded; (2) Insane (including the psychopathic); (3) Criminalistic (including the delinquent and the wayward); (4) Epileptic; (5) Inebriate (including drug-habitués); (6) Diseased (including the tuberculous, the syphilitic, the leprous, and others with chronic, infectious, and legally segregable diseases); (7) Blind (including those with seriously impaired vision); (8) Deaf (including those with seriously impaired hearing); (9) Deformed (including the crippled); and (10) Dependent (including orphans, ne'er do wells, the homeless, tramps, and paupers.[72]

Although Hooton would occasionally have disagreements with Eugenics organisations, notably the American Eugenics Society, in general his publications, research papers, and correspondence shows him to be closely tied to, indeed often directly supportive of, eugenicist campaigns in the United States.

In Ireland, in the 1930s, how might a study of the country's population which detailed racial types and linked those types to biologically determined capacities for intelligence and economic success have been used to influence state policy? Perhaps it is unlikely that the American eugenicist arguments concerning birth control and sterilisation would have found favour in a state dominated by Catholic social policies,[73] and immigration was rarely of significant concern in a state which regularly haemorrhaged its 'surplus labour' overseas. This is not to say, however, that Irish state policies were free from racial bias. Bryan Fanning has argued persuasively that the implementation of Irish policies regarding refugees and asylum seekers in the aftermath of the Second World War were both exclusionary and racist.[74] These policies were not influenced by the scientific research of the Harvard anthropologists, however, but by prevailing political, religious, and cultural prejudices against non-Catholics, and Jews in particular. There were local, mainly religious, pressures on the formation of Irish state policies which perhaps militated against the kind of influence with which the research of physical anthropologists found political and legislative expression in the United States. It is important not to overstate this, however. Pope Pius XI denounced eugenics on a regular basis, but his denunciations were often articulated so as to acknowledge that eugenics had validity in seeking to procure the 'strength and health of the future child'.[75] So too, the Irish Free State may have adhered to Catholic social policy, but it was also keen to join the league of modern, progressive nations, and to use modern scientific methods to develop its own economy, society, and culture.[76] So why not also its people? And why, if there were entrenched religious objections to physical anthropology and eugenics, did the leaders of the Catholic church in Ireland, from the Primate, Cardinal MacRory, down to the parish priests, not only welcome but actively assist the work of the Harvard anthropometrists?

The Harvard Irish study promised the Irish state a more complete racial survey of its population than almost any other modern country. That promise, however, was, perhaps crucially, not fulfilled until almost twenty years after the research had been conducted. *The Physical Anthropology of Ireland* was published in 1955, having been delayed first by minor errors in the tabulation of measurements when Hooton first organised the data for publication in 1940, and then by Hooton's commitments to serving the American war effort, which involved him in military anthropometry for some eight years.[77] By 1955, the horrors of the Nazi programme of racial selection and extermination had turned the tide of social and political thought against eugenics (and, to a lesser extent, physical anthropology). What had seemed the basis for sound scientific research and sensible social planning in the 1930s became ethically and politically unconscionable in the 1950s. Many of the men and women involved in physical anthropology and racial surveys in the 1930s retreated from the racial and eugenicist dimensions of the subject, absorbed into departments of anatomy, physical science or education, turned to social anthropology, or to archaeology, or revised the terms of their studies. Hooton described his own research in 1951 as having moved from matters of race to 'the study of individual constitution'.[78] He died before *The Physical Anthropology of Ireland* was published. Dupertuis remained an anthropologist also, but was employed in the Department of Medicine in Western Reserve University, Ohio, and his publications tended to lie in physical science and clinical medicine. Michael MacConaill became Professor of Anatomy in University College Cork in 1942, and became a recognised expert in biomechanics. He abandoned the ethnological focus of his earlier research, a move which Prendergast and Lee suggest was probably the result of the pejorative connotations the study of racial types had begun to acquire.[79] David Gamble subsequently became renowned for the cultural and linguistic research he published on the Gambian people, and not on the correlation of Irish racial types with kinds of mental illness. These changes of direction are indications of a much more general shift, after the Second World War, away from eugenics and scientific racism, but that physical anthropologists were less willing or able to defend and continue the racial element of their studies is not just a sign of an ethical reaction to Nazism. It is also the case that the scientific basis for such study was beginning to unravel. One of Hooton's research students. Edward Hunt, writing an overview of anthropometric methods in 1959, urged physical anthropologists to 'divorce trait combinations, or morphological types, in a population from faraway geographic subraces or conjectural history'.[80] When MacConaill reviewed *The Physical Anthropology of Ireland* in 1956, he commended the anthropometrical results, largely for their value to archaeologists, but stated that the sociological inferences were 'worthless as they stand' and 'should have been omitted'.[81] MacConaill gives as reasons for this suggestion that the sample upon which sociological inferences were made was not sufficiently large, and that the authors made some errors in their sociological profiles (e.g. 'To group "tinkers" with "hired labourers" is a major error in Irish sociology'), but one senses in his insistence on omitting the sociological profiles that MacConaill had become uncomfortable with the racial determinism implicit in the connection between morphological types and sociological characteristics.

In recent years, there has been a resurgence of interest in defining and identifying race scientifically, largely linked to, and as a result of, developments in genomic research. Such interest tends to crystallise around social and political concerns about health and crime. As Robert Carter argues, this resurgence resembles closely the scientific racism associated with earlier attempts to link race and crime on the basis of physiognomic features, and also receives its justification from the belief that establishing physical or genetic characteristics for racial groups can be beneficial in a biomedical setting.[82] The social concept of race has largely remained intact, despite the scientific advances of genomics research, according to Carter, because 'genomics dissolves race categories (by undermining the link between somatic appearance and group) only to reconstitute them at a deeper genetic level (by suggesting that our most significant connections to other human beings lie in our genes'.[83] If the notion that race has a scientific basis is, as Carter describes, a recurrent fantasy, the anthropometric surveys of Irish people conducted in the 1930s were founded upon a particularly virulent form of this fantasy, one which emphasised the illusion of knowing racial identity through facial biometrics. This is not, however, an obsolete or undermined facet of scientific racism, for it has re-emerged in the security paranoia of post-9/11 western states in the conviction that new digital 'facial recognition technologies' have a key role to play in counter-terrorism.[84] As Kelly Gates argues, these technologies function to produce the face as an index or trace of individual identity, but in the context of security threats which are intensely racialised, the face becomes an archetype, 'and one for which racial categories still deeply matter despite the absence of overtly racist references'.[85] For physical anthropologists writing about Ireland in the 1930s, it is especially the case that the face was an archetype, not simply an index of individual identity and biological inheritance, but a cipher of racial identity and racial history. In the measurements, descriptions, profiles, and photographs they produced, the evidence for distinctive characteristics of race, and the social efficacies of race, was shown to be plainly readable in the features of the face.

We can return now, albeit briefly, to the work of W. B. Yeats, and his remarkable invitation to read the lineaments of the portraits of his friends in order to judge him properly. To say that Yeats is alluding in his poem, specifically in his use of the word 'lineaments' to denote a facial register of racial identity, to the common practices of anthropometric science as it was being conducted around him in Ireland in the mid-1930s would be mistaken. This would fail to take proper calibration of the relationship between literature and science, or more broadly between literature and its cultural-political contexts. If the recurrent figure of reading the face as a racial cipher shows us anything, it is that both Yeats and the physical anthropologists were drawing from the same cultural well of racial classification, and that both understood race as a bodily practice, cipherable and decipherable on the body. That the reading of the face entails a concomitant, yet paradoxical process of individuation and racialisation may have broader significance in the work of Yeats, and not just in the poetry. I am thinking especially here of Yeats's theory of masks, and his deployment of masks in theatrical performance, which insist on the negation of facial readability in order to disengage from place and history, or to disengage 'soul' from 'self'. However, I want to turn now to a contradictory process at work in Irish literary and visual modernism, especially in its later stages from the 1920s to the 1940s. In the work of Liam O'Flaherty, Jack Yeats, and Samuel Beckett, I will argue that there is a progressive de-figuration of the face, which we should read as a critical negotiation of contemporary racial tropes. Specifically, it is the very modernism of their art which accounts for this process, and so what follows is also an argument concerning the cultural and political dynamics of Irish modernism.

With the honourable exception of the vast body of work on W. B. Yeats and James Joyce, of course, the critical record on Irish modernism remains slight, although in tandem with the impact of the new modernist studies of the 1990s, a more capacious and geo-political definition of modernism has given rise to revived interest in the forms and fortunes of modernism in Ireland.[86] Beyond the work of Yeats and Joyce, the meaning and extent of Irish modernism is uncertain, but the reasons for that uncertainty are significant. Terence Brown, for example, who notes the 'paucity of an explicit, developed interest in modernism in Ireland in its post-independence phase', attributes this paucity to the fact that 'in Ireland impulses which elsewhere could find expression in reactionary modernist stances and polemics were channelled into nationalist feeling and the exposition of its sustaining ideology'.[87] Tim Armstrong qualifies that argument in explaining what he sees as 'the defining uncertainty in the Irish modernist tradition', albeit in an essay addressing specifically the question of Irish Catholic modernism. Armstrong concludes that modernism in Ireland did not simply fall prey to the greater pressure of

conservative nationalism, but that '(Irish) Catholic modernism remains
. . . most productive when most an oxymoron'.[88] The degree to which
nationalism and modernism are confluent movements has been the
subject of much debate in Irish cultural studies, usually centring upon
the literary revival, of course. In post-revival Ireland, arguably an
even more complicated relationship develops between modernism and
nationalism. On the one hand, as Armstrong suggests, modernist poets
such as Thomas MacGreevy, Brian Coffey, and Denis Devlin share a
'Catholic lexicon', while, to different degrees, remaining more ambivalent about the cultural project of Catholic nationalism. This implies
a degree of confluence, at least, between modernism and the nation
state after the revival. On the other hand, both Gerardine Meaney and
Anne Fogarty have called attention to the androcentric narrative of
Irish cultural history, that leaves little space for the recuperation of the
dissidence articulated in and by the work of Irish female modernism.[89]
The marginalisation of Irish women writers during this period and since
is a lesson, Meaney writes, in 'what dominant historical forces do to
dissident cultural spaces'.[90] The complication between modernism and
nationalism emerges because, as Alex Davis points out, the nation-state
formed in 1922 was in some respects the autonomous 'high modernist
artwork' of the revival generation, which in turn for Davis explains the
antipathy felt towards nationalism by later writers, who 'tended to con-
flate the revival's representation of Ireland with the more obviously ideological national self-images promoted by Irish Ireland and de Valera'.[91]
That antipathy is certainly registered in the work discussed below, but it
is most evident, I will argue, in the formal tendencies of the work, in its
foregrounding of the processes of figuration and de-figuration.

Faciality in the Novels of Liam O'Flaherty

As J. Hillis Miller writes, the novel is interpreted 'in part through the
identification of recurrences and of meanings generated through recurrences', so that what may appear trivial or insignificant in a single
instance becomes a 'salient motif' when repeated.[92] The repeated word,
scene, or image becomes charged with significance, although it may
form neither a recognisable pattern nor discernible meaning within a
novel. What, then, might we understand to be significant about the
recurrence of lengthy descriptions of facial morphology in the novels
of Liam O'Flaherty? In O'Flaherty's short stories, the face is sometimes
used to define or distinguish a character, but in an unremarkable and
wholly economic manner. In the novels, however, the face takes on a

peculiar, extraordinary significance of its own, commanding a degree of narrative attention which I will argue often goes beyond the formal requirements of character depiction, scene setting, or even expressionist style. This is the case in every one of O'Flaherty's novels, from *Thy Neighbour's Wife* (1923) to *Insurrection* (1950), although the intensity of focus and the extent of repetition differs in degree between the novels.

It must seem obvious, of course, that the face should command the attention of any depiction of character in a novel. The face is the primary site of human organs of communication, and any, perhaps every, novel is likely to expend some portion of its narrative indicating facial gestures, expressions, and complexion. In some fewer cases, the face will be described and represented as the readable surface of character, the external sign of what is mysteriously contained within, or perhaps merely as the sign of how a character appears to others. This is the sense that O'Flaherty uses in the first instance of facial description we can isolate in his first novel, *Thy Neighbour's Wife*, in which the narrative depicts the face of Fr O'Reilly, the parish priest:

> His head was firmly placed on his shoulders and always thrown back at a decorative angle, showing his firm jaw, piercing blue eyes and broad forehead to perfection. His hair had turned grey, but it was a greyness that suited the rest of him, a greyness that could be associated with a well-fed body, and the due respect given to fifty-one years of age, by a parish priest who knew that his reputation for sanctity was secure, as secure as his bank account, which ran well into four figures sterling. His rosy cheeks showed that he had good health. His fleshiness, which was not too apparent, showed that he had a good appetite, and the reddish tinge of his nose, and the pimple on the tip of it, showed according to his enemies that he was a 'little fond of the bottle'.[93]

O'Flaherty's depiction of Fr O'Reilly focuses entirely on his outward appearance, and what this shows to others. We might be especially sensitive, in the light of the preceding section, to what might be implied in the 'firm jaw, piercing blue eyes and broad forehead', but in this instance I would suggest there is no context provided in the novel for understanding these details as racial markers. They function in conglomeration with the ensuing details merely to indicate rude health. The purpose of this description of his facial and bodily visage is not only to fix an image of character for the reader, but also to anchor the narrative point of view firmly on the outside, judging only by appearances and speculation. The narrator is omniscient – the four-figure bank account is a matter of authoritative knowledge, not idle speculation – but that omniscience is used here sparingly, and does not disturb the smooth surface of character evident in the outward appearance of the priest. No doubt one could find passages such as this in many novels. In O'Flaherty's novels, however, the face is increasingly represented and understood as an intricate and enigmatic morphology, the function of which in relation to character, scene, or narrative perspective becomes more difficult to discern.

This becomes most evident in O'Flaherty's best known novel, *The Informer* (1925). For instance, here is the description of the face of the character Francis Joseph McPhillip:

> His face was thin and sallow. His hair was black and cropped close. His eyebrows were black and bushy. His eyelashes were long and they continually drooped over his eyes. When his eyelashes drooped his eyes were blue, sharp and fierce. But when he raised his lashes for a moment to think of something distant and perhaps imaginary, his eyes were large, wistful and dreamy. They were soft and full of a sorrow that was unfathomable. His jaws were square, sharp and fleshless. His lips were thin and set tightly. This gave the lower part of his face a ferocious appearance. His nose was long and straight. His cheeks were hollow and on the cheekbones a bright flush appeared when he was seized with a fit of hard, dry coughing which he tried to suppress.[94]

Frankie McPhillip has committed a political murder, and he dies in trying to escape from the police at the beginning of Chapter 2 of the novel. For a character who is so short-lived in the novel, this passage provides us with too much information. It would possibly be too much information even about a character who stayed with us for the whole novel. It is too much because so much of this description seems redundant, beyond our capacity to use it in understanding the character or the novel. What matter that his 'nose was long and straight', or that his 'eyebrows were black and bushy'? Are these physical features code for personality characteristics? In the earlier passage from *Thy Neighbour's Wife*, the narrator told us clearly what each facial feature 'showed' about the priest, but here there is the assumption that such facial details are significant, without an indication of their meaning. What should we read into this 'thin and sallow' face, and the too many features of this face which follow? Some features are evidently described as a way of telling us something else. That 'a bright flush appeared' on the cheekbones 'when he was seized with a fit of hard, dry coughing which he tried to suppress', for example, gives us an indication of McPhillip's failing health, the cost of his recent time spent as a fugitive in the mountains. Yet even this detail is somewhat overdone. We could be told of his hard, dry coughing without this seemingly additional information that it registers as a 'bright flush' on his face. The face alone seems to be the focus of our interest, and not just as a vehicle for expression.

The description of McPhillip's eyes may also serve to tell us something useful about his character, and here the drooping or raising of the eye-lashes reveal two sides to his personality: the sharp, fierce, blue eyes of the man who has committed a murder and is now a fugitive, and the 'large, wistful and dreamy' eyes which signify 'a sorrow that was unfathomable'. 'Unfathomable' itself plays upon a dual meaning, at once suggesting unknowable depths, impossible to exhaust, and denoting a failure to understand (the fathom is a measure of the arm, so 'unfathomable' is to say 'beyond one's reach'). The eyes are the key to the consciousness here, the 'windows of the soul', yet we learn nothing of the character's 'distant and perhaps imaginary' thoughts, and cannot reach or ascertain the depths of his sorrow. Hence, as with the 'bright flush' on his cheekbones, the eyes also tell us nothing more than their own appearance, and return our attention to the face as surface. This catalogue of facial features thus seems to tell us everything about the face, but at the same time nothing very much beyond the face. How are we to know McPhillip? Through his face, this passage seems to suggest. The description of his face consists of description of all of its parts, and yet each part yields little or nothing to the whole. Even the 'ferocious appearance' is readable only in the lower half of the face, specifically in the lips, as if the features fail to assemble into a coherent whole.

We could attribute the excesses and anomalies of this passage to O'Flaherty's shortcomings as a novelist. In a review of the Wolfhound edition of *The Informer*, published in 1999, Liam Harte reflects, for example, on the obvious 'stylistic crudities, heavy-handed characterisation, and frequent lapses into overwrought, melodramatic prose' which mar O'Flaherty's novel, and which Harte suggests may account for the critical neglect of O'Flaherty's work in recent years.[95] The acknowledgement of such weaknesses is common among O'Flaherty scholars. We might think of such long pieces of facial description as exemplary of what Paul A. Doyle identifies as O'Flaherty's 'too frequent tendency to explain his characters' actions in lengthy expository passages', for example.[96] John Zneimer sees this tendency as symptomatic of the impatience O'Flaherty shows with the mechanical business of style, plot, or characterisation in his desperation to depict the 'soul's struggle', and admits that although the novels have 'unquestionable power', they lack the 'usual standards of craftsmanship'.[97] James O'Brien blames such excesses on O'Flaherty's failure to distinguish between 'scene and summary'.[98] Patrick Sheeran, perhaps O'Flaherty's most authoritative commentator to date, attends more closely to the particular problem of facial description, and observes of the depiction of Gypo Nolan, which I will discuss below, that 'the images fail to cohere – indeed they are only connected by occurring in successive sentences and by referring to the same object – products, in Coleridgian terms, of fancy rather than imagination'.[99] Such failures lead Sheeran to conclude that O'Flaherty 'lives more in the mind for what he tried to do rather than for what he actually accomplished'.[100] More generously, Terry Phillips has argued that we might understand the grotesque excesses of O'Flaherty's characterisation in terms of gothic style, and a stylistic search for sources of resistance to the dominant political and cultural narratives of Irishness after independence.[101] With similar magnanimity, Hedda Friberg argues that 'it is a manifestation of the compassion that marks O'Flaherty's approach to those who exist on the lowest rungs of society's ladder that he dwells for a moment longer than necessary' on the visible signs of their wretchedness.[102] In a telling observation, however, Declan Kiberd remarks that although O'Flaherty's 'movie-like reliance on sheerly external depiction' may yield occasionally convincing images, 'the narrative often lingers over surfaces that are never more than that'.[103]

Like many of these critics, I am conscious of O'Flaherty's weaknesses in terms of artistic control, although I tend to see many of these criticisms as the consequence of a misreading of O'Flaherty's novels as social realism. To attribute O'Flaherty's excessive depictions of facial morphology to lack of novelistic skill is to neglect the fact that such depictions are a consistent, purposeful component of every one of his novels. He may be in error in his consistency, of course, but I want to attend to what emerges when one considers the elaborate facial descriptions of O'Flaherty's novels as a 'salient motif' rather than a superfluous glut of prose. Let us return then to *The Informer* to the passage in which the eponymous informer, Gypo Nolan, is described:

> The man was dressed in a suit of blue dungarees, with a white muffler wound round and round his neck. He had a close-cropped, bullet-shaped head, fair hair and dark eyebrows. The eyebrows were just single tufts, one over the centre of each eye. They grew long and narrowed to a single hair, like the ends of waxed moustaches. They were just like ominous snouts, and they had more expression than the dim little blue eyes that were hidden away behind their scowling shadows. The face was bronzed red and it was covered by swellings that looked like humps at a distance. These humps came out on the forehead, on the cheekbones, on the chin and on either side of the neck below the ears. On close observation, however, they almost disappeared in the general glossy colour of the brownish red skin, that looked as if there were several tiers of taut skin covering the face. The nose was short and bulbous. The mouth was large. The lips were thick and they fitted together in such a manner that the mouth gave the face an expression of being perpetually asleep. His body was immense, with massive limbs and bulging muscles pushing out here and there, like excrescences of the earth breaking the expected regularity of a countryside. He sat upright in his seat,

with his large square head bolted on to his squat neck, like an iron stanchion riveted to a deck.[104]

The first thing to note about this passage is the abundance of similes. They are often unexpected, and perhaps even ineffective, however. To say that 'swellings . . . looked like humps at a distance', for example, adds very little to our conception of Gypo Nolan's face. To compare the tapered ends of his eyebrows to 'the ends of waxed moustaches' arguably confuses the mental image of the face, which apparently does not have a moustache. To compare the same eyebrows to 'ominous snouts' is even more disconcerting. What is an 'ominous snout', and what should we imagine an eyebrow in the shape of an ominous snout looks like? The phrase may be an example of catachresis, except that 'snout' was contemporary slang for 'informer', and this and Gypo's 'bullet-shaped head' are indeed ominous.[105] The whole of Gypo Nolan's face is a landscape of anomalous, disconcerting features, and the point of the above similes is not to provide us with a key to imagining Gypo Nolan's face, but to create the impression of a grotesque, malformed face, as Sheeran observes in his analysis of the same passage.[106] The failure of the similes is itself synecdochic of the grotesque, although it is the successful simile of Gypo's head being bolted to his neck 'like an iron stanchion riveted to a deck' which finally gives us a monstrous provenance for the image O'Flaherty is working to contrive.[107] Gypo is an assemblage of incoherent features, defined by 'excrescences' – swellings on his skin, scowling, protruding eyebrows more expressive than his eyes, and a head appearing to be riveted to his neck. What is interesting about this passage, however, is that, again, the attempt to describe and represent the face constantly loops it back to itself. The eyebrows are compared to a moustache, they are also compared to the dim eyes they hide; the skin looks as if it is 'several tiers of taut skin', and in two instances the face is described as 'covered' by skin; and, in an image which figures this return of the face to the face, we are told 'the mouth *gave the face an expression* of being perpetually asleep' [my emphasis]. This last phrase suggests that there is a prototype face, the faciality of the face, awaiting inscription from one of its expressive parts, the scowling eyebrows or the sleepy mouth. Yet this is an impossible object, a face without features awaiting the gift of those features, or a face beneath the bronzed red skin.[108] To separate the face from its expression, or the face from surface, as Wittgenstein argues, is an 'optical delusion which by some sort of reflection makes us think there are two objects when there is only one'.[109]

Wittgenstein's reflection on the problem of the face might remind us of another important modernist reflection on the problem of perceiving the instance from the archetype, or the action from the design, when Yeats asks rhetorically in 'Among School Children', 'How can we know the dancer from the dance?'[110] Yeats's question confronts us with the epistemological uncertainty of modernism about the paradoxical experience of the aesthetic as both the particular performance and the idea or prototype of that performance. For Jerry Gill, Yeats's question encapsulates a general problem of meaning for the arts: 'For meaning, or significance, always seems to transcend the empirical particulars that comprise it, but in a way which systematically eludes definition'.[111] The depiction of Gypo Nolan's face in *The Informer* embodies the same problem, of how to distinguish the aesthetic appearance of the face as a whole from the particular movements, excrescences, and shades of colour which comprise it. This is made especially evident in the catachrestic tropes recurrently introduced into the passage, which seem calculated to abrupt the process of comprehending the image of the face presented to us.

The problem of reading the face becomes a significant motif in *The Informer*. After Gypo Nolan decides to betray Frankie to the police, he stumbles forth through the streets of Dublin, increasingly tortured with fear for his safety and guilt for his betrayal. The psychological torment he experiences is conveyed principally through his recurrent face-to-face encounters with the slum-dwellers of Dublin's brothel district and with his former comrades in the revolutionary organisation who are now hunting him. So too, his face becomes the visible marker of his tortured emotions: 'his face contorted as if he were gazing at some awe-inspiring horror'.[112] Gypo's problem is that his face is all too readable, or at least that is what he comes to fear, while the faces of those who are pursuing him are opaque and illegible. Mulholland's face, for instance, wears 'that fixed grin of sardonic contempt that is nearly always seen on the faces of men who make a business of concealing their thoughts'. The face appears artificial, with hair like 'a dirty brown wig', eyes that 'stared glassily like a cat's eyes': 'These eyes are sometimes described as watery blue, but it is a totally wrong description. There was an indescribable coldness and depth in them which it is beyond the power of any colour to describe'.[113] The repetition of 'describe' as verb, noun and adjective here may be deemed clumsy, but it is consistent with the repetition of other words throughout the same paragraph, such as 'eyes', 'appearance', 'face', 'hair', and 'colour', which suggest a limited vocabulary, bare prose style, and expedient narrator. Moreover, it suggests both a striving for, and the unattainability of, the power to describe, and again casts up the problem of readability. These two types of face, the readable and unreadable, come face-to-face when Gypo is brought for interrogation to his superior, Gallagher:

> [He] was afraid of Gallagher's eyes into which he was looking steadily. He didn't like them. They were so cold and blue and mysterious. Goodness knows what might be hidden behind them. His face began an irregular chaotic movement. His jaws, cheek-bones, nose, mouth and forehead convulsed in opposite directions, as if a draught of wind had stolen in under the skin of his face and caused it to undulate.[114]

There are two instances here of the face imagined as a cover, concealing another surface behind it. The eyes of Gallagher are perceived as masks, the deceptive, unreadable surfaces behind which lurk the unknown face of Gypo's pursuer. Gypo's fear manifests itself as a facial movement, depicted here as an extraordinary detachment of the skin from its body, the tegument flapping in the wind like a flag, ungrounded from the solid bones of the skull. The scene implies the image of the *écorché*, the anatomical representation of the body without skin which, as Nina Jablonski observes, remains visibly human but no longer identifiable as a person.[115] It is at this very moment that Gypo's face comes alive, almost as something with a life of its own, animated by convulsions to resemble a flag in the wind, that it becomes figured as the mutilated, de-individualised face. Just as passers-by have gaped at Gypo's face, which they see ominously as 'so . . . so dead',[116] here the figurative separation of Gypo's face from his skull also symbolises perhaps his attendant fate.

Gypo's death at the end of the novel, like the murder of Teresa Burke in *The Puritan* (1932), is depicted as a kind of de-facement. In each case, it is significant that the corpse is depicted lying face down.[117] As Gypo nears his impending death, his face becomes glossy and impassive, 'like the features of a carved image', and when he dies he collapses face down on the floor of a church, his body in the shape of the crucifix. Much has been made of the image of Gypo, the informer, as the crucified Christ. The recurrent trope of the corpse face down, however, should also alert us to O'Flaherty's inversion of a vital component of Catholic ritual. The face of Christ on the cross is the ritual object of veneration, the icon of Catholic faith in redemption through sufferance, and as such the cross is always positioned so that the face is visible.[118] But Gypo falls forward onto his face as he dies, the culmination of the process shown through the novel of his face being gradually smoothed, glossed, and erased. In *The Puritan*, Ferriter's murder of a young prostitute, Teresa Burke, is also conceived in relation to Christian iconography, in that Ferriter believes in the necessity of a blood-sacrifice for puritan ideals. Teresa is that blood-sacrifice, through which redemption will be possible, thereby figuring her as the unwitting and unwilling Christ figure. Like Gypo, when she is murdered she falls face down, and Ferriter experiences a momentary 'childish curiosity to turn the corpse over on its back so that he could see its face'.[119] But the erasure of the face is central to Ferriter's motives, for he has conceived of his plan to murder Teresa when he compares a photograph of her face when she was a child with her face as a drunken and debauched prostitute. He steals the photograph after he has murdered her, indicating that the face of the child is a fetish object for Ferriter, the purity of which can only be safeguarded by the obliteration of the face of the woman. Ferriter is a symbolic figure for puritanical discourses in 1930s Ireland, undoubtedly, fusing together the iconography of Catholicism and nationalism. But his personal religious beliefs are hardly orthodox in this context. In his final confessional statement, he explains his crime as an act of 'revolt against a false idea of God': 'There is no God, but man has a divine destiny. It is the duty of each man to become God'.[120] Ferriter's beliefs echo the Nietzschean *übermensch*, as Gallagher voices Nietzschean ideas in *The Informer*. But locked in his prison cell, and tormented by visions of his crime, Ferriter's words ring hollow against the recurrent image of Teresa lying face down with a dagger in her back. The hidden or concealed face is the central topos around which *The Puritan* is organised, for not only is Teresa's corpse always remembered lying face down, but Ferriter's guilt and shame manifests itself in the recurrent gesture of hiding or covering his face.

One could argue that the refusal or inability to see the face in this instance is a manifestation of what Ferriter, as a representative figure of 'the puritan', cannot face. In *The Informer*, the prostitute characters are noted also for their facial morphology: from the drunken prostitute with 'debauched face and melancholy eyes', and 'ragged teeth', who seems to curse Gypo after he emerges from the police station, to Katie, who serves both as friend and betrayer to Gypo in the course of the novel:

> Traces of her young beauty still remained in the deep blue eyes, that were melancholy and tired and twitched at the edges, in her long lean figure now grown emaciated, in her black hair that strayed carelessly about her face from beneath the rim of her ragged red hat. But the mouth, that tell-tale register of vice, had completely lost the sumptuous but delicate curves of innocent girlhood and blossoming maturity. The lips hung down at the sides. They were swollen in the middle. Their colour had died out and had been renewed with loud vulgarity by cheap paint. The poor tormented soul peered out of the young face, old before the years had time to wrinkle it, sad, hard and stupefied.[121]

In this passage we encounter again the figure of the face with memory, the palimpsest face which records the contours of its past. We might say that Katie's face is figured both as a literal face, and the figure of faciality itself, the potential of the face to have been and become other faces. We come close to Deleuze and Guattari's concept of the abstract machine of faciality here, that system by which the face enables individuality, conformity, and deviance.[122] In the case of the above description of Katie, it is clear that only in deviating from the face of the child does Katie's face show its figural significance, and reveal the potential of the face for difference. For the puritan, however, the face of the prostitute registers not the potential for faciality, but the disfigurement or defacement of the face, and thus Ferriter's dream of puritanism, of the *übermensch*, is a dream or, as it turns out, a nightmare, of facelessness.

Mr Gilhooley (1926), in similar fashion, concludes with a death scene in which the face is covered. Gilhooley throws himself into a canal, ridden by guilt for having murdered Nelly, the woman he has fallen in love with. He falls into the canal backwards, covering his face with his hands, and in doing so literalises the painful desire to hide his face from other people that he feels after the murder.[123] Gilhooley's relationship with Nelly, his murder of her, and its consequences are all in fact organised around the topos of the face. It is Nelly's 'tiny and very white' face, 'like the face of a child that has lost its way and cannot find its mother', that first appeals to Gilhooley.[124] In the scene in which Gilhooley becomes besotted with Nelly's 'very white' face, his changing feelings towards her are signalled by the movements of his 'white eyebrows'. O'Flaherty's use of colours for facial depiction is analogous to the expressionist impasto technique, with strong, recurrent application of white, black, yellow, and red.[125] The strong use of such colours renders O'Flaherty's faces always artificial, as if they are masks, as if faces are in fact layers of colour. In all of his novels, O'Flaherty's faces become associated metonymically with a particular colour or striking facial feature. Mr Gilhooley has his white eyebrows, and pockmarks on the tip of his nose. Nelly is known by her very white face, and magnificent blue eyes, the same eyes which bear a look of terror and which Mr Gilhooley finds are unpleasantly appealing.[126] Their ill-fated relationship is foretold in the look of terror in Nelly's eyes. In the murder scene, it is again the face which remains the central figure. Nelly has driven Mr Gilhooley mad with jealousy, courting other lovers, and constantly talking about her previous lover, Matt. 'You never saw his face. His face is beautiful', Nelly tells Gilhooley, as he begs her for one last kiss, in a scene in which faces become symbolic of psychological states, his face becoming more ghoulish as hers becomes contorted with fear. When she shows him a photograph of Matt, 'smiling coldly at him', Gilhooley becomes violent, and feels that 'a strange man brandishing a club' has entered the room, a figure evidently of his own dissociated state as he murders her. His response thereafter, from the murder scene to the final scene of his suicide, is to cover his face, 'to prevent the people who passed from seeing his face', for 'he felt sure there was something in his face which they would all recognize'.[127] As he nears the canal, this fear of the mark of guilt on his own face, which would make him different from others, is recast as the fear that 'in all faces he saw his own face, horrible with the mark of guilt. In all faces he saw the ugliness of his own face'.[128] This synecdochic vision of his face becoming all faces is a clear sign of narcissism, just as his murder of Nelly is prompted by the fact that the photograph she holds up to him returns not his own image, but the image of another man, 'smiling coldly'. The face of the other is either impossible for him to see, or if seen, it strikes him as 'unpleasant', until finally it is own face which is horrible to see. If Mr Gilhooley gives a face to love, it is his own face, and when he cannot bear the face of the other, he becomes another in his dissociated state, erasing his own face, and, in murdering Nelly, effacing her. She is figuratively de-faced, as he cannot bring himself to look upon her after he has killed her, and exits the room with his hands over his face. When he sees her apparition at the canal bank, she has her back turned to him, moving away from him until she vanishes. His final words, 'There is nothing. Nothing at all', echo the famous final words of Kurtz in Conrad's *Heart of Darkness*: 'The Horror! The Horror!', and share the same sense that the world is godless, that there is neither good nor evil. When he looks upon other human beings he sees not the face of the divine, and not as beings with names and personalities, but as living parts of himself, 'each with a face like his own'.[129] At this moment, his face also becomes repulsive to him, and he is compelled to hide it behind his hands, and ultimately then to take his own life.

Like *The Puritan* and *The Informer*, then, *Mr Gilhooley* is organised around the central topos of the face, and more significantly, around the topoi of effacement and facelessness.[130] The face is a salient motif in O'Flaherty's oeuvre as a whole, as I have been arguing, but in these three novels in particular, the face becomes the dominant trope, and it repeatedly comes to represent opacity, unreadability, and effacement. If the face, as in the figure of prosopopoeia, should bring presence, a readable, recognisable, knowable surface to stand for all that is concealed and mysterious, in O'Flaherty's novels, it becomes repeatedly a figure of absence, of the indecipherable and the unknowable. Clearly, this has important implications for the discourse of phenotypology and its constitutive assumptions of facial readability and racial signification, but I will suspend discussion of these implications until we have established that the readability of the face is not the preoccupation of Liam O'Flaherty alone.

'Our Own Faces Made All Awry': Art and Anthropology in the Work of Jack B. Yeats

In May 1934, C. W. Dupertuis gave as a preliminary insight into the findings of his research 'that the farther West he went the less mixture of racial types did he find, which pointed to the fact that the purest types were found in that part of the country'.[131] The published results of the study, as interpreted by Hooton, didn't quite confirm this early impression, although there was a higher incidence of 'blondness' west of the Shannon, a slightly heavier concentration of 'pure Nordic', and the Aran Islands were said to constitute a distinctive ethnographic area, perhaps because of their isolation and hence relatively high level of inbreeding. Dupertuis spent much of the early part of his field work in Ireland in the west, especially in the Aran Islands, while his later collaborator, Helen Dawson, collected anthropometric data on Irish females entirely in the west. The west had been extensively mythologised in Irish culture in the late nineteenth and early twentieth centuries as a physical and symbolic repository of a Gaelic people and way of life untrammelled by the metropolitan and industrial habits which were understood to have corrupted the urbanised eastern seaboard of Ireland. From its inception, the Harvard study was interested in Ireland as an 'outpost', as an island with relatively well-known patterns of historical migration, and which was relatively isolated, with fewer 'subracial' strains to identify and track. This made the west of Ireland an especially apt focus for much of the field work, as the literary, mythological, and historical writings of the revival period identified the west as almost a living museum of an ancient peasant people. Although *The Physical Anthropology of Ireland* could hardly be described as romanticising the west, part of its origins lay precisely in these revival myths of the west. One of the key figures in the romanticising of the west during the revival period was J. M. Synge. Synge did more than most of his contemporaries to promote an ideal of the west as untarnished by commercial and industrial influence in his plays, *Riders to the Sea* (1904) and *The Playboy of the Western World* (1907), and in his prose, *The Aran Islands* (1907) and a series of articles he wrote for the *Manchester Guardian* on life in Connemara (1905). It is not Synge's work I wish to examine in this chapter, however, but the work of the illustrator for much of Synge's work in the west, Jack B. Yeats.

Jack Yeats accompanied Synge on his expedition to Connemara in 1905, drawing the illustrations for the sketches penned by Synge of the life of peasants in the most impoverished areas of the west. He also provided the illustrations for Synge's publications on Kerry, Wicklow, and for Synge's most successful work of prose, *The Aran Islands*. Although he had not accompanied Synge on the five summers he spent on the islands, Synge had contemplated asking Jack to illustrate the book as early as 1900.[132] Jack Yeats's collaboration with Synge formed the nucleus of a body of work which would gain him a reputation as the illustrator of revival Ireland. As Bruce Arnold writes, he was 'not being admired simply as an artist', but because he had become 'programmed to deliver a collateral visual message about the progress of Ireland's life and spirit'.[133] His work with Synge consisted of drawings of the people, activities, and landscape of the various parts of Ireland they visited, together or separately, although some of Yeats's drawings for *The Aran Islands* were based on Synge's photographs. In these illustrations, Hilary Pyle argues, Yeats 'concentrated on the wild, uncompromising nature of the existence' of 'a noble if poverty-stricken race'.[134] Beside drawings of kelp-burning, thatched cottages, and evictions, therefore, Yeats provides studies of the people, in which it is understood that they are 'types', or 'characters', the fruits of an anthropological expedition to the wilds and margins. Synge had reservations about the anthropological nature of their work in Connemara, writing in a letter that 'in certain ways I like not lifting the rags from my mother country for to tickle the sentiments of Manchester', and perhaps Yeats shared these reservations too.[135] Synge suffered from the accusations hurled at him in reaction to the production of *The Shadow of the Glen* that he was indeed tickling colonial sentiments by depicting Irish life as exotic, and he reacted defensively by suggesting that *The Aran Islands* might be best 'published and printed in Dublin on Irish paper'.[136] The relationship with Synge, according to Bruce Arnold, had also transformed Jack Yeats's outlook, and his view of the relationship between his art and his subject matter: 'He no longer looked at "Life in the West of Ireland" from the outside; it was becoming part of him'.[137]

Yeats moved to Ireland in November 1910, having lived in England for much of his life until then, and immersed himself in the Irish cultural scene. He held a number of exhibitions in Ireland, and sold many paintings, based on the sketches he drew in the west of Ireland with Synge. In 1912 he published *Life in the West of Ireland*, an album of forty illustrations of life and people in the west, together with sixteen reproductions of some of his recent oil paintings.[138] He also gave permission for five of his illustrations to be used in Robert Lynd's *Rambles in Ireland*, and in the following year, he produced twelve colour illustrations for George Birmingham's *Irishmen All*, and five illustrations for Pádraic Colum's *A Boy in Erinn*.[139] Many of the illustrations commissioned or requested from Yeats reflect his talents for strong line drawings of incident and action which were developed while working for newspapers and serial publications in England, but in several books, including his own *Life in the West of Ireland*, and the collaborations with Synge and Birmingham, Yeats was developing a talent and a reputation for depicting Irish 'types'.

In his work with Synge, it was perhaps inevitable that the types depicted were associated with a particular region. So illustrations entitled 'A Wicklow Vagrant', for example, or 'A Man of the Glens', or, in *The Aran Islands*, illustrations entitled 'An Island Man', or 'An Island Horseman', suggested that the dress, posture, or physical features of each subject were representative of their locality. For Birmingham's *Irishmen All*, Yeats produced twelve illustrations on the basis of Birmingham's chapter headings, all of which suggested a social type: the higher official, the minor official, the policeman, the squireen, the politician, the country gentleman, the farmer, the publican, the exile from Erin, the parish priest, the minister, and the young lady and gentleman in business. Of these, the squireen is the most obviously satirical of the illustrations, depicted wearing a gaudy red waistcoat, and flashy chequered trousers. The image of the farmer is perhaps the most strongly racialised face, made suggestively distinctive by thick sideburns which protrude almost to the nose, by the eyebrows which meet in the middle, and by a thin angular face. There are similar facial features, and faces which appear to be racially distinctive, in some of the character sketches in *Life in the West of Ireland*. On the basis of such work, Pádraic Colum praised Yeats for 'having discovered a new world for the painter – his pictures reveal the race – a race that has still vigour and personality with something of "the playboy" in every character'.[140]

Colum's praise for Yeats, published in 1914, is perhaps indicative of Arnold's argument that Yeats was becoming 'programmed' as an artist serving the nationalist cause, which is to say that the nationalism of his art lay in its reception perhaps more than its conception. How Yeats's pictures 'reveal the race' is worth considering. It is perhaps to be inferred from his commitment to drawing and painting subjects in Ireland, to exhibiting and publishing in Ireland too. It is perhaps to be inferred also from his contribution to the wider mythologising of the west as a distinctive, 'wild' space, which was believed to retain more of the culture of pre-colonial Ireland than the east. His choice of subject matter may define him as a national artist. But can it be read, or judged, from the pictures themselves, in their form and treatment, that Yeats's art represented 'the race'? When we look at Yeats's treatment of western 'types', for example, are those faces racially coded? To compare Yeats's illustrations of life in Manchester with those of life in Carraroe, or the Aran Islands, it is not particularly apparent that there is an 'Irish face' in Yeats's work. The differences between his paintings of English and Irish subjects – incidentals of facial shape, for instance, or the style and condition of dress – might be more easily attributable to social conditions, rather than race. And yet, there are some distinctive features of Yeats's Irish faces which become almost metonymic.

In the paintings of the teen years, this is especially apparent. The eyebrows meet, or to use the term common in physical anthropology, the eyebrows are concurrent. In *The Maggie Man* (1912), *The Barrel Man* (1912), *The Circus Dwarf* (1912), *The Farmer* (1913), *The Exile from Erin* (1913), *Before the Start* (1915), *The Public Speaker* (1915), *The Double Jockey Act* (1916), *On Drumcliffe Strand* (1918), and *Off the Donegal Coast* (1922) (and perhaps half a dozen other paintings in which it is difficult to discern the difference between eyebrow and nasion depression), the eyebrows are concurrent in the subject, or some of the subjects, of each painting. *Before the Start* is perhaps the most notable among these, because all three jockeys depicted in the painting display this feature prominently and clearly. It may also be significant that it is a discernible trait in *The Public Speaker*. *The Public Speaker* is based on sketches Jack Yeats made of Patrick Pearse speaking to Irish volunteers in Dundrum, but a comparison of the sketch of Pearse with the painting shows that Yeats replaced the observed Pearse with an imagined, or invented subject, whose eyebrows meet in the middle.[141] This indicates that the prevalence of concurrent eyebrows in Yeats's work may be a matter of conscious design, rather than the accidental consequence of having met many people with concurrent eyebrows. The monobrow, as it is sometimes known, has been the subject of various superstitions in European cultures, and is usually taken as a sign of bad luck, hereditary illness, ugliness, or untrustworthiness. It is highly probable that Yeats had something of this context in mind when painting his circus subjects, I would suggest, because in such paintings as *The Barrel Man* or *The Circus Dwarf* Yeats is drawn towards the image of the social scapegoat, the circus 'freak' who is marked physically with the sign of his difference. It is possible, thereafter, to suggest that the artist developed concurrent eyebrows as a leitmotif for such figures, and that *The Public Speaker* uses this leitmotif to mark the orator with the

Figure 2.8   Jack B. Yeats, *Before the Start* (1915). Courtesy of the National Gallery of Ireland. Photo © National Gallery of Ireland

sign that he too is something of a circus performer, or social freak. This argument would not explain Yeats's depiction of concurrent eyebrows in *The Farmer*, or *The Exile from Erin*, or the woman in *On Drumcliffe Strand*, however.

Is this motif of concurrent eyebrows a racial marker, therefore? We need to return to the physical anthropology at this point to place this question within the context of contemporary scientific raciology. There are some disagreements between the physical anthropologists in their interpretations of the data, but in general they agree on one thing. As a population group, the Irish show relatively high instances of eyebrow concurrency. Hooton and Dupertuis argue that, among Irish males, 'eyebrow concurrency is prevailingly medium (64.7 per cent), but oftener submedium (23.2 per cent) than pronounced (10.3 per cent)', and that the highest frequency of eyebrow concurrency was along the eastern seaboard, and the lowest in the west.[142] It was less pronounced as a feature among the west coast females in Helen Dawson's survey, this sex difference confirming what was 'usual and expected' for facial hair, but still relatively high.[143] Coon, reviewing the same data from Dupertuis's sample, of course, came to much the same conclusion, but stated it slightly differently, 'eyebrows show some degree of concurrency

Figure 2.9   Jack B. Yeats, *The Public Speaker* (1915). © Estate of Jack B. Yeats. All rights reserved, DACS 2009

in all but 2 per cent of the group'.[144] This placed the emphasis on the very small percentage of Irish men who showed no sign of eyebrow concurrency, rather than the varying degrees of submedium, medium, and pronounced evident in Hooton's analysis. Coon also confirmed that 'the greatest concurrency is found in the north and east, the least in the south and west'. Coon believed, or rather assumed, that concurrent eyebrows were a feature inherited from 'the older Mesolithic strain', and therefore another mark of the ancient lineage visible on the Irish face, although Gamble, who also noted high incidences of eyebrow concurrency, attributed this feature among Northern Irish subjects to the Dinaric sub-racial type.[145] For the physical anthropologists, clearly, eyebrow concurrency was one among the many facial markers that comprised the racially distinctive strains of the Irish. Jack Yeats may go slightly off the mark in that the anthropology showed greater prevalence of concurrent eyebrows in the east than in the west, but it seems likely, given the corroborating evidence from physical anthropology (albeit twenty years later), that Yeats was indeed using this as a visual cue of racial identity. Just as in the case of O'Flaherty's morphological descriptions, it is the recurrence of these facial features in the paintings of Jack Yeats which should alert us to their significance.

    The paintings in which concurrent eyebrows feature belong, however, to a distinct phase in Jack Yeats's work, what Hilary Pyle calls the 'descriptive' work.[146] This broadly conforms to the period of cultural and political revival, and includes the illustrations and paintings which, for the most part, reflected various aspects of Irish life and 'character types'. It was during this phase that Yeats acquired a reputation as a national artist, a reputation which Thomas MacGreevy would exaggerate further in his argument that Yeats was in fact a nationalist and republican artist.[147] Arnold disputes this view of Yeats's work, finding no evidence of an explicit political dimension in the paintings, and charting instead an artist who developed 'an understanding of many different strands of human motive which were clothed in emotional purpose often too deep to fathom'.[148] But Arnold over-stretches this argument at times, particularly in his reading of Yeats's lecture at the Irish Race Congress in Paris in January 1922, his only lecture on record. Arnold suggests that the lecture shows Jack's awareness of 'the danger of racial exclusiveness in the arts', but there is little evidence for this, other than perhaps a misreading of Yeats's advice that artists should not be considered as 'a wonderful and mysterious race' standing apart from the people, which is part of his democratic call to anyone to begin to draw or paint what they see.[149] In turn, Arnold makes little of the following passage, in which it is clear that there is an implicit national, and possibly even racial, meaning:

> When painting takes its rightful place it will be in a free nation, for though pictures speak all languages the roots of every art must be in the country of the artist, and no man can have two countries; and this applies with greater force to the artist than anyone else, for the true painter must be part of the land and of the life he paints. The artist may travel all the roads of the world, and may paint pictures of what he sees, but he can never be part of these roads as he can of the roads of his own land. His pictures will tend to be nothing but the dead skins of what he sees. . . . We must look to ourselves for the springs of our art. We must not look to Paris or London for a pace-maker.[150]

Arnold suggests that listeners such as de Valera 'would have been reassured by Jack's dedication to the new state' evident in this passage, but the politics of the passage go beyond this.[151] Yeats was endorsing the idea of a national art, certainly, and, in places, couching his lecture in the rhetoric of political nationalism. There is the echo of Emmet's 'Speech from the Dock' in the first line of this passage, and the organic metaphors for the nation, and for the relationship between the intellectual and the nation. Jack Yeats was born in London, and spent much of his childhood and adult life prior to 1922 living and working in England, for the most part happily it seems, so to argue that 'no man can have two countries' was perhaps to invalidate some of his own experiences. More pertinently, in his own case, it might be said to raise the question of how one determined the source of his art. If it was determined by choice, then surely an artist could bring to life the roads of any country he saw fit to pledge allegiance to, except that Yeats saw in such pictures the mere 'dead skins' of life. If it was determined by birth and experience, then surely his own hyphenated existence between Ireland and England made it eminently possible, even likely, that an artist could have two countries. Instead, and in keeping with the spirit of the Irish Race Congress as a whole, Jack Yeats was defining 'ourselves', and the springs from which his art flowed, in inherently racial terms.

Yeats's lecture was delivered and published at a time when a distinct change was about to become visible in the style of his art. The 'descriptive' phase was coming to an end, and although his subject matter for the most part would draw from the same Irish sources, and although in retrospect one can discern a 'gradual change in an artist outgrowing his old manner' as early as 1915, he was about to become the expressionist painter for which he is now most renowned.[152] 'In 1923 the outline vanishes', Pyle writes: 'At this point a painterly quality commences in representational works which have a freedom and a lyricism that is new, rich broad strokes hinting the colour to come, with soft expressive power rejecting the former constrictive outline'.[153] The change in style may be gradual, but to compare a Jack Yeats painting from 1915 with one from 1925 is to observe a fundamental change in the nature of his art. In 1915, in a painting such as *Before the Start*, Yeats was recording and describing cultural customs, character types, and, if we understand the concurrent eyebrows as racial markers, then racial types too. His work had a strongly referential quality, and implicit in his treatment of his subject matter was a cultural-political claim for its validity and distinctiveness. In 1925, in paintings such as *O'Connell Bridge* or *The Donkey Show*, although the source of subject matter remains recognisably, explicitly Irish, the lines and strokes which make up the faces of Yeats's subjects are becoming indistinct, indecipherable. In *O'Connell Bridge*, the grey faces of the men suggest stony impassivity, perhaps, whereas the two women's faces wear vibrant pink, yellow, and red tinges. We are drawn to the ways in which colour and line suggest mood, or psychological condition, to the ways in which faces are patterns of emotional meaning.

The comparison is even more acute when we have nominally similar subject matter, but treated in contrasting styles, as for example when we compare *The Exile from Erin* (1913) and *The Emigrant* (1928). *The Exile from Erin* depicts a man sitting beside a window, an urban landscape of flat-roofed houses visible beyond him, while he is focused upon the newspaper bearing news from Ireland in front of him, with more newspapers and books surrounding him, and a noticeboard studded with letters behind him. His downcast eyes, concentrated on reading, imply nostalgia for home, and a sense of alienation from his present surroundings. Arguably, the painting makes a similar point to the one Yeats was making in his 1922 lecture about the artist, that separated from his people, and the land of his origins, the man was merely a dead skin. His concurrent eyebrows, coupled with this sense that he has been cut off from the sources of his vitality, suggest again the potential for racial meaning. In *The Emigrant*, no such reading is possible. The emigrant figure certainly appears alienated, lonely, and mournful. The face and body are painted in grey with red streaks, with slapdash brush-strokes providing a rough shape and outline, and red splodges marking the eyes, mouth, and nostrils. But the figure is of indeterminate gender, or race, and although it is possible to surmise that he or she is stand-ing on a train, tram, or possibly in a bar, the surroundings have been stripped for the most part of reference points. It is impossible to say that the figure is Irish, let alone infer any political or cultural meaning from the painting. In both paintings, the face is everything, conveys everything, but in *The Emigrant*, Yeats has refined his technique of facial depiction to dissolve the racial and cultural markers evident in the earlier work.

As David Lloyd has recently argued, the aesthetics of Yeats's expres-sionist work go beyond this, however. In the work produced from 1923 onwards, we encounter the 'rigorous foregrounding of the technical problems of representation',[154] so that paintings such as *The Emigrant* draw attention to their own artifice, to splodges of colour, and thick, seemingly careless brushstrokes, and barely delineated shapes. The surface texture of Yeats's oil paintings after 1923 are pock-marked with thick impasto layers, paint applied directly from the tube, slapdash brush strokes, bare areas of canvas hardly even touched by paint, and layers of paint scratched and scored with a palette knife or brush handle. If the early work was too easily appropriated for political purposes, or viewed as a kind of anthropological window upon the west of Ireland, the later work resists the illusion of transparency, and makes even symbolic and figurative readings – of emotion, memory, or psychologi-cal states – impossible to ground. Lloyd's argument is similar in many ways to that made by Tricia Cusack, who sees the 'opaque facture' of Yeats's later paintings as undermining the security of national identity evident in his earlier work.[155] For Lloyd, the work becomes about 'the enactment of failure of representation, a failure either to retrieve or to abandon the object', an interpretation which does much to explain the influence of Jack Yeats on the work of Samuel Beckett.[156]

This goes some way to explaining what happens to the face in the later work of Jack Yeats too. To compare the faces of Yeats's work pre-1923 and post-1923 is to see the dissolution of the strongly delineated morphological features, and an increasing concern with minimalist techniques of facial figuration. In paintings such as *The Breaker Out* (1925), *The Bar* (1925) and *Fair Day, County Mayo* (1925), faces retain discernible features such as brow ridges, hair colour, nasal profile, but the surface texture of the paint becomes more striking than the facial features. The faces begin to appear like masks of paint. The paint ceases to figure as skin, and itself becomes a skin. The tendency towards abstraction, while not free to abandon the object or figure, means that increasingly the faces are revealed as patterns of marks, codes which signify only their codedness. They expose the 'abstract machine of faciality', as Deleuze and Guattari describe, in some cases almost literally 'composed by a black hole/white wall system', as monstrous and grotesque as the faces in O'Flaherty's novels.[157] In *The Bar*, for example, the barmaid's face is a thick, pasted white surface, upon which two eyes, two eyebrows, the nostril line, and the mouth are smeared and smudged strokes of red, black, and grey paint. It closely resembles the face of a clown. The clown face became a leitmotif in Yeats's late work, undoubtedly a continuation of his abiding fascination with the circus and performers, but it was also a significant development in his expressionist figurations of the face.

In a series of paintings beginning with *Johnny Patterson, or The Singing Clown* (1928), and including *The Clown Among the People* (1932), *They Come, They Come* (1936), *Alone* (1944), and *They Love Me* (1950), Yeats paintings of clown faces foreground the technique of faciality, crafting the painted surface of a painted face with strong use of impasto, signifying the face with dots and dashes of black and red. The clown face projects an image of faciality by, in effect, erasing the face of the performer. It is a figure of groundlessness, of the free-floating signifier, which replaces the readable anthropometric signs of a racially encoded face with the simulated marks of bare faciality. In these paintings, emotion is discernible. Indeed, one might say that Yeats is most concerned in the clown paintings with the juxtaposition of the counterfeit face and the implicitly real emotions. In *Alone* and *They Love Me*, for example, we are invited to see the face of the clown contorted in emotional pain, a view unseen by any of the clown's spectators. But the artificiality of the face begs the question of how can we read such emotions abstracted from the performance of the face? We are returned again to the problem of distinguishing the dancer from the dance, the figure from its grounding, especially also because of the formal

Figure 2.10   Jack B. Yeats, *The Exile from Erin* (1913). © Estate of Jack B. Yeats.
All rights reserved, DACS 2009

techniques in both paintings which foreground the medium. In contrast
to the earlier work in which the face could function as the promissory
of ethnographic meaning, in the later work faces become dis-figured,
incapable of sustaining any such ethnographic reading. Yet this disfiguration itself is only made possible because of the assumption of whiteness as universal, a point easily grasped when contrasting the clown
paintings with Yeats's paintings of Christy Minstrel shows, such as
South Pacific (1937) and *Singing 'Way Down Upon the Swanee River'*
(1942). Yeats's interest in the blackfaced minstrel performer shares
with his clown paintings the focus on the face as a cosmetic construction, an artifice of faciality, with the face of the performer erased by the
face of the performance. Yet it could hardly be claimed that blackface

Figure 2.11   Jack B. Yeats, *The Emigrant* (1928). © Estate of Jack B. Yeats. All rights reserved, DACS 2009

minstrelsy exceeded or evaded ethnographic meaning, although it undoubtedly complicates and problematises it. This is because, of course, blackface performances depend already upon the audience's understanding of an ironic play between the visual racial signifier of blackness, and the whiteness underneath, whereas the whiteness of the clown's face assumes the freedom of the blank canvas, but is nevertheless inscribed implicitly within a racial politics in which whiteness is the norm, the sign of universal humanity.

In the explanation Yeats gives in *Sligo* for his fascination with minstrel shows, this play of racial identification and difference, the ironic doubling of racialised faces, is made clear, although he is too quick to dismiss the symbolic potency of blackness:

> I think the fact that their faces are black is the least ingredient in the goblet. Blue, green or purple would be just as exciting. The main joint in the joinery is that the Minstrels are disguised in a frightening way. Oh, don't say 'Masks': Oh Masks, such a lot of talk about Masks – everyone knows about Masks just being about the last thing but three. . . . Christy Minstrel faces with the great pink mouths are not Masks, they are the faces of our brothers, our own faces made all awry.[158]

The point about blackface is to make both 'frightening' and 'exciting' that awry-ness, that performance of deviation from whiteness, in an ironic performance of affinity with the humanity of 'our brothers' which yet at the same time disavows affinity. Like the circus, blackface performance licenses the enjoyment and thrill of the spectacle of deviance, and in the process reinscribes the sense of 'ourselves' as spectators, as those who control and commodify the performances of others. If there is a sense of community with 'our brothers', it is produced within the confines of a spectacle designed for the consumption of self-consciously white people. That spectacle, however, is predicated upon a paradoxical situation, in which blackface is simultaneously an artifice dependent upon a material body and performance, and a reproducible sign, floating free of its material context. Like the clown paintings, then, the blackface paintings remark upon the indeterminacy of the face as a signifier of the real, mobilising the reproducibility of the face in performative gestures of emotion and identification to problematise the aesthetics of representation.

The face ceases to be the promissory of ethnographic meaning in Yeats's late work, but it is not simply the case that the modernist paintings exceed or transcend racial and national figuration. Indeed, one might recall *Men of Destiny* (1946), with its two central figures made translucent against the land and seascape, almost dissolving into insignificance and invisibility, which, by virtue of its title articulates a critical response to the nationalist iconography of Sean Keating's *Men of the South* (1921) and *Men of the West* (1915). It is possible too that Yeats made reference to his own appropriation into the national story in *Flower Girl, Dublin* (1926), which may be interpreted as an ironic counter-point to his earlier painting of a flower girl, *Bachelor's Walk, In Memory* (1915): the earlier painting suspends time at a poignant moment of commemoration for three victims of a British army shooting, when a Dublin flower seller stops to drop some of her wares at the place of the shootings, while the later painting depicts a flower girl doing nothing more significant than talking to a friend in a street at night, the people painted sketchily, their faces barely perceptible, the whole scene rendered almost carelessly. If they are companion pieces, the later painting seems to be robbed of poignancy, a study not of a moment of national significance, of the tragic deaths from which will emerge a heroic struggle for national self-definition, but instead of a people and a scene still-born, without the capacity for meaning, or struggle. As the later paintings complicate and criticise the nationalist iconography which was too easily read into the earlier work, so too the increasing indecipherability and imperceptibility of the face in Yeats's late paintings problematise the role of the face as a racial marker. The faces dissolve, almost indiscernible, against the dissolving figures of the body and the landscape, while the landscape itself becomes in painting after painting translucent and opaque, unable to sustain the markers of place, time or identity. Far from the national artist of renown, then, what we see in the paintings of Jack Yeats after 1923, which takes place under the name of expressionism, is a formal undoing of the capacity of the face to fix racial identity, a de-figuration of the face, and it is with this movement of de-figuration that I want to conclude the chapter.

'Balls, all balls': Effacement in the Novels of Samuel Beckett

The apotheosis of this process of facial de-figuration can be found in the novels of Samuel Beckett. In *The Unnamable*, the narrator describes himself as 'a great smooth ball . . . featureless, but for the eyes, of which only the sockets remain', or as a featureless egg: 'No, no, that's the old nonsense, I always knew I was round, solid and round, without daring to say so, no asperities, no apertures, invisible perhaps, or as vast as Sirius in the Great Dog, these expressions mean nothing'.[159] The narrator must reach for analogies – with the star, with the egg – to describe what is indescribable, a face without features. Does the face without features remain a face? The analogies are also rejected, however, as meaningless expressions, for the face without features is indefinable and intransitive. As Steven Connor argues, the imagination of a face without features is a form of longing for 'a disfiguration that will erase – but visibly erase – the apparatus of figurality itself'.[160] Later in the novel, the narrator dreams of the reassuring presence of a face:

> A face, how encouraging that would be, if it could be a face, every now and then, always the same, methodically varying its expressions, doggedly demonstrating all a true face can do, without ever ceasing to be recognizable as such, passing from unmixed joy to the sullen fixity of marble, via the most characteristic shades of disenchantment, how pleasant that would be. . . . A presence at last.[161]

The face is the illusion of presence, then, comforting and familiar, even if also here recognised as a machine, producing this illusion. The face is not the promissory note of human presence or relation, not the Levinasian sign of ethical being, but closer to Wittgenstein's conception of the face as a mathematical sign or system of signs. We see the face only because we see these signs *as a* face, in Wittgenstein's conception. Beckett's unnamable ceases to will these signs into a face, proclaiming the face 'Balls, all balls':

> I don't believe in the eye either, there's nothing there, nothing to see, nothing to see with, merciful coincidence, when you think what it would be, a world

without spectator, and vice versa, brrr! No spectator then, and better still no spectacle, good riddance.[162]

Without spectacle, there are only the words, and the silence, and the uncertainty of the unnamable at the end of the novel as to whether 'they' will 'say me', or 'perhaps they have said me already'.[163] *The Unnamable* is thus poised between preface and effacement, between the imagination of the featureless face awaiting inscription, and the dream of de-figuring or de-facing the face.

If the absence, or absenting, of the face is a central topos in *The Unnamable*, this is the culmination of a process which can be traced through Beckett's earlier novels. In some of the novels, the face is recognisable by distinctive features, even if those features tend to be depicted in grotesque and disfigured forms, reminiscent (perhaps surprisingly) of the facial descriptions we encountered in O'Flaherty's novels. I am thinking here of Mr Endon's face in *Murphy*, the big red nose and enigmatic smile of Watt, or Mary's mouth in the same novel, or, again in *Watt*, the ever-variable features of Mr Knott's face.[164] So too, the face is figured in various leitmotifs running through the novels, such as the four instances of characters falling on their faces in *Murphy*, and the several face-to-face exchanges, imagined exchanges or indeed, failed exchanges, as is perhaps most memorable in the comic committee scene, in *Watt*.[165] There are moments in which the face is understood to offer some sense of security or comfort, as at the beginning of *Murphy*, in the fitful and puzzling conversation between Murphy and his mentor, Neary:

> Neary came out of one of his dead sleeps and said:
> 'Murphy, all life is figure and ground.'
> 'But a wandering to find home,' said Murphy.
> 'The face,' said Neary, 'or system of faces, against the big blooming buzzing confusion. I think of Miss Dwyer.'[166]

But if the face functions in this instance as a figure of homeliness, of meaning and sense in a world of confusion, it is displaced at the end of the novel when Murphy's corpse is identified not by its distinctive facial features but by the 'extensive capillary angioma' on his arse. This scene is echoed at the end of *Watt*, where in trying to identify Watt, Mr Case tells us 'I cannot say that I recognize the face. . . . And yet I have a great memory for faces as a rule. . . . And for arses, added Mr Case as an afterthought. Let me once catch a fair glimpse of an arse, and I'll pick it out for you among a million'.[167] The repetition of this incidence of making the arse the primary site of human identification, or at least making the face and arse interchangeable as 'faces' of recognition, should alert us not just to Beckett's scatological propensities, but also to the motif of de-figuring the face.

More pertinent to our discussion here, of course, is the recurrent theme of the face being expressionless, enigmatic, or difficult to read. This is particularly acute in *Molloy* and *Malone Dies*. The smile that might have crossed Malone's face had he realised that he would still 'feel myself living as I do today', 'would not have been noticed, but I would have known that I was smiling'.[168] Even a 'little smile' has to be qualified as 'a little rictus rather', later in the novel, while Sapo's face is also described as 'always grave, or rather expressionless'.[169] The face ceases to wear emotion, or expression, or even to be capable of bearing recognition or resemblance. Molloy's failed pursuer, Moran, for example, contemplates the opacity and disappearance of his own face as reflected in water on two occasions. First, he merely notices that as the reflected image 'trembled towards an ever increasing likeness', 'a drop, falling from my face, shattered it again'.[170] In the second scene, however, preoccupied with imagining himself ageing, Moran is beset by a vision in which his reflected face is:

> a little globe swaying up slowly from the depths, through the quiet water, smooth at first, and scarcely paler than its escorting ripples, then little by little a face, with holes for the eyes and mouth and other wounds, and nothing to show if it was a man's face or a woman's face, a young face or an old face, or if its calm too was not an effect of the water trembling between it and the light.[171]

This vision Moran reads as an index of his 'growing resignation to being dispossessed of self'. In each case, the allusion to the 'trembling' of the water in which the face is reflected may conjure up the same sense of spiritual and metaphysical crisis which is articulated in W. B. Yeats's *The Trembling of the Veil* (1922), and indeed in Stéphane Mallarmé's famous remark that 'the trembling of the veil of the Temple troubled my epoch', from which Yeats takes his title.[172] For Yeats, this meant that 'the world was now but a bundle of fragments', in contrast to the ancient ideal he aspires towards in his art, that 'in man and race alike there is something called "Unity of Being"', and that 'there could be no aim for poet or artist except expression of a "Unity of Being" like that of a "perfectly proportioned human body"'.[173] Yeats describes a disagreement with his father on this very idea, when the son wished to extend the meaning of the 'Unity of Being' beyond the self to the state, 'to argue for a law-made balance between trades and occupations'.[174] And, of course, it is worth noting here our return to the link between race and the physical proportions of the body, as we traced earlier in the recurrence of a racial meaning in Yeats's use of the word 'lineaments'.

If the trembling of the veil in his epoch drove Yeats towards the notion of a subjective and racial ideal, however, it has a different resonance in Beckett. In *Molloy*, the 'trembling' is not troubling, but instead gives the illusion of likeness and calm. Moran confesses he 'attended but absently to these poor figures'. He refuses, in other words, the Yeatsian sense of anguish for the age, or indeed for his self, and the trembled images of his face are read as not unwelcome signs of the disappearance of the self.[175] That process continues to find its locus in the face as the novel continues, with Moran 'becoming rapidly unrecognizable': 'when I passed my hands over my face, in a characteristic and now more than ever pardonable gesture, the face my hands felt was not my face anymore'.[176] And, indeed, it finds its ultimate expression of the face without features, 'no asperities, no apertures', in *The Unnamable*, in which the face becomes either meaningless or invisible.

Beckett's technique of rendering visible the erasure of the subject may be attributed to the influence of Jack B. Yeats, whose late work in the subjective mode, as Gordon Armstrong argues, 'finally demanded the elimination of all but a trace of the subject itself, a trace of both the coming and going of forms of consciousness'.[177] Armstrong takes as the title of one of his chapters considering the relationship between the work of Beckett and Jack Yeats, 'stages of an image', from Beckett's argument that Yeats's paintings showed the image through various stages of construction, blank or barely washed canvas here, thickly layered impasto there. The phrase might be fitting as a description of Beckett's prose representations of the face too, the topography of the face rendered into stages of dissolution, the bare construction or recognisable outline in the early novels, thinning into indecipherability and invisibility in *The Unnamable*. 'The artist that stakes his being comes from nowhere', wrote Beckett in his 'Homage to Jack B. Yeats'.[178] 'And he has no brothers', he added, a remark which we cannot help but read as a wry tilt at the very divergent forms and implications of the work of the Yeats brothers.[179] Beckett's admiration for Jack B. Yeats's paintings focuses on the painter's rendering of 'desperately immediate images', on the 'violence of need which not only unleashes them but disrupts them beyond their vanishing lines'.[180] Beckett is drawn, then, not just to the immediate, vibrant impact of Yeats's technique on the canvas, but to the disruption of these images 'beyond their vanishing lines'. In assessing the influence of Jack Yeats on Beckett, David Lloyd points up this question of how an aesthetic of disruption and erasure in the works of both might be understood as 'a deeply implicit political affair'.[181] 'Precisely the tension between the act of figuration and its formal questioning . . . prevents the dimension of the political in either artist's work from ever congealing into a concrete utopian project', although Lloyd detects in the preoccupation of both artists with the limits and ruins of representation 'the anticipatory trace of a republic' (that is, a 'republic' understood in capacious and utopian terms).[182] To describe any political implication in the aesthetics of disruption in Beckett or Jack Yeats as an 'anticipatory trace' is as far as one could go, however, and it is far from clear, other than the inclusivist commitment of both artists to the representation of tramps and misfits, what such a trace anticipates. Perhaps the very least that could be said of Samuel Beckett, Jack Yeats, or Liam O'Flaherty, indeed, is that their work could be read, as W. J. McCormack playfully suggested of Beckett's boils and cysts, as 'symptoms of non-integration displayed on the Irish body politic in its first decade or so of institutional independence'.[183]

McCormack locates Beckett's refusal to integrate with the racial and nationalist politics of Ireland and Europe in the thirties in his 'self-effacing translations' for Nancy Cunard's *The Negro Anthology*, to which Beckett was the most abundant contributor.[184] My argument above is that effacement, of an altogether more general form, is a salient motif in Beckett's novels, as it is in the work of Jack Yeats and Liam O'Flaherty, and that in each case effacement is, in effect, a clandestine articulation of *non serviam*. 'If the face has a politics', write Deleuze and Guattari, 'dismantling the face is also a politics involving real becomings, an entire becoming-clandestine'.[185] The face will not bear the projected markers of racial typification, and will not yield to the formal demand for character, likeness, or readability. In the overde-termination, disruption, and erasure of the facial figure, each of these artists, however consciously, shows a critical point of departure from the bodily practices and aesthetic ideologies which make race a visible and knowable object. The de-figuration of the face in Irish modern-ism is neither a direct nor necessarily even a conscious response to the racial discourses of anthropology and eugenics. Aside from the complex dynamics between cultural texts and historical forces, one reason for this is that the sub-racial categories and sociological profiles invented by physical anthropologists had no discernible social effect. There is no evidence to suggest that the term 'Dinaric', or 'Nordic Mediterranean', or even 'Keltic', became part of the social formation of any subjects in Ireland, although the pervasiveness of the anthropological quest to establish the physical grounds of racial difference would lead to the justifiable supposition that race was a significant factor in the social consciousness of the Irish peoples in the decades after independence. Instead, we must conceive of the contradictory readings of the face, and contradictory readability of the face, as being simultaneously available, or latent perhaps, in the racialising culture of Ireland in the first half of the twentieth century.

The face was a central figure in the cultural imagination of Ireland, both in the revival period, and more significantly (because more ambivalently) in the post-independence period. The face was associated not just with a racial idea of physical appearance and proportions, with the political aesthetics of race, but also with the very landscape and topographical image of the nation.[186] But as Wittgenstein reminds us, the face is indistinguishable from what we read into the face, from the impression we allow the face to make upon us. Crucial to both racialising discourses, and our critical resistance to such discourses, is the act and form of reading, whether that 'reading' takes the form of measuring, looking, judging, deciphering, or indeed effacing. Wittgenstein visited and lived in Ireland sporadically through the time surveyed in this chapter, preoccupied largely with the ideas which were published in *Philosophical Investigations*. As an Austrian Jew living abroad first by choice, and later by necessity, he would also have spent much of this time anxious about the fate of his family and homeland. In the midst of his work and this anxiety, we might recall the story of how on an excursion near his home in Rosroe, accompanied by his friend, Con Drury, Wittgenstein stopped suddenly to look at a five-year-old girl sitting outside a cottage, and said, 'Drury, just look at the expression on that child's face. You don't take enough notice of people's faces; it is a fault you ought to try to correct'.[187]

Notes

1. W. B. Yeats, *Yeats's Poems*, pp. 439–40.
2. R. F. Foster, *W.B. Yeats: A Life, II*, p. 598.
3. W. J. McCormack, *Blood Kindred*, p. 383.
4. McCormack states that these imperatives are benign in 'The Municipal Gallery Revisited', or modulated, as the addressee is clearly identified as anybody who might go to the gallery (p. 382), but he finds the imperative in Yeats's grammar in other poems more troubling.
5. For a brief overview of various visual and artistic representations of the Irish face, see Noel Kissane, *The Irish Face*.
6. See Fintan Cullen, *The Irish Face*, pp. 11–12, for comment on the relationship between portraiture and national historical significance. Cullen notes that John Lavery donated thirty-four paintings to the gallery in 1935 (p. 216), which included portraits of the major figures involved in the 1921 treaty negotiations. The gallery already had portraits by, among others, John Butler Yeats, including the one of Synge (1905) and Antonio Mancini's portrait of Lady Gregory (1908).

7. Yeats's famous description of Maud Gonne in his *Memoirs* acknowledges this influence explicitly: 'I had never thought to see in a living woman so great beauty. It belonged to famous pictures, to poetry, to some legendary past. A complexion like the blossom of apples, and yet face and body had the beauty of lineaments which Blake calls the highest beauty because it changes least from youth to age, and a stature so great that she seemed of a divine race'. *Memoirs*, pp. 40–1.

8. *Yeats's Poems*, pp. 283, 337.

9. Ibid., p. 411.

10. Ibid, p. 461.

11. Richard Ellmann, *The Identity of Yeats*, pp. 188–9.

12. See Miriam Claude Meijer, *Race and Aesthetics in the Anthropology of Petrus Camper.*

13. This controversy about scientific racism, and the supposed link between cranial shape, race, and intelligence capacity, has re-ignited several times in recent decades. See Stephen Jay Gould, *The Mismeasure of Man* and Richard J. Herrnstein and Charles Murray, *The Bell Curve*. Nobel prize-winning geneticist, and director of the Cold Spring Harbor laboratory, Dr James Watson made comments recently to the *Sunday Times* about African people that 'all our social policies are based on the fact that their intelligence is the same as ours – whereas all the testing says not really'. Watson has also been controversial for promoting eugenicist solutions to some healthcare problems. See 'Black people "less intelligent" scientist claims', *The Times*, 17 October 2007: http://www.timesonline.co.uk/tol/news/uk/article2677098.ece

14. The influence of Petrus Camper on the caricatures of the Irish as simian-featured is indeed discussed by L. Perry Curtis Jr in the authoritative study of these caricatures: *Apes and Angels*, p. xix.

15. F. A. C. Wilson, 'The Statues', in Jon Stallworthy (ed.), *Yeats: Last Poems*, p. 179.

16. That supposed phenotypical differences between the English and Irish were used to define and bolster nineteenth-century justifications of English racial superiority has been examined within the field of Irish studies for some time, but interestingly this is a major focus also of Robert Young's recent book, *The Idea of English Ethnicity*. Young is wholly persuasive about the shifting emphasis of racial theories in nineteenth-century England, but somewhat more problematic in asserting that Englishness became an identity characterised by its inclusiveness in the twentieth century, and that contemporary England exemplifies a successful multi-cultural nation.

17. The work most closely associated with Yeats's enthralment to fascist and eugenicist arguments is, of course, *On the Boiler*, in which Yeats bemoans the degeneration of modern European civilisation (as a result of the overpopulation of the poor, where Yeats understands poverty as the result of hereditary inferiority), and praises fascist governments. Although he credits peasants, and specifically a little negro girl whom he had played with as a child, with precious faculties of clairvoyance, he suggests that such people are 'Among those our civilization must reject', and that in the new era, 'the best bred from the best shall claim again

their ancient omens'. See *On the Boiler* in W. B. Yeats, *The Collected Works of W.B. Yeats, Vol.5*, pp. 220–51.

18. See Paul Scott Stanfield, *Yeats and Politics in the Nineteen-Thirties*, Elizabeth Cullingford, *Yeats, Ireland and Fascism*, Marjorie Howes, *Yeats's Nations*, and most recently, W. J. McCormack, *Blood Kindred*.
19. Seán Hand (ed.), *The Levinas Reader*, p. 82.
20. Gilles Deleuze and Félix Guattari, *A Thousand Plateaus*, p. 196.
21. Ludwig Wittgenstein, *Philosophical Investigations*, p. 144.
22. Ludwig Wittgenstein, *The Blue and Brown Books*, pp. 162–3.
23. Roger Scruton, 'Wittgenstein and the Understanding of Music', p. 7.
24. Wittgenstein, *The Blue and Brown Books*, p. 165.
25. Earnest A. Hooton and C. Wesley Dupertuis, *The Physical Anthropology of Ireland*, p. 42.
26. Michel Foucault, *History of Sexuality, Vol. 1*, p. 140.
27. The financial records of the Harvard Irish Study, kept in the E. A. Hooton papers, were consulted in the Peabody Museum of Archaeology and Ethnology, Harvard University, accession no. 995–1.
28. E. A. Hooton, 'The Harvard Study of the Irish Free State'. E. A. Hooton Papers, Manuscripts Box 21. Interestingly, Hooton misspells several of these names.
29. Letter from Lloyd Warner to E. A. Hooton, 26 July 1932. E. A Hooton Papers, Manuscripts Box 21.
30. Hooton and Dupertuis, *The Physical Anthropology of Ireland*, p. viii.
31. Letter from Seósamh Ó Neill to E. A. Hooton, 15 June 1936. E. A. Hooton Papers, Manuscripts Box 21.
32. Hooton and Dupertuis, *The Physical Anthropology of Ireland*, p. v.
33. Noel Ignatiev, *How the Irish Became White*, passim.
34. Hooton, 'The Harvard Study of the Irish Free State'.
35. See Hooton and Dupertuis, *The Physical Anthropology of Ireland*, pp. 192–247.
36. T. F. O'Rahilly, *Early Irish History and Mythology*, passim.
37. Hooton and Dupertuis, *The Physical Anthropology of Ireland*, p. 141.
38. The record cards for all of the measurements undertaken in the Harvard study are kept in the Peabody Museum of Archaeology and Ethnology, Harvard University: Irish Study Records, Boxes 1–3.
39. Dupertuis describes how the anthropometric survey was conducted in *The Physical Anthropology of Ireland*, pp. 4–11.
40. Hooton and Dupertuis, *The Physical Anthropology of Ireland*, p. 8.
41. See E. A. Hooton, *Up from the Ape*.
42. See also E. P. Stibbe, *An Introduction to Physical Anthropology*, especially 'Examination of the Living Subject', pp. 183–91.
43. It is obvious why the face would attract the greatest attention, and numerous studies have concentrated on the mechanics and dynamics of facial recognition and facial communication. For a concise and lucid overview, see Vicki Bruce and Andy Young, *In the Eye of the Beholder*.
44. E. A. Hooton, 'The Evolution and Devolution of the Human Face'. E. A. Hooton Papers, Manuscripts Box 1.
45. Hooton and Dupertuis, *The Physical Anthropology of Ireland*, p. 181.
46. Ibid., p. 171.

47. Letter from Helen Dawson to E. A. Hooton, 30 August 1941. E. A. Hooton Papers, Correspondence Box 13.
48. Hooton and Dupertuis, *The Physical Anthropology of Ireland*, p. 137.
49. Ibid., p. 137.
50. T. Walmsley, J. M. Mogey, and D. P. Gamble, 'The Peoples of Northern Ireland'. For an overview of Thomas Walmsley's career, see W. R. M. Morton's brief biography in *The Anatomical Record*, pp. 266–9.
51. MacConaill indeed refers to this work in 'The Physical Anthropology of Ireland', pp. 47–8.
52. Michael A. MacConaill, 'The People of Rachrai', pp. 4–7.
53. Michael A. MacConaill, 'The Correlations of Length, Breadth and Height in Forty Mixed Crania'. MSc thesis, June 1928, Queen's University of Belfast.
54. 'Post-Natal Development of Hair and Eye Colour with Special Reference to Some Ethnological Problems', pp. 218–25, and 'Normal Proportions of European Calvaria', pp. 23–32.
55. The essay had been sent in draft form to E. A. Hooton in 1943, seeking advice about how to get it published, a difficult task given war-time restrictions on paper in Britain. With Hooton's help the essay was published under the title 'Physical Type and Mental Characters' in the *American Journal of Physical Anthropology*. The draft version is stored among E. A. Hooton's papers, Peabody Museum, Manuscripts Box 13.
56. David P. Gamble, 'Physical Type and Mental Characters', p. 199.
57. Ibid., pp. 217–8.
58. Carleton Stevens Coon, *The Races of Europe*, p. 384.
59. William Z. Ripley, *The Races of Europe*, p. 301.
60. David H. Price, *Anthropological Intelligence*. Hooton and Dupertuis are among the anthropologists cited by Price as involved in 'race-specific' war-time planning of the OSS, the forerunner of the CIA, and were specifically consulted on biological means of waging war against Japanese soldiers and civilians (p. 223). Price also quotes from a paper Hooton published in 1943, which advocated similar measures to be taken against the Japanese as a 'race' in the aftermath of war as he advocated against the Germans (see below), namely that of sterilisation, hybridisation, and the colonisation of Japan with 'other Asiatics' (p. 192).
61. E. A. Hooton, 'The Wages of Biological Sin'. E. A. Hooton Papers, Manuscripts Box 1.
62. Hooton and Dupertuis, *The Physical Anthropology of Ireland*, p. 171.
63. E. A. Hooton, 'Should Racial Differences be Denied or Disregarded in a Democracy?'. E. A. Hooton Papers, Manuscripts Box 1.
64. E. A. Hooton, 'Should Racial Differences be Denied or Disregarded in a Democracy?'. E. A. Hooton Papers, Manuscripts Box 1.
65. E. A. Hooton, 'An Anthropological Appraisal of the Jewish People'. E. A. Hooton Papers, Manuscripts Box 1.
66. E. A. Hooton, 'A Scientist Looks at the Race of Supermen'. E. A. Hooton Papers, Manuscripts Box 1.
67. Letter from Edmond J. Donlan to E. A. Hooton, 19 January 1943. E. A. Hooton Papers, Correspondence Box 7.

68. Letter from Marvin Green [or Treen], forwarded from Ales Hrdlicka to E. A. Hooton, 4 May 1939. E. A. Hooton Papers, Correspondence Box 13.

69. E. A. Hooton, 'The Wages of Biological Sin'.

70. Diane Paul, *Controlling Human Heredity*, p. 21.

71. Brian Friel's *The Home Place* (2005) includes an English colonial figure, Dr Richard Gore, who busily and boisterously measures the head and facial features of the Irish, primarily in the service of identifying racial characteristics. He is clearly the butt of the play's satire of English colonial and racist attitudes The appendix to the play provides details of an anthropological expedition to the Aran Islands, as the historical basis for the play's representation of anthropometry as the instrument of colonial power. The Harvard Irish Study was the most extensive such expedition to Ireland, and covered the whole island, but unlike the subject of Friel's play, it was entirely conducted with the assistance, knowledge, and gratitude of both the Irish Free State and the government of Northern Ireland.

72. Joseph L. Graves, *The Emperor's New Clothes*, p. 119.

73. For an overview of the pronatalist policies of the Irish Free State and Republic, see Noel Whitty, 'Law and the Regulation of Reproduction in Ireland: 1922–1992', pp. 851–88.

74. Bryan Fanning, *Racism and Social Change in the Republic of Ireland*, pp. 76–101.

75. See, for example, the fourth instalment of the 'Encyclical Letter of His Holiness the Pope on Christian Marriage', as reported in the *Irish Independent*, 23 January 1931, p. 6, under the heading 'Pernicious Practices Condemned'.

76. A Dáil Éireann motion to support Dr Dupertuis's racial survey was proposed by the Minister for Education, Mr Derrig, as 'of very considerable national and scientific importance', and was agreed by the Dáil finance committee on 23 July 1935. Dáil Éireann, Vol. 58, 23 July 1935, Committee on Finance, Vote 49 – Science and Art.

77. Some findings of the study were published earlier than 1955, however. Coon published his conclusions from Dupertuis's data in *The Races of Europe*, of course. Hooton and Dupertuis also published 'Age Changes and Selective Survival in Irish Males', as a monograph of the *American Journal of Physical Anthropology* in 1951. Hooton had also published an essay, 'Stature, Head Form, and Pigmentation of the Adult Male Irish', in the *American Journal of Physical Anthropology* in 1940, pp. 229–49.

78. Letter from E. A. Hooton to George C. Dowd, 31 May 1951. E. A. Hooton Papers, Correspondence Box 7.

79. P. J. Prendergast and T. C. Lee, 'Walking on Water: The Biomechanics of Michael A. MacConaill (1902–1987)', p. 73.

80. Edward E. Hunt, 'Anthropometry, Genetics and Racial History', pp. 64–87.

81. M. A. MacConaill, 'The Physical Anthropology of Ireland', pp. 47–8, and 'The Physical Forms of Irishmen', pp. 92–101.

82. Robert Carter, 'Genes, Genomes and Genealogies: The Return of Scientific Racism?', pp. 546–56.

83. Ibid., p. 554.

84. The anthropometric measurement of the face for biomedical purposes is also not obsolete and is in fact experiencing a resurgence, as a result of new 3-D imaging techniques which enable researchers to identify facial gestalts specifically linked to genetic disorders. See Peter Hammond et al., 'Discriminating Power of Localized Three-Dimensional Facial Morphology', pp. 999–1010. Professor Hammond also presented his research findings at the British Association Festival of Science 2007, widely reported in British media on 10 September 2007. Hammond's techniques show how the technologies of face measurement have advanced, with the digital imaging devices able to record 25,000 points on the face, compared to the 125 measurements and observations made by Dupertuis in Ireland from 1934–6.

85. Kelly Gates, 'Identifying the 9/11 "Faces of Terror"', p. 435.

86. In this respect, one volume of critical essays stands out as a major endeavour to reassess the fate of modernism in Ireland in the wake of Yeats and Joyce: Patricia Coughlan and Alex Davis (eds), *Modernism and Ireland*. This has been followed by Alex Davis's admirable contextualisation of the work of Denis Devlin in *A Broken Line*.

87. Terence Brown, 'Ireland, Modernism and the 1930s', *Modernism and Ireland*, ed. Coughlan and Davis, pp. 38, 41.

88. Tim Armstrong, 'Muting the Klaxon', *Modernism and Ireland*, ed. Coughlan and Davis, pp. 70–1.

89. See Anne Fogarty, 'Gender, Irish Modernism and the Poetry of Denis Devlin', *Modernism and Ireland*, ed. Coughlan and Davis, pp. 209–31, and Gerardine Meaney, 'Regendering Modernism', *Women*, pp. 67–82.

90. Meaney, 'Regendering Modernism', p. 81.

91. Davis, *A Broken Line*, pp. 11–12.

92. J. Hillis Miller, *Fiction and Repetition*, p. 1.

93. Liam O'Flaherty, *Thy Neighbour's Wife*, p. 10.

94. Liam O'Flaherty, *The Informer*, p. 9.

95. Liam Harte, 'Free State Interrogators', p. 233.

96. Paul A. Doyle, *Liam O'Flaherty*, p. 117.

97. John Zneimer, *The Literary Vision of Liam O'Flaherty*, pp. 188–9.

98. James H. O'Brien, *Liam O'Flaherty*, p. 56.

99. Patrick F. Sheeran, *The Novels of Liam O'Flaherty*, p. 274.

100. Ibid., p. 301.

101. Terry Phillips, 'A Study in Grotesques', pp. 41–52.

102. Hedda Friberg, *An Old Order and a New*, p. 93.

103. Declan Kiberd, *Irish Classics*, p. 493.

104. O'Flaherty, *The Informer*, p. 16.

105. The OED cites an example of 'snout' as slang for 'informer' from C. E. B. Russell's *Young Gaol-Birds* in 1910.

106. Sheeran, *The Novels of Liam O'Flaherty*, pp. 273–4.

107. With his bolted neck, Gypo Nolan might bring Frankenstein's monster to mind, if it were not for the fact that this feature of the monster was only established by Boris Karloff in James Whale's 1931 film, six years after O'Flaherty published *The Informer*. Mary Shelley's novel contains no such description of the monster, although the novel does contain a description of the monster's face which raises interesting questions about

the monster's racial composition. For a discussion of the racial contexts and racial interpretation of Shelley's *Frankenstein* in both the Romantic and Victorian periods, see H. L. Malchow, *Gothic Images of Race in Nineteenth-Century Britain.*

108. Steven Connor inverts this relation between skin and face: 'The skin is, so to speak, the body's face, the face of its bodiliness. The skinned body is formless, faceless, its face having been taken off with its skin'. See Connor, *The Book of Skin*, p. 29.
109. Wittgenstein, *The Blue and Brown Books*, p. 162.
110. Yeats, *Yeats's Poems*, p. 325.
111. Jerry H. Gill, 'On Knowing the Dancer from the Dance', p. 125.
112. O'Flaherty, *The Informer*, p. 65.
113. Ibid., pp. 69–70.
114. Ibid., p. 84.
115. Nina G. Jablonski, *Skin*, p. 5.
116. O'Flaherty, *The Informer*, p. 34.
117. This may also be the case in *Insurrection*, in which Bartly Madden dies lying 'prone', which although not specified clearly, would suggest face down.
118. The cross is, however, sometimes veiled in 'Holy Week', beginning on Passion Sunday, and unveiled on Good Friday. Despite this, the cross remains facing the worshippers.
119. Liam O'Flaherty, *The Puritan*, p. 19.
120. Ibid., p. 248.
121. O'Flaherty, *The Informer*, p. 37.
122. Deleuze and Guattari, *A Thousand Plateaus*, p. 196.
123. Liam O'Flaherty, *Mr Gilhooley*, p. 288.
124. Ibid., p. 42.
125. This expressionist use of primary colours can be traced back to, and perhaps remains most notable in, *The Black Soul* (1924), a novel influenced by and dedicated to Edward Garnett.
126. O'Flaherty, *Mr Gilhooley*, p. 43.
127. Ibid., pp. 280–1.
128. Ibid., p. 287.
129. Ibid., p. 286.
130. I am struck by the similarities between Hillis Miller's reading of Hardy's *The Return of the Native* in *Topographies*, and the reading I have developed here. In the figures of the face and effacement Miller traces in Hardy's novel, and in terms of Hardy's depiction of a 'universal emptiness', there may be grounds here for considering Hardy a possible influence on the work of O'Flaherty. See J. Hillis Miller, *Topographies*, pp. 9–56.
131. 'Purest Types in West', *Connacht Tribune*, 26 May 1934, p. 8.
132. Bruce Arnold quotes from Lady Gregory's diaries from 1900 to support the statement that Synge had intended Jack Yeats to do the illustrations for *The Aran Islands*. See Bruce Arnold, *Jack Yeats*, p. 145.
133. Ibid., p. 161.
134. Hilary Pyle, *Jack B. Yeats*, p. 89.
135. Arnold quotes from this letter, addressed to Stephen McKenna, in *Jack Yeats*, p. 134.

136. J. M. Synge, *Collected Works, Volume 3: Plays, Book One*, p. xxvii.
137. Arnold, *Jack Yeats*, p. 152.
138. Jack B. Yeats, *Life in the West of Ireland*.
139. G.A. Birmingham, *Irishmen All*; Pádraic Colum, *A Boy in Erinn*; Robert Lynd, *Rambles in Ireland*.
140. Quoted in Arnold, *Jack Yeats*, p. 183.
141. Jack B. Yeats, 'Pearse Addressing a Volunteer Rally in Dundrum', *Dublin and Greystones, 1914*, Sketchbook 110, 1914, pencil on paper, National Gallery of Ireland.
142. Hooton and Dupertuis, *The Physical Anthropology of Ireland*, p. 58.
143. Ibid., p. 267.
144. Coon, *The Races of Europe*, p. 381.
145. Gamble, 'Physical Type and Mental Characters', p. 15.
146. Pyle, *Jack B. Yeats*, p. 167.
147. Thomas MacGreevy, *Jack B. Yeats*, passim.
148. Arnold, *Jack Yeats*, p. 205.
149. Ibid., p. 214.
150. J. B. Yeats, 'Modern Aspects of Irish Art', pp. 4–5.
151. Given de Valera's recent resignation as President, and the formation of the provisional government, this is perhaps not the best way of articulating the sense that both pro-treaty and anti-treaty delegates at the Congress may have been pleased to find that Jack Yeats was representing art and the role of the artist as essentially national. Jack Yeats, of course, differed from his brother in siding with the anti-treaty or Republican side during the Irish civil war, and as such was opposed to the Irish Free State in the form it took in 1922.
152. Pyle, *Jack B. Yeats*, p. 127.
153. Ibid., p. 128.
154. David Lloyd, 'Republics of Difference', p. 467.
155. Tricia Cusack, 'Migrant Travellers and Touristic Idylls', p. 202.
156. Lloyd, 'Republics of Difference', p. 471.
157. Deleuze and Guattari, *A Thousand Plateaus*, p. 196.
158. Jack B. Yeats, *Sligo*, p. 132.
159. Samuel Beckett, *The Unnamable, The Grove Centenary Edition*, p. 299.
160. Connor, *The Book of Skin*, p. 71.
161. Ibid., p. 356.
162. Ibid., p. 368.
163. Ibid., p. 407.
164. Beckett, *Murphy* and *Watt, The Grove Centenary Edition*, pp. 149, 184, 187, 189, 211, 274.
165. See *Murphy*, pp. 20, 60, 65, 88 for the leitmotif of falling on the face; see *Watt*, pp. 287, 294, 312 for the face-to-face motif.
166. Beckett, *Murphy*, p. 5.
167. Beckett, *Watt*, p. 367.
168. Beckett, *Malone Dies, The Grove Centenary Edition*, p. 178.
169. Ibid., pp. 199–200.
170. Beckett, *Molloy, The Grove Centenary Edition*, p. 140.
171. Ibid., p. 143.

172. W. B. Yeats, *Autobiographies*, p. 109. Stéphane Mallarmé, 'Variations sur on sujet', *Oeuvres Complètes*, p. 360.
173. Yeats, *Autobiographies*, pp. 189, 190, 246.
174. Ibid., p. 190.
175. For an interesting reading of the figure of the face, and the aesthetics of disappearance and flight, in Beckett's *Film*, see Alice Gavin, 'The "Angle of Immunity"', pp. 77–89.
176. Beckett, *Molloy*, p. 164.
177. Gordon S. Armstrong, *Samuel Beckett, W.B. Yeats, and Jack Yeats*, pp. 222–3.
178. Samuel Beckett, 'Homage to Jack B. Yeats', p. 9.
179. Seán Kennedy examines Beckett's 'cultural positioning' of Jack B. Yeats as an artist from nowhere, in contrast to MacGreevy's situation of Yeats as a republican artist, in 'The Artist Who Stakes His Being is from Nowhere', pp. 61–74.
180. Beckett, 'Homage to Jack B. Yeats', p. 9.
181. Lloyd, 'Republics of Difference', p. 473.
182. Ibid., p. 474.
183. W. J. McCormack, *From Burke to Beckett*, p. 390.
184. Ibid., p. 390.
185. Deleuze and Guattari, *A Thousand Plateaus*, p. 208.
186. Among the publications of the time which use this idea of the nation as a face are Michael Lloyd's *The Face of Ireland*, Arland Ussher's *The Face and Mind of Ireland*, and Josephine Hunt Raymond's book of verse, *The Remembered Face of Ireland*.
187. Quoted in Richard Wall, *Wittgenstein in Ireland*, p. 15, from Rush Rhees, ed., *Ludwig Wittgenstein: Personal Recollections*, p. 141.

Chapter 3

'Aliens in Ireland': Nation-building and the Ethics of Hospitality

In the opening scenes of John Ford's classic film, *The Quiet Man* (1952), the quality of hospitality appears to be conditional upon protocols of familial and communal recognition.[1] As Sean Thornton emerges from his train – three hours late – on to the platform of Castletown, a crowd of railway staff and bystanders react with puzzlement to his arrival, anxiously querying his intentions, and mistaking him for a foreign tourist bent on fishing. It is only when he reveals to his hired driver, Michaeleen, the identity of his father and mother, and that he was born in the local village of Innisfree, that it is clear he is a returning migrant, and not an American tourist. The passage from foreigner to native is repeated in the scene in the bar in which Thornton's greeting and offer to buy drinks is met with hostile silence until a village elder establishes Thornton's local pedigree. As a native, Thornton is immediately re-integrated into the rituals of the community. A crowd instantly gathers around him singing the Irish-Australian rebel song, 'The Wild Colonial Boy', and stands by him against the seething hostility of the local 'squireen'. The parish priest, too, welcomes him back into the community upon learning of Thornton's genealogy by telling him to be at mass the following morning at seven. Ford's film goes on to dramatise the struggle between Thornton and the squireen to be the local *übermensch*, one forged in the steel factories and boxing clubs of Pittsburgh, the other in the agrarian labour of an Irish farm. Thornton's right to own his familial home, to take a local woman for his wife (the squireen's sister), and to partake of communal rituals is, however, clearly dependent upon first establishing the bonds of patrilineal descent. There is a clear distinction between the somewhat bemused 'welcome' extended to the visiting foreigner and the 'welcome home' by which Thornton is 'naturalised' as an insider, entitled, on the basis of *jus sanguinis*, to the rights of communal citizenship. As such, then, Thornton's arrival serves both to show the boundaries of communal belonging, and to imply an entirely different set of conditions of hospitality for the arrival of someone from outside those boundaries. The anxious welcome of the foreigner on the railway platform functions all the more clearly to delimit and fetishise the foreigner as foreigner, as one who is made conspicuous in his difference. The platform itself is envisioned as state border, as the point at which the foreigner arrives and is recognised as an identifiable subject, but both the border and the delimitation of the foreigner are dependent upon recognising the pact which binds the host society as one. Thornton's passage from foreigner to native exposes the patrilineal and racial bases upon which this pact is based, and from which the 'real' foreigner, the foreigner who does not alight at Castletown station, is implicitly excluded.[2]

The history of the Irish state, as indeed the history of every state, is a history of self-constitution determined not just through acts of assertion and definition but also exclusion and rejection. There is no state, no 'home', without the foreigner, without the one who is defined legally or culturally as other. In this sense, as Jacques Derrida argues, 'the relationship to the foreigner is regulated by law, by the becoming-law of justice'.[3] The arrival of the foreigner, whether tourist, migrant, or refugee, always invokes the law, and entails a passage through the juridical and regulatory apparatus of the state. At the same time, the arrival of the foreigner is also a question of ethics, the ethics of hospitality, intimately related to the issue of sovereignty, since as Derrida writes, there is 'No hospitality, in the classic sense, without sovereignty of oneself over one's home, but since there is also no hospitality without finitude, sovereignty can only be exercised by filtering, choosing, and thus by excluding and doing violence'.[4] Every state not only places a limit on hospitality (through specific constitutional, political and civic apparatuses) but is in itself a limit on hospitality, as Kant recognised in 'Perpetual Peace' (1795).[5] The universal right to hospitality, by virtue of common inhabitation of the earth, was paradoxically enshrined within the sovereign domain of nation-states, and so, as Hannah Arendt explained in *The Origins of Totalitarianism*, 'man had hardly appeared as a completely emancipated, completely isolated being who carried his dignity within himself without reference to some larger encompassing order, when he disappeared again into a member of a people'.[6] The nation-state is thus constantly constituted as both the guarantor of universal rights for its own citizens and the arbiter of the terms upon which citizenship is conferred. Membership of a nation-state, however conferred, becomes the *a priori* condition upon which access to human rights is determined. The right to hospitality, then, in the Kantian sense, is always a matter of relation between nation-states, and this co-dependence of hospitality and sovereignty makes the nation-state constitutively opposed to cosmopolitanism, to the possibilities of iterative, itinerant, and alterative subjectivities within (but not of) the state.[7]

The Irish state as formally constituted in 1922, and reconstituted in 1937 (Bunreacht na hÉireann) and 1949 (Republic of Ireland Act), was the product of a nationalist struggle to wrest the integrity of a presupposed racial and territorial identity from foreign domination and influence. The political claim to legitimacy and authenticity rested upon a conflation of the *ethnos* and the *demos*, so that sovereignty was not simply the product of a democratically expressed will, but was projected as the ancient and inalienable right of a pre-defined, historically continuous 'people'. States founded on such conceptions tend towards the fetishisation of homogeneity, as Seyla Benhabib makes clear from her reading of Hannah Arendt's work: 'The more that nationalist ideologies stressed aspects of identity which preceded the political, the more they based the equality of the citizens on their presumed commonality and sameness'.[8] Religion and race were the most prominent ingredients in the nationalist conception of Ireland's difference from Britain and the British Empire, and, as race did not necessarily or even easily articulate itself as a practice, the conspicuous Catholicism of Ireland became the defining feature of the post-independence state.[9] The Eucharistic Congress hosted in Dublin in 1932 was only the most spectacular demonstration of the interdependence of religious and nationalist fervour, which was also manifest, in sometimes more insidious ways, in state policies on education, health, welfare, justice, and even foreign relations. While Catholicism ought to, and in some ways did, foster a sense of transnational identification, it also converged neatly with cultural nationalism in its strictures against 'foreign' forms of entertainment, dress, speech, and behaviour, which could be variously denounced morally as either 'unCatholic' or 'unIrish', or both. 'Cosmopolitanism' was thus as derogatory a term in Catholic discourse as in nationalist discourse, and for both the foreigner was associated with the contagion of a cosmopolitanism which knew neither home nor faith, which represented instead the secular and the itinerant.

Partition certainly curtailed the aspired sovereignty of the state, but as J. J. Lee argues, it nevertheless eased the convergence of religious and political interests in the Irish Free State to enable a greater sense of ideological unity:

> partition . . . saved the South from the most explosive internal problems subverting new states, race and religion, by the simple device of exporting

them to the North. However objectively mongrel its genes, the Free State was subjectively virtually 100 per cent homogeneous.[10]

In what has become known as 'the age of de Valera', from the 1930s through to the late 1950s, the exigencies of both national and international politics served to intensify this perception of Irish society and culture as homogeneous. The Censorship Act of 1929 prohibited the publication, sale and distribution of many foreign publications (mainly from Britain and the US), as well as Irish publications which were deemed to have transgressed accepted moral and religious values. The protectionist policies of the new Fianna Fáil government, which led to the 'economic war' with Britain in the 1930s, sought to foster economic self-sufficiency by cutting off or curtailing dependence upon foreign goods. The vigorous pursuit of neutrality during the Second World War also entailed isolation from the wider world, and, as Claire Wills has recently shown, was denigrated by its critics, within and without Ireland, as escapist provincialism, and promoted by its advocates as 'a battle for Ireland itself', or 'Ireland versus the foreigner'.[11] In the aftermath of the war, and into the 1950s, the Irish state continued to manifest this sense of repulsion from 'the foreigner', through what Bryan Fanning has charted as 'overt racial discrimination within Irish refugee policy', especially against Jewish refugees, even those who were victims of the Nazi concentration camps.[12] The admission of refugees in response to various humanitarian and political crises after the war was usually severely limited, and in some cases, disastrous, such as the inhospitable accommodation of Hungarian refugees in an internment camp in Knocknalisheen between 1956 and 1958. Fanning attributes the material and conceptual inadequacies of the Irish state's response to refugee crises to 'an institutional monoculturalism which identified difference as a threat'.[13]

The end of 'the age of de Valera', when de Valera left his fifth term of office as Taoiseach in 1959, and was succeeded by Seán Lemass, is conventionally associated with a more liberal and internationalist outlook in Irish politics. Ireland first contributed to the United Nations Peacekeeping Mission in 1958, applied to join the European Economic Community in 1962, and abandoned protectionist economics for Keynesian free-market policies. The advent of RTE television in 1961, the relaxation of film censorship, and the impact of reform in the Catholic church after 'Vatican II', as Dermot Keogh suggests, all served to bring an insular, isolated Ireland into closer contact with the social and cultural changes which were sweeping through the western world.[14] The Fianna Fáil party which had exhibited 'a fierce suspicion of cosmopolitanism', and raged against industrialisation and urbanisation in favour of 'cosy homesteads' in a new agrarian order, in the 1930s, had by the late 1950s embraced (at least as aspirations) the technologies of industrial modernity, the economics of international capitalism, and the emergent ethics of international justice and peacekeeping.[15] None of these changes necessitated a revision of the conception of the state as the political expression of a sovereign, homogeneous, and distinctive *ethnos*, however, but rather entailed a revision of how to imagine and regulate the relationship between the state and other states. As we will see, the 'foreigner within' was still made conspicuous as the fetishised object of both exotic fantasy and moral suspicion.

The history of intellectual responses to the myths of cultural homogeneity and the suspicion of cosmopolitanism in the mid-century decades often seems to be one of a besieged and despairing minority. Terence Brown depicts the 'country's most gifted writers' as doomed to 'public indifference or misunderstanding', and stifled by cultural provincialism (most obviously through censorship).[16] Emigration or exile represented not just an economic necessity, which it was for many Irish people, but also a cultural necessity, since the state seemed incapable of supporting the material or artistic life of its people.[17] The best journals of the period – *The Bell*, *Kavanagh's Weekly*, and *Envoy* – looked upon Irish cultural life with almost unremitting gloom. The despondency appears to have its source both in the perception that Ireland was too insular and inward-looking, wallowing in some auto-erotic obsession with its own distinctiveness, and in the presumption of cultural homogeneity, of a people united in their satisfaction with frugal tastes, devotional pieties, and moral conservatism.

While this idea of a distinctive and homogeneous people inspired some degree of admiration and a greater degree of approbation among Irish writers and artists, the premise of this chapter is that the figure of the foreigner, and the cosmopolitan body, became a recurrent and ideologically significant trope in some of the most renowned literary writing of the period. The foreigner proves to be impossible to contain at the border, but instead trespasses across, and necessitates a reconstruction of, presumed models of community, sovereignty, and identity. In particular, it seems, the cosmopolitan body – usually the female body, marked in specifically visible and performative ways as cosmopolitan – threatens to denaturalise the seemingly most intimate communal bonds of racial and religious affiliation. As such, these writings serve to undermine the nationalist antipathy towards cosmopolitanism, and to announce the project of re-imagining community beyond this dichotomy.

'Ireland her own, and all therein'

The Yeatsian vision of Ireland as a spiritual oasis offering sanctuary from the ravages of rationalism and materialism persisted in the strange fictions of Francis Stuart in the 1930s, with the embattled heroes of *Pigeon Irish* (1932), for example, seeking to establish secret colonies or 'arks' of chosen people to preserve the best of Irish civilisation from the threat of 'an Ireland rationalised, mechanised, hygienised'.[18] The threat in Stuart's novel is understood to come from an inner corruption, from the cities especially, as well as invading forces. Hence, Ireland's last defenders resort to using pigeons as a means of communication with their front lines, rather than the 'defeated' and 'useless' machines like the 'wireless' and 'airplanes' invented by modern science.[19] It was, perhaps, a strangely prescient vision of some of the rhetoric associated with Ireland's policy of neutrality during the Second World War, with its improbable casting of 'Ireland's destiny as the saviour of humanity', in preserving the vestiges of early European civilisation from the ruins of war.[20] It was also, however, a close approximation of the spiritual vision of Ireland proffered by the newly elected government, and particularly its charismatic leader, Eamon de Valera.

De Valera used his earliest radio broadcasts as Free State President to appeal to 'the people of our race' across Ireland and the USA. The synchronised broadcast of the first of his St Patrick's Day speeches in 1932 to 'the Irish people at home and in America' provided the technical means for articulating a racial community beyond the disputed boundaries of national sovereignty,[21] a 'people' brought together in the experience of 'temporal coincidence' which Benedict Anderson argued constituted the basic structure of modern imagined community.[22] Nevertheless, the pronouns used by de Valera specify the necessary limits of the racial imaginary, and the pragmatic convergence of territorial and political integrality: 'For us here in Ireland the National Feast Day is now drawing to a close. For you who are listening to me beyond the ocean . . . the day is still young'.[23] The vision de Valera proceeded to set out for his new government was also necessarily bound to the image of territorial and bodily unity:

> The aims of the new Government are simple. I know no words in which I can express them better than those of Fintan Lalor:
>
>> Ireland her own, and all therein, from the sod to the sky. The soil of Ireland for the people of Ireland, to have and hold from God alone who gave it – to have and to hold to them and their heirs forever, without suit or service, faith or fealty, rent or render, to any power under heaven.

> We desire to pursue these aims without ill-feeling towards any Irishman, without injury to any Irishman, without injury to any nation.[24]

There were specific political contexts which made de Valera's chosen quotation meaningful – namely, the grievances which persisted from the treaty of 1921: the oath of allegiance, the land annuities, and partition. In the ensuing months and years of his office, de Valera worked to rid the country of these betrayals of sovereignty. But de Valera was also setting out an ideological vision here, which purported to represent a nation and race appointed by God, and with a historical destiny to fulfil into the future. The touchstones of de Valera's nationalism are in these key words, 'soil', 'people', and 'God', and in the relationship between them in which the convergent soil and people hold their sovereignty forever as the gift of God. This is not, then, a polity, established and maintained through consent, free to cede the sovereignty of its borders up to foreign powers, or indeed to join in treaties with other states which compromise that sovereignty. The image is one of a homogeneous, inalienable people, living in and on an inviolable territory, bound by divine ordinance. It is sacred land, populated by a sacred people. The ethical orientation of this vision, however, is worthy of some analysis.

De Valera's aim to govern 'without ill-feeling towards any Irishman, without injury to any Irishman, without injury to any nation' reveals its own bias, most obviously in terms of gender, but also in the way in which ethical value is entirely weighted upon nationality, and upon a presumed homogeneity of nationality. At the risk of taking de Valera too literally, is ill-feeling or injury permissible towards an Irishwoman, or a Frenchman living in Dublin, or minority communities which have not formed nations, or stateless refugees? It may well be naive to believe that government can be pursued without causing ill-feeling or injury to anyone, but de Valera's implicit exemptions here raise important questions not just about when and to whom it is possible or desirable for national governments to cause harm, but also about the imagined constituency of the nation.

Lalor's words, however, seem to have a different bearing: 'Ireland her own, and all therein'. 'All therein' may simply be an allusion to the totality and integrality of the island and its people, but following from 'her own', it also seems to raise the prospect of people who are *in* Ireland, but not 'owned' by or belonging to Ireland. It suggests a distinction between 'her own' and 'all therein' which invites consideration of a cosmopolitanism within the territorial bounds of the nation. Yet, de Valera's explanation of how his aims will be pursued glosses away the image of the foreigner within Ireland, and restores the unambiguous sense that the Irishman and his relations with other nations are the only terms worthy of ethical value.

The status of foreigners or 'aliens' in Ireland was, however, a significant and persistent topic during the 1930s, and emerged in a different form after the Second World War in relation to various refugee crises. On 10 April 1935, de Valera's government passed into law two acts which served to regulate the inclusionary and exclusionary powers of the state. The Irish Nationality and Citizenship Act (1935) set out to define natural-born and naturalised citizens of the state, and the terms in which citizenship was acquired, forfeited, or lost. On the same day, the Aliens Act (1935), which superseded the 1925 Aliens Act, defined how 'aliens' within the state were to be controlled, and prescribed measures to be taken should aliens contravene those state controls. Aliens were required to register their presence in the state, and notify the Gardaí of change of residence, travel, employment, occupation, 'and other matters'. The number of aliens entering the country each year was relatively small, and in general very few aliens were refused entry, or deported. In 1937, for example, 11,176 aliens entered the country, whereas only six were refused entry.[25] The Minister for Justice, who regularly reported to the Dáil on the alien population in Ireland, also specified the nationalities of aliens registered in Ireland: in 1939, for example, of 2,620 aliens then registered, 1,297 were Americans, 326 Germans, 189 Italians, 160 French, 126 Russian, 123 Belgian, with various other western and eastern European nationalities in some dozens, and then single figure numbers of Egyptians, Chinese, Iraqi, Palestinian, and other nationalities, and just six stateless persons.[26] The numbers involved were hardly likely to disturb the hegemony of Irish racial and religious ideologies in defining the interests and identity of Free State citizenship (and, as Bryan Fanning has argued, the exclusionary processes of nation-building in Ireland tended to have particular ramifications for Protestant, Jewish and Traveller minority communities, rather than aliens).[27] Yet, the issue of alien 'invasion', domination, or penetration of the state was raised with surprising regularity throughout the 1930s.[28]

It was raised particularly in relation to employment in trades and industries. *The Cross*, a journal published by the Passionist Fathers, made a particularly scandalous accusation in 1934, for instance, that aliens, 'mostly Jews', were being 'favoured to an unbelievable extent' with import licences, resulting in a monopoly in the distributive trades 'with disastrous consequences to the plain people of Ireland'. Moreover, 'The growth of subversive doctrines, of non-Christian morality, and of anti-Christian teaching may in many cases be traced to the activities of alien immigrants'.[29] The *Irish Times* reported this accusation without much comment, nor much sign of evidence to justify the accusation. Although it quoted official figures for alien immigration which showed quite clearly that there was no mass invasion, it also acknowledged that no figures were available for immigration from Britain, and a key part of the allegation in *The Cross* was that Jews were coming *en masse* to Ireland as 'naturalised Englishmen', and therefore evading alien immigration laws. *The Cross* was not exceptional in complaining about alien invasion of industries, however. The Electrical Trades Union complained of 'excessive German labour' being employed in the construction of Ardnacrusha power station on the Shannon in 1932.[30] Bricklayers and Hotel trades unions were also reported to be considering the question of alien labour in 1932. In 1934, the Dublin Trades Union Council protested against the number of 'engineers, bottlemakers, bricklayers and several other trades' being employed in Irish industries, and reasoned that 'strangers imported on what seemed the most logical grounds have invariably killed our industries and sent them back to the countries from whence the strangers came'.[31] Protests were made, and questions raised in the Dáil, about the employment of 'foreigners in sugar factories' in 1936, particularly concerning graduate-level jobs, with the perception that foreign graduates were taking jobs away from Irish graduates.[32] The Irish Cinema and Theatre Association also protested in 1936 against the prospect that Irish cinemas were about to be taken over by foreign companies (mainly English) which would employ alien managers to run them.[33] The government had already passed legislation to attempt to stop the infiltration of foreign industries into Ireland. The Control of Manufactures Act, passed on 29 October 1932, had forbidden Irish industries or businesses to be owned by non-nationals. It was an important part of de Valera's protectionist policies, ensuring that foreign transnational corporations could only trade in Ireland through Irish-owned subsidiaries.

It should be noted here, of course, that anxieties concerning English influence, and the pernicious immigration of foreigners through England, were tied up with these issues of alien invasion. The connection between the two was made explicit in a Convention of National Manufacturers meeting in Dublin in 1934, in which the resolution to maintain the control and ownership of Irish industries in Irish hands was broadly supported as a way 'to stop the onward flow of alienism threatening the rightful heritage of the Irish people'. After all, as a Mr Walsh of the Killeen Paper Mills explained, 'They were not in their present mood, and particularly after recent events in the country, in any frame of mind to accept another phase of alienism. They had not exported the foreigner in one guise to admit him in another. The country was theirs'.[34] It is probably the case that comments such as these about 'alienism' still referred to the English, and to the necessity for Irish nationalists to remain as vigilant against English influence in the process of nation-building as they had been in establishing the right to nationhood in the first place. But references to 'the foreigner', 'the stranger', or 'aliens' also illustrated a broadening of the nationalist war against English domination to a war against foreign influence of all kinds. A war between two peoples, races or nations became a war against 'alienism' *per se*. The post-independence decades witnessed a shift of focus in Irish political rhetoric from blaming the British empire for stunting Irish industrial and economic growth to blaming foreigners and aliens of all kinds for taking Irish jobs, inhibiting opportunities for Irish workers and graduates, dominating trades and business sectors, and siphoning Irish profits abroad.

This shift has obvious ramifications in the ambivalent response of Irish governments during and after the Second World War to various refugee crises. Dermot Keogh argues that government responses to crises involving refugee children were generally liberal, for example, but not in the case of Jewish refugee children, including most notoriously, the refusal of entry to 100 orphans from Bergen-Belsen in 1946 on the grounds that 'any substantial increase in our Jewish population might give rise to an anti-Semitic problem'.[35] In terms of refugees of all ages, and particularly Jewish refugees, in the early years of the Second World War especially, Ireland is one of the countries Keogh describes as 'illiberal', which 'could have done much more'.[36] This was a trend which continued, as Bryan Fanning argues, for even after Ireland ratified the UN Convention on Human Rights (1951), its response to Hungarian refugees after the political crises of 1956 was 'characterised by an exclusionary pre-Convention ethos with much in common with the problematic responses to Jewish refugees' of the wartime years.[37] That it was an ethos should be stressed. It was not a matter of the predilections of one particular minister or official. De Valera was known to be predisposed towards the plight of Jewish refugees, for example, while his ambassador in Berlin throughout the 1930s, Charles Bewley, was notoriously supportive of Nazi persecutions of the Jews, and seems to have been personally responsible for refusing or deterring Jewish asylum applications.[38] The policies and debates concerning aliens and refugees, and more particularly the xenophobic and exclusionary practices which followed from these policies and debates, were less the effect of individual influence than systemic bias. An ethical orientation towards the needs of the alien or the refugee was discernible in various voluntary organisations, and individuals, but not in the purview of the state. The ethics of the state were still very much bound up in a sense of obligation to 'ourselves', with little sense of a humanitarian responsibility towards the needs of others (either within or outside the state).[39]

The ethical basis of Irish nationalism is in many respects no different from the ethical basis of emergent European nationalisms more generally in the nineteenth and twentieth centuries, and was strongly influenced by the philosophical foundations laid by J. G. Herder. Herder argued that the nation-state was the natural expression of a distinctive cultural identity, and had profound ethical significance in providing human beings with a positive sense of connection.[40] This positive ethical value of nation-states contrasted with states or empires which were the product of 'the wild mixing of various races and nationalities under one sceptre', which were 'mechanical contrivances instead of bonds of sentiment', and were too 'weak' and 'devoid of inner life' to form the basis for human morality.[41] The true cosmopolitan, freed from the entanglements of nationality, was for Herder a 'shadow' being, who had no home to offer as shelter to anybody in need.[42] There is an echo of this understanding of nationalism as the proper foundation for the ethics of hospitality to others in Declan Kiberd's essay, 'Strangers in Their Own Country' (2001), which, stringent in its condemnation of racism against recent immigrants, argues for Irish political leaders to 'outline a national philosophy', for 'only a people secure in their national philosophy are capable of dealing confidently with those who come among them with deep commitments to alternative codes'.[43] Kiberd's solution to the dangers of racism in Irish society is broadly in keeping with a number of contemporary political theorists, including Ernest Gellner, David Miller, and Dominique Schnapper, who have argued for the necessity of cultural nationalism to the success of liberal democracies.[44]

But would not such a 'national philosophy' simply repeat the sense of division, already presupposed in Kiberd's sense of a people dealing separately and distinctively with those others who come among them, between one homogeneous national group and immigrants coming from other homogeneous national groups? As Arash Abizadeh argues, 'faced with cultural heterogeneity, state-sponsored nationalist projects of cultural assimilation, speciously justified by reference to some supposed need for homogeneity, have increasingly proven to be not just ineffective, but positively counterproductive to the goal of integration', citing the French republican version of cultural nationalism as a case in point.[45] It could be argued that in the early decades after independence, the Irish state had embarked on such a programme of cultural assimilation, not directed towards the integration of immigrants, of whom as we have seen there were not vast numbers, but directed towards the integration of its own 'nationals' into a coherent sense of shared cultural values and practices. The compulsory teaching of the Irish language in primary and secondary schools, the language require-ment for civil service and teaching appointments, the various attempts to shape a common culture, and, concomitantly, the various attempts to prohibit or restrict 'foreign' cultural influences, were just some of the ways in which the cultural identities and practices of its own nation-als were subjected to state manipulation and control. Consequently, a process of nation-building orchestrated by the state to regulate the cultural values of its own nationals is unlikely to provide a secure basis for an ethics of hospitality to others, either within or outside the state. Indeed, 'others' are perceived to be the very obstacle to national self-definition. 'The ethical problem with nationalism', as Dan Smith argues, 'lies at its heart, in the project of forming a state. . . . It is because of that project that the national group is likely to fail to grant to others what it claims for itself'.[46] It is perhaps of little wonder that, in the midst of debates about aliens and naturalisation in Ireland in the 1940s, Myles na gCopaleen (alias Flann O'Brien) protested that it was not fair that any foreigner could become an Irish national, when there was no 'comparable concession . . . whereby an Irish person can divest himself of Irishry'.[47]

To what extent, then, could a state founded upon hostility to 'the stranger' embrace an ethics of hospitality to 'the foreigner'? Paradoxically, of course, this is exactly what the state set out to do, in one sense, as one of the few industries which it succeeded in developing was the tourism industry. The idea of Ireland as specifically a culture of hospitality was marketed aggressively by the Irish Tourist Board as a way of countering the association of the country with political violence, which one newspaper report attributed to 'the continued tendency on the part of a limited section of the British Press'.[48] Indeed, in 1952, the same year as *The Quiet Man* was first shown, the Tourist Board launched its journal, still in existence today, entitled *Ireland of the Welcomes*. Kiberd begins his essay by lamenting that 'a céad mile fáilte ['a hundred thousand welcomes'] is not extended to all new arrivals any more'.[49] But, notwithstanding the efforts of the tourist industry, it is unlikely that it ever had been. The representation of foreigners, and the political rhetoric surrounding aliens, suggests that Irish hospitality was usually conditional, and often problematic in terms of how the foreigner was marked out as the symbolic embodiment of exoticism, immorality, or rootless modernity.

To understand the conditions of Irish hospitality, and the processes within nationalism which determine how the culture responds to the perceived threats of 'alienism', it is important to historicise the intensification of anxieties concerning cosmopolitan interdependencies. Denis Johnston's *The Moon in the Yellow River* (1931) illustrates such a moment in dramatising the tension surrounding German involvement in the construction of Ardnacrusha hydro-electric power station on the river Shannon in the late 1920s. We have already seen how the number of German workers employed by the Siemens-Schuchertwerke company in building Ardnacrusha raised objections from Irish trades unions. In Johnston's play too, tension exists between the Irish characters and the German engineer, Tausch, not just for the reason that he may be employed in a job which could be occupied by an Irish worker, but also for more symbolic reasons. Ardnacrusha was built as a model engineering project which would supply electrical power to the entirety of the Irish Free State. It was therefore highly symbolic of the promises of technological modernity. Tausch believes in progress, in the capacity of engineering to improve the social and economic welfare of human beings, and envisions that his power station will help to make 'a happy nation of free men'.[50] His happy vision is soon interrupted by a small group of dissidents intent on blowing up the power station, however, and its leader, Darrell Blake, pricks Tausch's naivety by objecting to the 'ludicrous machinery' which threatens to turn 'us all into a race of pimps and beggars'.[51] Blake also articulates a sentiment which we find echoed in Stuart's *Pigeon Irish*, when he tells Tausch that 'we intend to keep one small corner of the globe safe for the unfortunate human race', by protecting it from the globalising processes of modernity. Aunt Columba also joins in this attack on Tausch, explaining that the power plant will breed dependency, which in turn means that they would be 'expected to bow the knee to some place-hunting industrialist with a small technical education and with neither culture nor religion to guide them'.[52] Blake's rebellion is, of course, against the Free State which sponsors the modernising project, and to which he has the usual anti-treaty objections, but the focus and target of his rebellious act is the symbolic location of foreign cooperation with the state.

By the end of the play, Blake has been murdered by the Free State troops Tausch has secretly telephoned, and Tausch's beloved power station has been blown up, its turbines made silent. Johnston makes clear that the *kulturkampf* symbolised by Tausch and Blake has deadly consequences. The play might be argued to be recasting the civil war and its aftermath as the ideological conflict between a civic, modernising nationalism and an ethnic, recalcitrant nationalism, but this is to gloss too easily over the centrality of Tausch as a foreigner within this conflict. Blake asks rhetorically of Tausch: 'Why can't you just go away?'[53] Even the resigned former engineer, Dobelle, who has renounced the vision of progress he once worked to build, jeers at Tausch as a foreigner, refers to him as a 'Moor', and tells him to 'Take your works where they belong'.[54] It is Dobelle who counters the idea of modernity he has lost faith in with the mystical and enigmatic vision (which forms the play's title, and is borrowed from Ezra Pound) of the ancient Chinese poet, Li Po, trying to embrace 'the Moon in the Yellow River', a river he blames Tausch for muddying with his turbines. It is a romantic vision of purity and harmony with nature, yet already conscious of its absurdity in a world defined by enlightenment ideals and technological inventions. Tausch is not just a German engineer. He is the play's only exponent of cosmopolitanism, of a world beyond the possessive and divisive methodologies of nationalism. 'This world is neither yours nor mine', he tells Blake, 'It belongs to all these people'.[55] Yet his cosmopolitanism seems as dangerous to nationalist pastoral ideals as his power plant, for he is in Aunt Columba's eyes someone 'with neither culture nor religion to guide them'.[56] The presence of Tausch, as indeed the presence of German engineers at Ardnacrusha, was a significant marker of the cosmopolitan interdependencies of the newly founded state, and more broadly of the processes of cosmopolitanisation immanent in modernity itself. Daniel Levy describes these processes, in reference to contemporary social changes, as '*internalized* globalization, globalization *from within* the national societies'.[57] Tausch is not simply the scapegoat for internal divisions about state legitimacy and social change, but is himself symbolic of the processes of modernisation and cosmopolitanisation which challenge the very ethos and ethics of nationalism. As we shall see in the next section, the foreigner or alien as pariah in the nation-state becomes a significant trope in Irish fiction in the mid-century period.

The Alien as Bio-Poetical Pariah

'Given the complexity and heterogeneity of modes of national belonging', writes Judith Butler, 'the nation-state can only reiterate its own basis for legitimation by literally producing the nation that serves as the basis for its legitimation'.[58] This process, Butler argues, is 'stipulative and criterial', by which she means that nationality becomes the material and cultural product of the nation-state, defined and achieved as a result of ideological labour, with some of those contained within the borders of the nation necessarily found 'wanting' in relation to the stipulations and criteria of nationality.[59] In an age in which rapidly expanding, transnational, mass entertainment technologies made it increasingly difficult for nation-states to control and manipulate their own cultural borders, those borders became all the more clearly the focus of defensive and often chauvinistic attempts to stipulate the distinctiveness of national identity. In the Irish Free State, as Michael Mays argues, the 'pervasive obsession with national regeneration', a feature common to many countries in the 1920s and 1930s, was particularly acute.[60] The vigorous defence of the family as the basic and analogous unit of the state, the enshrinement of the primary role of women as mothers, the prohibition of all forms of contraception, and the social stigmatisation of childbirth outside marriage were the most obvious ways in which efforts were made to influence biological regeneration. But related to the biological concerns of the state were also what I discuss below as the biopoetical practices of national identity, which relied upon the development of codes of physical and aesthetic conduct in relation to bodily practice. The process by which the body was to be disciplined and trained as a specifically national body, exemplifying national criteria of morality, taste and beauty, depended upon the cultivation of affects of revulsion from deviant bodily practices. Lipstick applied too thickly, dresses worn too high to the knees, or swimming too near to members of the opposite sex – these were the signs of moral and sexual degeneracy, which were not just anathema to Catholic social teaching, but also to the biological imperatives of the nation-state. In several fictions of the mid-century period, these marks of degeneracy are shown to be projected on to the foreign female body, which is the subject of hysterical, xenophobic anxieties about the threat of contamination and corruption of native purity and integrity.

Angèle Maury, the central character in Kate O'Brien's *The Last of Summer* (1943), ought not to be considered a foreign body. She is, after all, a Kernahan, who has chosen her mother's surname, Maury, because it is better suited to her acting career. When she decides to visit her father's family home in Ireland in the autumn of 1939, however, it is with some apprehension that the relatives might be 'inhospitable', and that her father may have been right to live in exile in Paris.[61] Even before she sets foot in the Kernahan home, Angèle learns what it means to be a pariah, to be marked symbolically as an outsider and outcast in the land of her father's birth. As she walks past some children, a young girl sneers at Angèle's lipstick, 'What happened your lips?' Angèle feels the rebuke with greater force than could have been intended; she felt an accidental expression of something which had vaguely oppressed and surprised her, these ten days, in the Irish air – an arrogance of austerity, contempt for personal feeling, coldness and perhaps fear of idiosyncrasy. . . . She hated the rudeness and she heard the insult to her reddened mouth symbolically – so self-conscious was she. She heard it as an ignoble warning from the people of her father.[62]

The redness of Angèle's lipstick is the sign both of difference and injury here. In the child's sarcastic question, it denotes disfigurement, a mark on the body which draws attention to the body, and which signifies deviation from a socially policed norm. That the child is the agent of social prohibition, the arbiter of social axioms of physical appearance, is shocking to Angèle, because the child is all the more likely to reflect the mores of this austere, insular society with rude candour. Angèle begins to laugh at the child, delighted by the girl's 'nerve', but she is chastened by the abrupt and immediate ways in which she stands out as an alien, one who not only is made to feel physically idiosyncratic but also that she does not belong. She has experienced 'yokeldom' in other societies, she recalls, and the feeling of being a stranger, but this is more startlingly exclusionary, not just because of Angèle's rebuked sense of familial history and connection, but also because of the particular uniformity of contempt and oppression she senses 'in the Irish air'.

The lipstick which for Angèle means an attempt to control her looks, to exude confidence, to present a mask behind which she can be herself, is for the young girl, and by association the community to which she belongs, the mark of a loss of control, a slippage or accident, beneath which lies the weakness of foreign character. As Angèle learns later in the novel, what is at stake in this reading of her body, of the marks upon her skin, is the contested biopoetics of national and racial identity. As she observes, with some ambivalence, a skilful performance of Irish dancing, with 'a cold, fanatical character all its own', her cousin Martin tells her 'This national dancing blows the gaff on us, I always think. If you like it proves why Dev. is making a success of us. We're a prim, stiff-backed lot'.[63] For all that Angèle is half-Irish by birth, she exhibits none of the disciplinary biopoetical practices of 'stiff-backed' Irishness. Martin presents this stiff-backed image of Irishness as essential, or ahistorical, but it was an image carefully cultivated through the formalisation of Irish dancing in the early twentieth century, and more generally in modern forms of 'conduct literature', especially for girls. *Our Irish Girls*, for example, a monthly magazine for 'young Irish ladies' published in 1936–7, formed a club in which members were encouraged to pray 'for the progress of clean literature in Ireland', speak Irish wherever possible, wear their membership badge and salute other members, 'avoid the company of those who swear, blaspheme or use evil language', and 'be modest in their dress, remembering that the best dressed persons never go to extremes, and that to be vulgarly dressed is a certain sign of bad personal taste'.[64] Like the girl who sneers at Angèle's lipstick, these girls served to police the boundaries of national virtue, upholding as 'Irish' that which was clean, Gaelic, and modest, demonising as 'foreign' anything which fell short of these standards.

'Our Irish Girl' was ideally 'honest and obedient', modestly dressed, devoted to prayers and regular church attendance, and scrupulously shy of male company.[65] In contrast, Angèle is described as 'the very twentieth-century *essence*' of 'sex appeal',[66] and her complexion, movement, and looks are frequently observed and admired as 'exotic' by her Irish family and their neighbours. It is by appealing to her exotic looks that Dr O'Byrne hopes to persuade Angèle's Aunt Hannah that Angèle is 'very, very dangerous'. No one except the young girl in the opening scene of the novel is overtly rude or unwelcoming to Angèle. The most serious accusation she can make against her Irish family is that she has only been 'half welcome'.[67] She brings no injury or insult to the family, but instead two of her cousins fall in love with her, one proposing marriage, and the prospect of becoming Mrs Kernahan, and living the rest of her life in the Irish home of her father appeals to her greatly. It gives her the hope of a sense of belonging, a sense of place, a small knowable community of which she believes she might be a part. She dreams of fitting in, but this is dashed in the conclusion to the novel when even her fiancée pleads with her to return to her 'own people' in France instead of being trapped in Ireland. As a foreigner, and as an artist, Angèle is believed to be incapable of settling into the austere routines of village life in Ireland. Marriage, which Aunt Hannah understands as involving 'some sacrifice of self', would be too much of a sacrifice, it seems, in the lonely isolation of neutral Ireland. Angèle leaves for France at the end of the novel, abandoning her brief dream of finding a home and a sense of belonging, instead saying politely, 'It's been a lovely holiday'.[68]

What makes Angèle so 'very, very dangerous' is not what she says or does, but how she looks. It is nothing so discernible as skin colour, although she is lighter in complexion than her country cousins. It is not bone structure either, although she is noted for her thinness. Nor is it so obvious as her use of cosmetics, although one character's distrust of Angèle's 'face painted so that you can't see it rightly' is a revealing insight into how she generates anxiety not just as a foreigner but also as an actress.[69] Instead, in the ease of her movements, the lightness of her body, in the very absence of 'stiff-backedness', Angèle poses a biopo-etical challenge to the bodily practices of Irishness. More significantly, despite her professed attachments to France, and her desire to belong equally to Ireland, Angèle is constantly regarded as cosmopolitan, as being attached to no specific place or identity. Hannah remarks that Angèle 'belongs to the world',[70] and later refers to her as a 'poor root-less, wandering waif'.[71] Dr O'Byrne, too, says that 'she would be exotic and distinguished anywhere'.[72] This emphasis on Angèle's lack of place, on her world-citizenship, makes it clear that the antipathy towards her is not the consequence of prejudice against some specific foreign national type, but rather against an imagined dissolution or unbinding of national identity. As Giorgio Agamben argues, following Badiou:

> The State . . . is not founded on a social bond, of which it would be the expression, but rather on the dissolution, the unbinding it prohibits. For the State, therefore, what is important is never the singularity as such, but only its inclusion in some identity, whatever identity (but the possibility of the *whatever* itself being taken up without an identity is a threat the State cannot come to terms with).[73]

The Last of Summer does not divide characters along racial lines. Angèle's Irish paternity makes her, by right, an Irish citizen as well as of Irish descent. Instead, the novel stages a contest between cosmopoli-tanism and nationalism, or more specifically, the insular de Valerean nationalism which believed in the virtues of self-sufficiency, frugality, and 'modesty'. As such, Martin's cosmopolitan past as a student in Paris, as well as Angèle's father's exile, indicate their shared inability to live within the confines of the cultural nationalist ideologies of the Irish state. But Angèle, as a woman, an actress, and, by appearance, a foreigner, symbolises this exclusionary process of national self-definition most clearly. Although 'France' is the name to which Angèle runs for safety, even at the time of its most imminent danger, the novel shows that this is because the possibility of what Jean-Luc Nancy calls the 'being-in-common' rather than the 'common being' is constantly refused.[74] Angèle may learn to love the house, the family, the farm, the village, even the country of her fiancée, but she will never belong. She will never be assimilated into the 'one true being' of Irish nationality, or at least so her detractors believe. What the novel exposes, in other words, is the reliance of Irish nationalist models of community upon the idea of the nation as a singular, homogeneous essence, incapable of being together with, or being-in-common with, the other.[75]

It was not enough then to simply 'be' Irish, or of Irish descent. Irishness was a specific bodily practice, a disciplinary mode of being, which was constantly worked out in relation to transgressive, cosmopolitan, and foreign others. The cosmopolitan body, which Angèle Maury exemplifies in O'Brien's novel, recurs in Francis MacManus's *The Fire in the Dust* (1950). Here again, a young woman, Maria Golden, symbolises an alternative and transgressive bodily practice. *The Fire in the Dust* is narrated by an Irish schoolboy, Larry, and is the story of his awakening to a cosmopolitan world beyond his insular Catholic upbringing, which is also in a sense his sexual awakening. The Golden family, specifically Larry's classmate, Stephen Golden, and Stephen's sister, Maria, represent a foreign and exotic influence on the 'small town' ethos of Kilkenny. One scene is especially instructive of the dynamics of this conflict between native and foreign bodily practices. Maria foists herself upon the company of Larry, Stephen, and their classmates in a boat on the river, but when the oar drops into the water, Maria strips herself of her frock and dives in to retrieve it. Her intrusion upon their boating party is itself unwelcome, and causes the boys anxiety about what should happen to them should this 'mixed' company be seen by one of the priests. Larry also worries about Maria's appearance: 'She was a woman who climbed over walls like a tomboy, laughed when her legs were bare to the thighs, wore lipstick red as blood on her mouth, and talked loudly'.[76] When the motion of the boat pitches Maria's body against Larry's, and he instinctively grasps her waist to stop himself from falling out, he responds angrily to her teasing, pushing himself away from her, and just managing to restrain himself from spitting 'vicious things' at her, 'that she was a painted strap, dolled up like a tinker woman in a flashy dress'.[77] The tinker reference is especially resonant, as Stephen's only experience of female nudity in any form has been to glimpse a 'tinker' woman breast-feeding her baby. When Maria dives in to the water to retrieve the oar, the schoolboys react venomously, partly out of fear that she is naked: '"The bloody scut of a tomboy," said the rower beside me, "she'll ruin us before the whole town" . . . "Oh, Holy Mary, this is going beyond the bounds" . . . "The foreign mongrel. Is she in her skin, Larry?"'.[78] Their anxiety is clearly related to the social stigma of being associated with 'loose women', or sexual immorality of any kind, but is also juxtaposed with schoolboy titillation. Maria Golden is half-Irish, half-Spanish, and has an 'illegitimate' daughter whom the Golden family passes off as her adopted sister. Larry is one of the few people in the novel to get close enough to the Goldens to realise the truth of Maria's past, but for most others, it is the fact of Maria's appearance and seemingly uninhibited tactility which prompts revulsion and fear. Like Angèle in O'Brien's novel, Maria Golden's father is Irish, and thus she is legally and racially defined as Irish, but her mother was a Spanish dancer, and this is seemingly sufficient to warrant the slur of 'foreign mongrel'. The irony of de Valera's mixed parentage, of course, may well be part of the novel's pointed critique of Irish xenophobia.

MacManus stages a direct contrast to Maria Golden's sensual and tactile form in the figure of Miss Dreelin, a pious Catholic who befriends Maria's father, with marriage in mind, but it becomes apparent that Miss Dreelin seeks to rescue the man from sin, especially, it seems, the sins of his children. Her piousness is recurrently exposed as dangerously fanatical obsession, however. This exposure also takes physical form, as Miss Dreelin's fanaticism is revealed through her 'over-bright eyes quivering in the sallow sockets, and the spittle dribbling and flicking from the mouth that opened like a hungry cat's with the delicate pink tongue lolling over the teeth'.[79] The contortions of the body here indicate that Miss Dreelin's puritanical obsession with sexual morality is a repression of the body and its desires to the point of self-wounding. Miss Dreelin is only the most extreme, perhaps even the most caricatured, exponent of a code of physical and sexual conduct which the novel shows to be deeply flawed. Moreover, the apparent interrelationship of pious sexual morality and xenophobia reveals that what is being policed by these disciplinary processes is not simply a code of behaviour derived from Catholic social teaching, but from a specifically Irish nationalist ideology, which binds together sinfulness and foreignness. Just as in O'Brien's novel, for MacManus the codes of sin and foreignness are etched on the cosmopolitan body. When Larry slaps Maria for kissing him, for example, he seeks to 'find an apology for my brutality in the scent, the powder, the lipstick, the short cotton frock, until a little more provocation would have made me shout that she was a bad woman'.[80] Larry presents his immersion in the domestic world of the Goldens as like visiting a 'foreign place, too strange to be told about or to be understood at home', as profoundly incommensurable modes of being and understanding the world.[81] Yet by the end of the novel, and occasionally glimpsed through the retrospective insight of his narrative, it is clear that the Goldens embody an altogether more natural, healthy, and liberal ideal of human existence than the cold, repressive atmosphere of Catholic Ireland. In Larry's dawning realisation of this ideal lies the seeds of a more liberal, cosmopolitan society of the future, so that whereas O'Brien's novel ends in Angèle's resignation in the face of Irish puritanism and xenophobia, MacManus's novel sketches a note of hope, even though the Goldens themselves suffer tragic fates.

The same cultural borders of sex and shame continue to be explored in John Montague's story, 'An Occasion of Sin' (1964). Françoise O'Meara, a Frenchwoman married to an Irishman and living in Dublin, is given a sharp lesson in the moral codes of Irish society at her favour-ite beach. Her positive, affable demeanour gets her into trouble when she is spotted talking to clerical students, and even swimming with them. 'You're giving bad example', warns a small fat man, 'Lots of people on the beach . . . are talking'.[82] When she explains her anger at this warning to her husband, he too becomes solemn and cautions that 'in certain circumstances you might be considered an occasion of sin'.[83] That such an attitude comes from her husband causes Françoise to despair of these cultural borders, these seemingly pervasive Irish repressions of sexuality and the body: 'Did everyone in this country measure things like this?' The social repression of the body is something she notes from her observations of her fellow beach-goers, particularly the embarrassed and suspicious manner in which the men would get undressed, at first appearing to her as a comic ritual involving con-vulsive wriggling behind towels, swift glances from side to side, and stealthy jerks and pulls of clothing into place. 'Why were they doing it?' she asks, whereas her own uninhibited dressing rituals attract a mixture of furtive and furious gazes.[84] Through Françoise's eyes, the seemingly proper codes of Irish social behaviour are seen as not only idiosyncratic or comic, but as tragic and wounding. Françoise is more than just an anthropological device through which Montague focuses a critical exposure of Irish social and sexual discourses, however. By the end of the story, she has been effectively ostracised from the other beach-goers, stigmatised as a corrupt, foreign influence. The clerical students whom she had befriended are themselves guilty of treating her disrespectfully, asking questions of her marriage and of love which they dare not ask of Irish people, and teasing her, knowing well that she would be ostracised by their doing so. The knowledge that she is a foreigner both makes Françoise more interesting to them, and also puts them at their ease to treat her more playfully, and less seriously than if she were Irish. There is, in other words, an element of both condescension and exploitation in the way they engage with Françoise. The story ends with Françoise deciding not to return to the beach. She has learnt the lesson, it seems, that there is little room for difference in Ireland, other than as an exotic curiosity. Even her husband coldly remarks, when she is baffled by the behaviour of the Irish beach-goers, 'You don't understand', meaning of course that she is an outsider and that the native codes will remain a mystery to her.[85] Thus, Montague's story comments as much on the fate of the foreigner, of the cosmopolitan body, in an apparently mono-cultural Ireland, as on the sexual repressions of Irish social life.

If, as Michael Mays has argued, 'stultifying conservatism' was the 'defining trait' of the Irish Free State, an argument he makes to counter recent attempts to qualify the image of de Valera's Ireland as unremittingly insular,[86] that conservatism was examined by some of the period's writers as a complex projection of anxieties about the legitimacy of the nation-state on to the figure of the female, cosmopolitan body. It is important to stress, however, that as much as these fictions told stories of the resignation, flight, or even defeat of foreigners in the face of a seemingly intractable and inhospitable culture of national chauvinism, their exposure of the operative significance of the stigmatised foreign body in national ideology was itself the product of a counter-cultural effort to liberalise Irish society. In some respects, what we witness in these fictions is also the reliance of liberal forces in Irish culture upon the stigmatisation of the foreign body, because the contaminative power of the foreign body, with its alternative bio-poetical practices, is itself conceptualised as the agent of social and cultural change in Ireland. This is most clearly exemplified in MacManus's novel in the figure of the narrator, Larry, who is only able to glimpse beyond the strictures and censures of his Irish Catholic upbringing once he has encountered, viscerally and conceptually, an alternative mode of being, embodied by the 'foreign' characters.

The same dynamic between illiberal, insular Irish society and cosmopolitan catalysts exists in Edna O'Brien's landmark novel, *The Country Girls* (1960), which Declan Kiberd characterises as proto-feminist.[87] Joe Cleary also associates O'Brien's fiction with a certain constitutive quality, suggesting that it might be rescued from the charge of defeatism with the argument that it 'releases disruptive energies that are never entirely contained by its deflated endings'.[88] But for Cleary the sexual revolution promised in O'Brien's trilogy is revealed to be 'a romance that cannot be realised', resulting in a rather dispiriting void.[89] What is noteworthy about this promise of sexual revolution in *The Country Girls* is the extent to which such hopes are pinned to relationships with foreign characters. Cait seeks to escape from the strict morality and insularity of rural life through romantic and sexual liaisons with the predatory middle-aged Frenchman, known as Mr Gentleman, who promises to take her on a romantic weekend in Vienna and make love to her there for the first time, but abandons her abruptly before they go.[90] When Cait and Baba move to Dublin, and are able to enjoy the greater liberty and pleasures of city life, this is because they board with an Austrian couple, Gustav and Joanna, whose tolerance of the girls' late nights and male friends differs greatly from the dreary regimen of the convent school or the stifling atmosphere of rural life. Gustav and Joanna also provide the girls with the stability and understanding of a cosy familial unit, in stark contrast to Cait's childhood spent under the constant threat of her father's drunken violence and abusiveness, and in the shadow of her mother's fear. The interdependence of the nation and the family in nationalist ideologies is here subverted by associating a foreign couple with the supposed moral virtues of Irish family life, even if what remains relatively unchallenged is the ideological vision of familial stability as the cornerstone of public virtue. Arguably too, the positive affirmation of the familial which Gustav and Joanna represent in surrogate form is checked by the depiction of Mr Gentleman, who only begins to prey upon Cait in the familial vacuum left by her mother's death, and her father's desertion.

The novel ends with Cait being introduced to the new lodger, whose only phrase is 'No English speak'. That the novel ends on this scene suggests that Cait is fully assimilated to the cosmopolitan world of strangers in the city, a move which Cleary seems to dismiss as simply a recurrent naturalist device to enable plot closure, but which ought at least to alert us to the formal significance of the cosmopolitan as a *deus ex machina* solution to the apparently ineluctable doom of Irish insularity. The role of foreign characters as catalysts of liberal social and sexual change may be a product of the novel's utopian investment in the promise of the romance narrative, but it also implies a revealing cultural critique of the impoverished condition of nationalism as a fund of ideational resources for imagining change. Just as in MacManus's novel, looking 'within' for the seeds of change, of regeneration, is by implication a futile gesture.

The romance of *The Country Girls* is a stark contrast, however, to the bleak vision of sterility and degeneracy in Aidan Higgins's *Langrishe, Go Down* (1966). Higgins's novel tells the story of Imogen Langrishe's ill-fated romance with Otto Beck, a German student who lives as an alien on the Langrishe estate in Ireland. The Langrishes were once ascendancy landowners, but the three surviving sisters, unmarried and childless, are now living in poverty on the estate, unable even to pay for the food they need. The novel begins in winter in 1937, and plays upon the imagery of sterility and death in ways consciously reminiscent of *The Waste Land*, and also, in figuring the imminent extinction of the Langrishe family, echoing Yeats's symbolisation of Anglo-Irish degeneracy in *Purgatory*. The Langrishes are, in fact, Catholic converts, but they remain stigmatised as Protestant landowners by their Catholic neighbours and tenants. Hence, even assimilation with the majority culture of 'Catholic Ireland', as one neighbour refers to it, fails to rescue the Langrishes from the apparently unavoidable fate of marginalisation followed by extinction. The bulk of the novel is set in the summer of 1932, however, when the youngest sister, Imogen, somewhat desperately throws herself into a problematic sexual relationship with Otto Beck. He lives rent-free on the Langrishe estate, poaches from the estate, and embodies in every way the figure of the parasite. He is also symbolically interconnected with the rising tide of militarism and racial mythology in Nazism, even though he disavows Nazism politically. Imogen is far from idealistic or romantic about her relationship to Otto, whom she understands as a man 'capable of committing violent depredations on the chastity of any female who might chance to take his fancy'.[91] He displays no manners as she conventionally understands them, and takes what she gives him in exchange for nothing but words and sex, neither of which prove 'productive' in any sense. Her desire for him is no more than a last attempt at self and possibly familial preservation, against the interminable sterility and impoverishment of the Langrishe line.

Otto is a cosmopolitan, who has visited many countries and cities, and who can talk knowledgeably about literature, philosophy, mythology, and travel, and thus represents a very different cultural inheritance from 'Catholic Ireland', which is symbolised early in the novel by the Keegan family reciting the rosary, 'an oratorio for the humble', at their fireside.[92] But he embodies none of the liberalising virtues of the other foreign characters we have noted in mid-century Irish literature. The relationship between Imogen and Otto becomes abusive, and ends in a still-born child of which he knows nothing. The novel concludes in 1938 with Imogen returning to the house that Otto rented, and finding the remnants of someone who had been sleeping there, a tinkerman, she surmises. The scene clearly symbolises the ghostly reminders of past loves, past hopes, all the more poignant because Imogen's life now seems destined to be loveless and hopeless. Caught between the indifference and intractability of 'Catholic Ireland', and the predatory manipulations of her foreign lover, Imogen has finally nowhere to go, and nothing to belong to. *Langrishe, Go Down* thus shows a growing discomfort, in comparison to the other texts we have considered above, with the exotic fantasy of the foreigner as the agent of liberal social and sexual change. If Otto has any sexual symbolism for Irish society, it is as a predatory and parasitical sexual conqueror, and certainly not as sexual liberator, although Mr Gentleman in *The Country Girls* is, of course, already an indication of this role. Higgins's novel may thus mark a critical point of departure from what we have been tracing as something of a leitmotif in mid-century Irish writing – the foreigner or cosmopolitan body as bio-poetical alternative and liberalising agent. Although all of these fictions in which the foreigner figures as liberal agent serve to critique the nationalist vision of community as repressively homogeneous and stiflingly insular, ultimately none seems capable of imagining alternative modes of community. The culmination of this trend, symbolically, is the still-born child of Otto and Imogen's ill-begotten relationship. In this poignant symbol, Higgins too stops deliberately short of the point at which alternative modes of community might be imaginable, and in the process scuttles the one device, the liberalising foreigner, Irish writings had begun to use routinely as the fantasy solution to the stultifying conservatism of the mid-century period. Only by returning the foreigner to the status of pariah is it possible for Higgins to show, in truly Beckettian mode, the exhaustion of imaginative and ethical resources in mid-century Ireland, with, by implication, its book bannings, its clerical *gauleiters*, its masochistic endorsement of the 'virtues' of frugality and frigidity, and its pervasive suspicion of 'alienism'.

The Refugee

In her essay, 'The Jew as Pariah' (1944), Hannah Arendt argued that it was the realisation of the full implications of the pariah status of Jews which made Kafka a Zionist:

> A true human life cannot be led by people who feel themselves detached from the basic and simple laws of humanity nor by those who elect to live in a vacuum, even if they be led to do so by persecution. Men's lives must be nominal, not exceptional.[93]

As Seyla Benhabib observes, however, Arendt was also deeply aware that the need for community, for belonging, and the community- and nation-building project which evolves from this need, 'establishes new "insiders" and "outsiders"', the Israeli state produced by Zionism being no exception.[94] What I have been arguing in this chapter is that the figure of the outsider (the alien, the foreigner, and, at times more specifically, the cosmopolitan body), is a recurrent preoccupation in Irish political discourse and literary representations in the mid-century period, and a significant site of contest between the state and its intellectual dissidents. That contest centres upon the exclusionary effects of a nation-building process premised upon what Nancy calls 'thinking of community as essence', or attempting to forge community into '*a single* thing (body, mind, fatherland, Leader . . .)'.[95] What we see in the writings discussed above, I would suggest, is an abiding concern with imagining the arrival (as a literal or figurative step) of the foreigner into the national community as a symbolic test of the capacity of that community to think itself beyond essence, beyond a presumed homogeneity.

That the national community repeatedly fails to do this is a measure of its ultimately self-degenerative paucity of imaginative and ethical resources.

The Irish state repeatedly presented the nation as an objective given, 'independent of the perceptions and feelings of the agent', but it is clear, as Margaret Moore argues, that the nation in general is instead 'contingent on its members' sustaining a certain image of it based on their perceptions and feelings', an image heavily influenced (but by no means pre-determined) by factors such as shared language, religion, law, geographical situation, and so on.[96] It is this imagined nature of the national community, the contingency of its very foundations and sovereignty, which draws our attention to the field of political and cultural representations, for the very sources I have sought to examine in this chapter – political speeches and constitutions, parliamentary acts, newspaper articles, films, plays, novels, and stories – are evidence of the public contest about the meanings of the national community they imagine. The foreigner marks the limits of the imagined national community, and thus becomes the symbol not only for the nation's figural opposite, but also for its dissolution, its unbinding, or for what simply cannot be absorbed or ingested into the body of the nation. Hence, the foreigner is also always likely to become the site of imaginative investment as the symbolic promise of a new community, a new mode of being beyond the existential limits of the nation, and therefore warrants our attention as an important figure of dissidence.

In the literature of mid-century Ireland, the figure of the foreigner clearly serves as a conduit for creative opposition to the restrictive forms of community embodied in the new state. This is to emphasise what may be an obvious point, that the imagined encounter between the foreigner and Irish insularity is really also the scene of a contest within the Irish polity itself, between the exponents of ethnic and civic nationalism, between protectionism and internationalism, between the rural and the urban, between the religious and the secular, and so on. In particular, it may be understood as a principal site of contest for the rising generation of educated middle-class urbanites, exposed to the cosmopolitan influences of television, cinema, and radio, able to avail to some extent of opportunities for travel, and perhaps also employed in the new manufacturing and services sectors with regular contact with international customers and 'non-national' workers. In the late 1950s, in response to shifting pressures within Irish society, and some international changes too, Ireland embarked on a process of modernisation, liberalisation, and secularisation which, even if, as Brian Girvin states, 'more traditional norms quickly reasserted themselves',[97] nevertheless

constituted what Tom Garvin calls the 'silent revolution', with profound 'consequences which involved the disappearance of an entire
social and political order that had grown up after the Great Famine of
the 1840s'.[98] The apparent cosmopolitanism of the new middle class
in this cultural revolution was not without its problems, however, as
James Plunkett's story, 'A Walk Through the Summer' makes clear.

Plunkett explores the social dynamics of a triangular relationship between the 'new' Ireland, typified by this cosmopolitan middle
class, the 'old' Ireland, defined by the twin poles of Catholicism and
nationalism, and the figure of the refugee, who is treated with either
condescension or contempt. The story was first published in the wake
of the Hungarian refugee crisis, in which the Irish government, keen to
be seen internationally as a liberal, modern society, adopted the UN
Convention on Human Rights in 1956, and welcomed Hungarians in
particular, but only within a tightly defined set of criteria for selecting
particular kinds of refugees who would easily assimilate into the conservative Catholic ethos of the state. The state proved inadequately pre-
pared for dealing with the new arrivals, however, as mentioned earlier
in this chapter. Hungarian refugees were encouraged to come to Ireland
in the first place, it seems, only because of popular support for a sense
of Catholic solidarity, so that Irish 'hospitality', such as it turned out
to be, was based upon the 'sameness' of the Irish and the Hungarians,
not their difference.

In Plunkett's story, the refugee character, Sara, is a Polish Catholic,
but her situation and her reason for coming to Ireland are broadly
similar to those of the Hungarian immigrants. She does not have to
suffer the hardships of internment, however, but is welcomed by a
middle-class family in the Dublin suburbs:

> She was a Pole, a refugee Barbara had offered to take care of. A couple of
> years before she had come from a world of devastated homes, a chaos of
> maimed people and orphaned children, so remote from the untouched safety
> of Dublin that few who met her realized that it had had any real existence.
> But they treated her with kindness. She was almost, but not quite, one of
> the family.[99]

The horrors of Nazi and then Stalinist regimes in Poland are barely conceivable in the bourgeois security of suburban Dublin, but nevertheless
are sufficiently understood to warrant a duty of kindness to Polish refugees. What Plunkett is tracing in the story, however, is the ambivalent
and conditional nature of such hospitality, precisely this sense that Sara
is 'almost, but not quite' welcomed by the host culture. 'Almost, but
not quite' is, of course, a phrase familiar from Homi Bhabha's studies
of colonial and racial mimicry, and signifies for him the tension in race

relations between the demand for identity or sameness and the inevitable counter-pressure of difference.[100] The 'Other' is always constructed as a partial presence within the authoritative ideological discourse, so that Sara, for example, is both legitimated and simultaneously displaced within Barbara's family. She is invited to join the family, but remains a kind of subservient, incomplete member. Barbara masks Sara's ambivalent status in the family with frail excuses for excluding her from family activities, or treating her as a servant. So too, in terms of her status within Irish society, her Catholicism is understood to warrant her inclusion in a gesture of pro-Catholic solidarity, but her ethnic difference precludes her from being treated as one of 'us'. This is made painfully apparent to her in her encounter with the blind man whom Casey, Plunkett's protagonist, brings to Barbara's house:

> 'You're a foreign Catholic. Brought up in indifference. Then taken into good homes where you get the height of good feeding. You never suffered.'
> 'I think we suffered.'
> 'No. You've a loose way of living, you foreign Catholics. Not like Irish Catholics. What about that cigarette?'
> The girl went out to empty the bucket, washed her hands and returned with a cigarette. She lit it for him and he rattled on. He talked about the great faith of the Irish and about all they suffered. Some people didn't appreciate how lucky they were, living free in comfortable Irish homes. As she tidied up he asked her questions. She made no answers. For some reason she had begun to weep. But quietly. She did not want him to know.[101]

There is a bitter irony in this scene in which Sara is quietly cleaning up the blind man's vomit, the result of his greedy indulgence in the hospitality offered to him in Barbara's house, while he demands of her the gratitude for hospitality which he has failed to show himself. Moreover, his identification of her as 'foreigner', and as part of an undeserving and over-indulged crowd, typifies the process of racialising refugees as undesirable in Irish society. Sara is never less than grateful and deferential, even and perhaps especially in silencing the ghosts of her suffering, but the hospitality shown towards her consequently appears ambivalent and strained.

Sara dominates Plunkett's story, and yet is one of the least exposed of the characters in terms of narrative perspectives. Casey's point of view tends to determine the focus of the narrative, and it is he who brings the blind man into fateful collision with the middle-class household of Barbara, Casey's secret lover, and with Sara. Casey is a liminal, bohemian figure, who shares the musical tastes but not the prosperity of Barbara and her philanthropic husband, John, and who lives 'on the fringes' of poverty, 'saved only from its indignity by youth and a touch of fastidiousness'.[102]

Even Casey is not above the casual indifference to the suffering of others which the story seems to indict as much as racism in both its latent and aggressive forms. Casey, we are told, 'knew something of Sara's background, things Barbara had mentioned to him from time to time. It was a topic he did not wish to pursue'.[103] But indifference may be preferable to the response of Casey's friend, Ellis, to Sara's suffering, who 'had been touched to the extent that he desired to seduce her'.[104] Plunkett's world is one of complicated morals, in which sympathy and hospitality are never quite free of social and economic interests, and in which tolerance is delicately balanced with indifference. This is particularly evident in his ironic depiction of the bourgeois cosmopolitanism of suburban Dublin. Barbara and John listen to Haydn, mix with businessmen, musicians, and scholars, discuss the problems of international business deals, and take in a Polish refugee, but this is a weak cosmopolitanism unfit to understand or deal with the force of cultural and political prejudice, as is evident in their uncomfortable encounter with the blind man:

> 'There's a lot of our people and when they get thrown in with moneyed people they lose themselves in embarrassment. But I'm an Irish Catholic and I'm not ashamed to be what I am whether I'm in the company of Protestants or Communists.'
>   Nobody answered, in the hope that in that way their desire to listen to the music might register most forcibly. It worked for some minutes. Then the blind man groped for his stick and made a fumbling attempt to rise.
>   'I can see I'm not wanted.'
>   John jumped up and went across. 'Please,' he said, pushing him back gently into the chair.
>   'Then why does nobody talk to me?'[105]

The music becomes the cover behind which the other characters hide to save themselves from confronting the racial pride and religious and political bigotry of the blind man. It is this embarrassed encounter between the bohemian bourgeoisie and the force of bigotry which leads Casey to relinquish his relationship with Barbara, as he seems to recognise the thinness of the suburban commitment to hospitality and cosmopolitanism. He contemplates how much his abandonment of Barbara might hurt her, and concludes that she will find other distractions. The implication, subtly suggested but surprisingly barbed, is that the liberal tolerance and graciousness of Barbara and John, their apparent generosity towards Sara, their polite forbearance of the blind man, and even Barbara's supposedly frivolous affair with Casey, are all the superficial and self-serving distractions of a bored and indifferent suburban middle class.

If the problem with the new, cosmopolitan Ireland is its failure to engage with otherness in a meaningful way, or to understand the racism

which it ought to counter, Plunkett's story also delineates the impoverished social and cultural conditions in which racism and bigotry fester.
The blind man's bigoted pride in his race and religion is shown to stem
from his determination to counter the force of colonial racism with that
of his own racial pride, like 'the citizen' of Joyce's *Ulysses*. Casey also
forgives or at least tolerates the blind man's stubborn ingratitude as
somehow excused by the indignity and helplessness of his social position. More strangely, when Barbara asks him why he brought the blind
man, Casey replies 'Love'.[106] This answer, brief and elusive, raises the
possibility that the story is centred on the ethical response and more
broadly ethical responsibility to the other.[107] Plunkett's story refrains
from mobilising any counter-arguments to the prejudices and racism
of the blind man. Whenever the blind man shows his bigotry and hate,
the key moral touchstones of the story, Casey and Sara, respond with
generosity. Sara's silence, or Casey's smile to himself, may appear to
abandon the blind man to his prejudices, and leave racism unanswered,
but both characters communicate the generosity implicit in the duty of
hospitality – Casey guides him through streets in which he is lost and
finally gives up his bed for the old man, Sara serves him with the food
and cigarette he desires and even clears up his vomit. Of course, it is
one of the telling strains in Plunkett's story that Sara is only permitted
to communicate her defiant, persistent presence, her right to belong,
through silence and compliance. But her silence throws the focus of
the text back on the question of response and responsibility. In this
way, Plunkett's story ranges from the specific dynamics of a racialised
encounter between competing versions of Irishness and the refugee to a
more general concern for the ethics and politics of hospitality. Perhaps
most obvious of all, the story recognises that the consideration of the
politics of Irish hospitality should not only centre on the refugee, but
also address the historical and contemporary forms of Irish racism.

The literary texts I have examined in this chapter point forwards
out of their own time toward the intensification of a relationship
between Irish modernity and racism in the present, and in this respect
they warrant our critical attention for the prescience with which they
envisage the attendant complexities of cosmopolitanism. But I have
also argued that they demand our consideration for their engagement
with cosmopolitical relationships in their own time, and for the ways
in which they imagine and animate the ethical, representational, and
political problematics of the interplay between 'Irishness' and its cultural others in the mid-century period. In particular, each of these texts
brings into focus the construction of Irish national identity through
racialised, chauvinistic encounters with figures of foreigners and

'alienism', and serves to critique the myths of Irish cultural homogeneity formed as a result. As such, they may be read as counter-texts to the contemporary fixation with imagining Irish society in the mid-century as a dark age of homogeneous and uncontested cultural nationalism. In *Outrageous Fortune*, Joe Cleary argues that a marked tendency in contemporary Irish culture is 'to cleave at the sensorial level' to 'the story of the death of de Valera's Ireland', and in doing so, to fail to give imaginative expression to the 'emergence of some new order'.[108] As a result, Cleary argues, we are no closer to understanding the cultural implications of 'the social world of financial services centres, computer industries, comfortable middle-class suburbs and golf clubs, designer boutiques, congested motorways or city-centre gay saunas, gyms or sex shops' of the so-called 'Celtic Tiger' Ireland than we are to understanding the complexities of modernity in de Valerean Ireland.[109] It should come as no surprise, then, that the fictions of the foreigner in Irish culture I have been examining in this chapter also stop short of imagining alternative forms of political community, and stop short of the full implications of their cosmopolitical critique of the insularity of the Irish nation-state. It is this failure to imagine post-nationalist community, to think beyond the long-sterile notion of cultural homogeneity, which, in the mid-century period as well as in more recent years, gave currency and legitimacy to the insidious ideologies of racial and cultural chauvinism. The romance of the foreigner in Irish writing of the mid-century decades may not be capable of sustaining any utopian project of re-imagining the nation-state from cosmopolitan perspectives, but in exposing the lie of Irish hospitality, and the figural limits of the nationalist project, these writings might serve to articulate, now as in the mid-century period, an ironic reply to racist discourses, for now as then, as Paul Gilroy argues 'the founding *absurdity* of "race" as a principle of power, differentiation, and classification must remain . . . persistently, obstinately in view'.[110]

Notes

1. *The Quiet Man*. Dir. John Ford. Perf. John Wayne, Maureen O'Hara, Barry Fitzgerald. Republic Entertainment Inc., 1952. DVD, Universal, 2006.
2. Luke Gibbons reads *The Quiet Man* as 'a western with an unusual ethnographic sensibility', in which Thornton as a returned emigrant 'can only survive by negotiating precisely the kind of cultural traditions emigrants were encouraged to jettison on their errand into the wilderness in America', and comes to symbolise an opening up of narrative space

to ethnic diversity. My reading above argues that the opening scene in particular embodies a more pointed reinscription of the ethnographic, and more particularly the figure of ethnographic borders, than Gibbons acknowledges. See Luke Gibbons, *The Quiet Man*, pp. 15–16.

3. Jacques Derrida, 'Foreigner Question', *Of Hospitality*, p. 73.
4. Ibid., p. 55.
5. For contrasting readings of Kant's thinking on the relationship between the state and hospitality, see the essays by Seyla Benhabib and Jeremy Waldron in Benhabib et al., *Another Cosmopolitanism*, pp. 13–101.
6. Hannah Arendt, *The Origins of Totalitarianism*, p. 291.
7. I am indebted here of course to Homi Bhabha's discussion of the cosmopolitan citizen as iterative and alterative in 'Unpacking My Library Again', pp. 5–18, reprinted in *The Post-Colonial Question*, ed. Chambers and Curti, pp. 199–211.
8. Seyla Benhabib, *The Rights of Others*, p. 62.
9. The Tailteann games of 1924, 1928, and 1932 were vaguely conceived as expressions of Irish racial traditions, and to some degree resembled the alliance between nationalism and physical culture movements in various European countries in the same period, but it is false to distinguish them from other forms of cultural practice, such as those orchestrated by the GAA, the Gaelic League, and the Irish Dancing Commission.
10. J. J. Lee, *Ireland 1912–1985*, p. 77.
11. Claire Wills, *That Neutral Island*, pp. 45–82, p. 92.
12. Bryan Fanning, *Racism and Social Change in the Republic of Ireland*, pp. 59–86.
13. Ibid., p. 90.
14. Dermot Keogh, *Twentieth-Century Ireland*, pp. 243–4.
15. R. F. Foster, *Modern Ireland, 1600–1972*, p. 547.
16. Terence Brown, *Ireland: A Social and Cultural History, 1922–1985*, p. 237.
17. Interestingly, even emigration, which reached very high levels throughout the 1950s, was conceptualised in contrasting ways in relation to notions of racial and cultural homogeneity. Dian Killian points to the likely racial undertones of Alexis Fitzgerald's response to the 1954 report on emigration that high levels of emigration might be 'a sign of our vitality', whereas John A. O'Brien, in a book entitled *The Vanishing Irish*, published in the same year, lamented Irish degeneracy (largely as a result of emigration) and prophesied that 'If the past century's rate of decline continues for another century, the Irish will virtually disappear as a nation and will be found only as an enervated remnant in a land occupied by foreigners'. See Dian Killian et al., 'What's White Got to Do With It?', p. 169, and John A. O'Brien, *The Vanishing Irish*, p. 7.
18. Francis Stuart, *Pigeon Irish*, p. 144.
19. Ibid., p. 33.
20. Ibid., p. 57.
21. *Speeches and Statements by Eamon de Valera, 1917–73*, pp. 193–6.
22. Benedict Anderson, *Imagined Communities*, p. 24.
23. *Speeches and Statements by Eamon de Valera*, pp. 193–4.
24. Ibid., p. 194.

25. 'Alien Arrivals Here Over Period of Nine Years', *Irish Times*, 16 May 1946, p. 7.
26. 'Aliens in Ireland', *Irish Times*, 20 October 1939, p. 5. The issue of the nationality of Ireland's aliens was bound to be of particular urgency given the recent outbreak of the Second World War, and Ireland's declared policy of neutrality.
27. Fanning, *Racism and Social Change*, pp. 30–58.
28. See Mary Daly's analysis of xenophobia in Irish society in her essay, 'Cultural and Economic Protection and Xenophobia in Independent Ireland, 1920s-1970s', in Faragó and Sullivan, eds, *Facing the Other*, pp. 6–18, and also her analysis of attempts to construct an indigenous Irish industrial sector in *Industrial Development and Irish National Identity, 1922–1939*, pp. 75–102.
29. 'Aliens in the Free State', *Irish Times*, 1 November 1934, p. 4.
30. 'Alien Labour in the Free State', *Irish Times*, 6 September 1932, p. 2.
31. 'Importation of Workmen', *Irish Times*, 9 January 1934, p. 5.
32. 'Foreigners in Sugar Factories', *Irish Times*, 12 May 1936, p. 7.
33. 'Free State Film Industry', *Irish Times*, 16 December 1936, p. 7.
34. 'The Free State's Economic Problems', *Irish Times*, 24 January 1934, pp. 11–12.
35. Dermot Keogh, *Jews in Twentieth-Century Ireland*, p. 210.
36. Ibid., p. 194.
37. Fanning, *Racism and Social Change*, p. 87.
38. See Keogh, *Jews in Twentieth-Century Ireland*, pp. 174–5, and Fanning, *Racism and Social Change*, pp. 75–6.
39. The ethics of nationalism have been the subject of considerable debate in recent years, especially perhaps in the light of resurgent nationalisms in Eastern Europe, and the fall of communism. See, for instance, Margaret Moore, *The Ethics of Nationalism* and Ronald Beiner (ed.), *Theorizing Nationalism*.
40. Herder defends nationalist community for it 'attaches people together into their center, makes them firmer on their tribal stem, more blooming in their kind, more passionate and hence also happier in their inclinations and purposes'. Quoted from Russell Arben Fox, 'J. G. Herder on Language and the Metaphysics of National Community', p. 253, in which Fox argues that Herder was not wedded to a racial or in any way fixed notion of national community, but instead was interested in the nation as an expression of linguistic and cultural bonds, through which we became fully human.
41. Quoted in Richard White, 'Herder', p. 172.
42. See Fox, 'J. G. Herder on Language and the Metaphysics of National Community', p. 257.
43. Declan Kiberd, 'Strangers in Their Own Country: Multi-Culturalism in Ireland', in Declan Kiberd and Edna Longley (ed.), *Multi-Culturalism*, p. 74.
44. See Ernest Gellner, *Nations and Nationalism*; David Miller, *On Nationality*, and 'The Ethical Significance of Nationality', pp. 647–62; and Dominique Schnapper, *Community of Citizens*.
45. Arash Abizadeh, 'Does Liberal Democracy Presuppose a Cultural Nation?', p. 508.

46. Dan Smith, 'Ethical Uncertainties of Nationalism', p. 501.
47. Myles na gCopaleen, 'Cruiskeen Lawn', *Irish Times*, 16 May 1944, p. 3.
48. 'The Tourist Trade', *Irish Times*, 25 April 1934, p. 4.
49. Kiberd, 'Strangers in Their Own Country', p. 43.
50. Denis Johnston, *The Moon in the Yellow River*, in *Selected Plays*, p. 121.
51. Ibid., p. 139.
52. Ibid., p. 147.
53. Ibid., p. 143.
54. Ibid., pp. 163, 168.
55. Ibid., p. 143.
56. Ibid., p. 147.
57. Daniel Levy, 'The Cosmopolitan Figuration', pp. 177–87.
58. Judith Butler and Gayatri Chakravorty Spivak, *Who Sings the Nation-State?*, p. 31.
59. One hyperbolic example of this ideological project of stipulating the criteria of nationality can be found in the short-lived newspaper, *The Gael*, which ran to just three issues in 1954. *The Gael* counselled its readers to aspire towards the epithet of 'Gael' as an ideal form of Irishness: 'A Gael inherits the tradition and heritage of the Irish race, he is ennobled and even spiritually elevated by that rich inheritance, he values things of the spirit far more than those of the world, just as did his forefathers when they freely gave all to attend the Mass during the Penal Days. The drunkard who curses and disgraces himself in our streets is no Gael, though he may be Irish. Certain low types of individuals who haunt certain types of dance-halls and streets, usually with their motor-cars, are no Gaels, no matter how many times they are born in Ireland. . . . Spivs, shysters, racketeers, low types, anti-nationals and all such ilk are no Gaels'. See 'What is a Gael?', *The Gael*, 17 April 1954, p. 4.
60. Michael Mays, *Nation States*, p. 91.
61. Kate O'Brien, *The Last of Summer*, p. 3.
62. Ibid., p. 5.
63. Ibid., p. 96.
64. 'All you want to know about the new "Our Irish Girls" Club', *Our Irish Girls*, 7 (Oct. 1936), p. iii.
65. Club membership was organised by 'Uncle Pat', however, and girls were encouraged to send their names, addresses, and sometimes photographs to 'Uncle Pat', as well as to contribute to 'Uncle Pat's Corner' of puzzles and jokes. The avuncular pseudonym was clearly intended to evoke the familial and avoid the issue of sexual identifications.
66. O'Brien, *The Last of Summer*, p. 149.
67. Ibid., p. 195.
68. Ibid., p. 242.
69. Ibid., p. 120.
70. Ibid., p. 19.
71. Ibid., p. 148.
72. Ibid., p. 149.
73. Giorgio Agamben, *The Coming Community*, p. 85.
74. Jean-Luc Nancy, *The Inoperative Community*, p. xxxviii, p. 29.
75. See Heather Ingman's Kristevan reading of two other novels by Kate

O'Brien, *Mary Lavelle* and *The Land of Spices*, as well as Elizabeth
Bowen's *A House in Paris*, and Polly Devlin's *Dora*, for interesting
overlaps with the concerns raised above: Heather Ingman, 'Translating
between Cultures', pp. 177–90.

76. Francis MacManus, *The Fire in the Dust*, p. 84.
77. Ibid., p. 86.
78. Ibid., p. 87.
79. Ibid., p. 132.
80. Ibid., p. 67.
81. Ibid., p. 77.
82. John Montague, 'An Occasion of Sin', p. 136.
83. Ibid., p. 138.
84. Ibid., p. 130.
85. Ibid., p. 131.
86. Mays, *Nation States*, p. 100. Mays responds critically in particular to
    Brian Fallon's *An Age of Innocence*.
87. Declan Kiberd, *Inventing Ireland*, p. 566.
88. Joe Cleary, *Outrageous Fortune*, p. 167.
89. Ibid., p. 168.
90. Edna O'Brien, *The Country Girls*, p. 173, p. 187.
91. Aidan Higgins, *Langrishe, Go Down*, p. 153.
92. Ibid., p. 18.
93. Hannah Arendt, 'The Jew as Pariah', pp. 88–9.
94. Benhabib, *The Rights of Others*, pp. 63–6.
95. Nancy, *The Inoperative Community*, p. xxxix.
96. Moore, *The Ethics of Nationalism*, p. 7.
97. Brian Girvin, *Between Two Worlds*, pp. 200–1.
98. Tom Garvin, *Preventing the Future*, p. 24.
99. James Plunkett, 'A Walk Through the Summer', p. 35.
100. Homi Bhabha, *The Location of Culture*, pp. 85–92.
101. Plunkett, 'A Walk through the Summer', p. 53.
102. Ibid., p. 37.
103. Ibid., p. 56.
104. Ibid., p. 58.
105. Ibid., pp. 46–7.
106. Ibid., p. 46.
107. This reply might approximate to what Derrida defines as the 'law of
     unconditional hospitality', an ethical responsibility towards the absolute
     other. See *Of Hospitality*, p. 79. For an interesting reading of Dickens' *A
     Christmas Carol* and Joyce's 'The Dead' in relation to Derridean notions
     of hospitality, see Paul K. Saint-Amour, '"Christmas Yet to Come"',
     pp. 93–117.
108. Cleary, *Outrageous Fortune*, pp. 229–31.
109. Ibid., p. 209n.
110. Paul Gilroy, *Between Camps*, p. 42.

Chapter 4

'Ireland, and Black!': The Cultural Politics of Racial Figuration

'Ireland, and black!', the title for this chapter, comes from the 'Occasional Discourse on the Negro Question', published anonymously in 1849, and attributed to Thomas Carlyle, in which Carlyle forewarns that the consequences of emancipating the West Indies would be a *black Ireland* – "free", indeed, but an Ireland, and black!' The punctuation of this phrase, 'Ireland, and black!', with caesura and exclamation registers the pathetic incongruity of the two terms, which are at the same time conjoined, and in each iteration in Carlyle's discourse the signification of black Ireland is marked textually or rhetorically as incompatible. Compared to 'our own white or sallow Ireland, sluttishly starving, from age to age', Carlyle says, 'a negro Ireland' would be beyond comprehension: 'Imagination cannot fathom such an object; the belly of chaos never held the like'.[1] Of course, Carlyle is using this impossible object, 'black Ireland', as a figure of inhuman depravity with which to attack philanthropic arguments about the West Indies, and the figure of 'black Ireland' is re-located to the Caribbean in ways which might lead us to pursue the same deconstructive reading as Colin Graham when he traces the tropological (and indeed tropical) flotation of 'Ireland' as a signifier in his essay, 'Ireland, East of Atlantis'.[2] One of the floating signifiers of 'Ireland' Graham reads in this essay is from John Mitchel's *Jail Journal*, published a year before Carlyle's text, in which Mitchel exclaims in surprise when discovering another island called 'Ireland' on his journey to Bermuda.[3] Whether it is black or free, Mitchel does not say, but here Graham's reading follows the disorienting doubling of 'Ireland', where, 'exiled from its grounded self', it becomes 'excessive', and 'topples into an Ireland of ceaseless reproduction and commodification'.[4] Carlyle's phrase, however, exerts pressure in different directions, not just to make Ireland available as a reproductive and commodified trope, but also to mark Ireland within a racist taxonomy in which the existence of 'black Ireland' is both deemed impossible, and paradoxically made imaginatively or figuratively indispensable. The caesura is followed by the conjunctive, and it is this paradoxical condition of 'Ireland, and black!' as a persistent figure in Irish culture, that I want to trace in this chapter.

To begin this chapter with Carlyle, of course, is to invoke those colonial discourses of race in which the Irish represented a particular threat as a debased or degenerated form of whiteness.[5] Thus, the spectre of 'black Ireland' which Carlyle raises in his essay is a double negative, conjoining the visible marker of black skin as a register of racial inferiority with the more elusive threat of white degeneration typified by the Irish, whom in the mid-nineteenth century had become, in Luke Gibbons's words, 'the simianized underclass that threatened the white Caucasian race from within'.[6] Gibbons builds upon Matthew Frye Jacobson's argument that the increasing trend in the nineteenth century towards biological explanations of race 'was motivated by an anxiety to distinguish *between* white races', to suggest that the Irish presented Victorian discourses of racial difference with the problem of an invisible, epidemiological 'other', 'a source of pollution in the body politic'.[7] The Irish were thus an anomaly, an aberration, in an otherwise effective visual schema of racial distinction, and it is this anomalous position – a 'white colony' in an empire premised upon white superiority, or as Gibbons memorably coined, 'a First World country, but with a Third World memory'[8] – which has absorbed the attention of some of the most astute analyses of Irish cultural history in recent decades. For David Lloyd, it is clear, particularly from the history of Irish immigrant society in the United States, that the relationship between Irish and black peoples has never been simply one of analogy and solidarity, but in relation to colonial discourse, it is one of equivalence: 'For Anglo-Saxons, "Celt" and "Negro" were a comparable threat to their society'.[9] It may well be, as Gibbons suggests, that the equivalence of the terms 'Irish' and 'black' 'threw into disarray some of the constitutive categories of colonial discourse'.[10] My intention in this chapter, however, is to analyse the 'afterlife' of that nineteenth-century history of black-Irish relations, specifically focused on the ways in which blackness has been figured within Irish culture since the mid-twentieth century.

In Chapter 1 we saw how the pariah figure of a 'black Ireland' lurked behind the nationalist demand for independence, since the claim to national distinctiveness was inseparable from the racial assertion that, in Douglas Hyde's words, 'the Irish are neither negroes nor mongrels nor castaways'.[11] Even in making connections with other national movements of liberation, de Valera appealed for American support on the basis that Ireland was 'the one remaining white nation in the slavery of alien rule'.[12] In this sense, the struggle for national self-determination re-enacted in conceptual terms the assertion of Irishness as a white ethnicity in the racial politics of nineteenth-century America, which Noel Ignatiev examined in *How the Irish Became White*.[13] Through the work of Eric Lott, Lauren Onkey, and Catherine Eagan, the complex ways in which Irish-Americans asserted their own 'whiteness' through cultural performances of blackface minstrelsy has become clearer, performances which, as Onkey writes, 'became a way for the Irish to both emulate African-Americans and distance themselves from them'.[14] Meanwhile, significant attention has been devoted within Irish studies to the ways in which twentieth-century black artists in the Harlem Renaissance, the Caribbean Literary Renaissance, and in a number of African cultural nationalist movements have been inspired or influenced by Irish cultural precursors.[15] Irish nationalist intellectuals and politicians have also sometimes alluded to the common causes of black and Irish peoples against oppression. Bill Rolston argues in his essay, 'Are the Irish Black?', that

> for every example of a revolutionary who was progressive on Irish affairs while being racist, there is another person who managed to generalise their opposition to imperialism and repression in order to identify with those in other struggles – from James Connolly and Roger Casement at the turn of the twentieth century to Bernadette Devlin

whom Rolston cites for her provocative act of passing on to the Black Panthers the symbolic key to the city of New York given to her by the city's mayor.[16] David Lloyd sees not so much a history of such solidarity, as an ethical imperative towards it, especially in Irish America:

> Our history is full of reasons to seek out both international and inter-ethnic connections, because of what we know and because of what we could know better of ourselves and of others. And because the struggle against injustice is not ended just by our own becoming 'legal'.[17]

As Michael Malouf has demonstrated in relation to de Valera's expressions of solidarity with other anti-colonial movements in 1920, however, such claims of inter-ethnic solidarity are often invested in complex strategies of acquiring legitimation or recognition, in which gestures of affiliation are never clearly distinguishable from acts of appropriation.[18]

One argument of this book is that the particularities of Ireland's anti-colonial, nationalist struggle, and the perceived need in the course of nation-building to forge a myth of cultural homogeneity, have militated in favour of insinuative forms of racism and raciology. The methodological nationalism of much Irish historiography and cultural criticism has also arguably privileged a monocultural narrative, in which *the* Irish have been victims of racism in the colonial past, and sometimes perpetrators of racism in other countries, but the history of racism in modern Ireland has only recently become the subject of academic and critical discourse.[19] Even Rolston in his essay, 'Are the Irish Black?', becomes mired in the exclusionary assumptions of methodological nationalism in his final summary: 'Are the Irish black? Of course not. But is our struggle like that of anti-colonial peoples elsewhere, despite the different colours of our and their skin? Yes'.[20] Although the emphatic denial of Irish blackness is accompanied by a footnote which avers that 'There are some people of colour in Ireland who, along with members of the Travelling community, are subject to racial abuse and attacks', Rolston's essay nonetheless concludes somewhat problematically with a simplistic equation of Irishness with whiteness, and the equally problematic assumption that there is one Irishness, and one struggle with which *the* Irish identify. There is, uncomfortably, little space for the relationship between the terms 'black' and 'Irish' other than through the anti-colonial solidarity of one monoculture with another.

The relatively small number of black immigrants in Irish society prior to the 1990s has led some commentators to portray Ireland as a broadly homogeneous state, untested in the complexities of multi-racial co-existence. In his book, *Ireland and the Irish: Portrait of a Changing Society*, published in 1994, John Ardagh wrote that 'the Republic is spared the racial problems found in so much of Europe today. . . . The Irish are not racist, and they even feel some solidarity with the Third World, in part because of their shared colonial experience'.[21] The evidence for this solidarity, perhaps predictably, is given as Irish contributions to charitable funds for Africa, and 'Irish Catholicism's strong missionary tradition'. But Ardagh asks, 'if Asiatics or Africans were ever to arrive in some numbers, would the Irish remain so tolerant? As yet they have no experience of living in a multiracial society'. Racism breeds only in multi-racial societies, according to this understanding. It arrives with the migrants, refugees, and asylum seekers. It is no surprise, especially in the light of many recent studies of racism in Ireland from sociological and historical perspectives, that racism in various forms precedes the recent influx of immigrants.[22] It is important, first of all, to take issue with the very notion of a multi-racial society, which presumes the actuality and stability of races *per se*, and to clarify that however one categorises population groups within a state – according to cultural affiliation, language, nationality, ethnicity (no less problematic than 'race'), skin colour, or any other supposed measure of identity – the population of the Irish state has always been heterogeneous and hybrid. My concern in this chapter, however, is to show that not only has Ireland experienced racism, and encountered social and cultural problems as a result of perceived racial differences, prior to the 1990s, but that the problematic conjunction of the terms 'black' and 'Ireland' has been a significant preoccupation in Irish writing and culture for quite some time. I shall focus in particular in this chapter on the 1960s and 1970s, a time of significant change in Irish society, when decades of isolationist policies were giving way to the political desire to foster international relations and indeed to seek analogies for Irish experiences. One further implication of Ardagh's question about the arrival of black and Asian peoples into Ireland, is that there is a blank space of representation when it comes to how that arrival might be conceptualised in Irish cultural and social narratives. What I am suggesting in this chapter is the opposite, that the political narratives and cultural productions examined here evince the existence of prescribed narratives of so-called 'multi-racial' experience in pre-'Celtic Tiger' Ireland, and that these narratives leave a problematic legacy for the attempt to recognise and celebrate a 'cosmopolitics' of heterogeneity in contemporary Ireland.

Legality, Racism, and the Black Presence in Ireland

The first reported deportation order in the Irish state was issued in Cork in 1925, to a 'black Prince'. On Monday 22 June 1925, a 'coloured visitor' who described himself as 'Prince Shervington of Abyssinia', appeared before Cork District Court, charged with having breached the laws governing aliens in the Irish Free State.[23] He had failed to register as an alien when he arrived in Cork two months previously, failed to register his address as a lodger in a house in Little William Street, and had no passport or any other form of identification. When arrested, he made a statement to the Gardaí that he was 'the recognised Prince of Abyssinia and heir to the throne', and was travelling *incognito*, but when asked for verification of his claims, 'he produced some telegrams in a foreign language', one of which he purported was from foreign royalty which when translated simply read 'Congratulations, Marie Christina'. The state solicitor prosecuting the case argued there was no 'bona fide' in the correspondence, nothing to support the 'Prince's' testimony. The 'Prince' stated that he had been born in Jamaica in 1897, emigrated to the United States in 1915, joined the US Army in 1917, and served in France, but was later discharged on declaring British citizenship. In 1922, he joined the Spanish Army and fought against the Rif tribes in Morocco, and when Gardaí initially approached him for his papers in Cork, he had referred them to the Minister of War in Madrid. He also claimed to own 'banana, coffee and fruit plantations' in Jamaica, and to have arrived in Cork with over £71, most of which he had now lost in gambling. When asked to swear upon oath as to his citizenship, the 'Prince' replied: 'Not to-day; I am a bit too sick to swear'. The *Irish Times* reported this reply without comment, as if there needed no editorial direction to see the painfully naive way in which the man was foiling his own attempts at deception.

On the basis of investigations made by the Gardaí, the state solicitor had not been able to prove the identity of the 'Prince', and there had been 'complaints from civilians' about his drunkenness, gambling, and debts, and reports from British police that he had obtained money from clergymen on the promise that when he was installed on the Abyssinian throne, he would make donations to their churches. He had even caused a newspaper scandal in England when he was mistaken for Sir Hari Singh, the Maharaja of Jammu and Kashmir, who had been the subject of intense newspaper speculation as to his whereabouts in late 1924 when he was the victim of a fraud case.[24] On his own merits, as it were, the 'Prince' acquired local celebrity in Cork as a result of his court appearances,[25] and the newspaper reports of his trial reveal an evident sense of ridicule about the man's testimony and his claims to be a 'Prince'. Behind the media delight in this courtroom farce, however, the 'Prince' was ultimately, and simply, 'undesirable'. The Garda superintendent who was called as a witness in the trial stated that 'the town would be better off by his absence', and that he was 'an unsuitable person'. The state solicitor argued on the basis of 'the conduct of this man in town' and of 'his character', that he should be deported. The judge ordered the 'Prince' to furnish the Gardaí with evidence of his identity under the Aliens Act within seven days. When he failed to do so, he appeared before the court on 30 June, and was sentenced to a fine of £5.[26] When he failed to pay the fine, he was imprisoned in Cork Male Gaol for six weeks.[27] He was also recommended by the judge for deportation, and was the first reported case of deportation since the Aliens Act was passed into law in January 1925, or indeed since the Irish Free State came into existence in 1922.

Paul Gilroy's influential chapter in *There Ain't No Black in the Union Jack* (1987) on the identification of black communities in Britain with criminality also begins with a courtroom anecdote, and argues that the courtroom itself has become an important site of contemporary racial discourses.[28] In the case cited by Gilroy, in which a young black man was tried in London in 1985 for possession of cannabis, both the judge's comments about 'your own people', and the media fixation with his lifestyle as an unemployed, 'pot-smoking rastafarian', reveal that the focal point of the trial was the ability of racially defined minorities to adhere to the law as a national institution. Racial stereotypes of young black men were openly articulated, and obviously at stake, both in the court room and in the media representation of the case. The young man was always symbolic of black settlement in white Britain, representative of a 'race' described by one of Britain's leading police commissioners as 'constitutionally disorderly', now resident in a nation which prided itself on its legal institutions and its defence of the rule of law.[29] The symbolism of the case heard in Cork District Court in 1925 is quite different, but no less instructive about the relationship between racial difference and the law as an instrument of national expression.

The 'Prince' was a curiosity, to the court and to the newspapers, not so much the object of racial or national fears, as the object of cultural ridicule. Race was never articulated in the court room, as far as it can be discerned from newspaper reports and court minutes, nor did it need to be. For the purposes of the trial, under the terms of the Aliens Order, he was simply a curious outsider, a 'colourful' visitor who had not obeyed the legislation governing his admission to, and permission to reside in, the Irish state. Yet in the newspaper reports of the case, it is clear that a familiar figure of racial representation is in play here, although it is a figure not recognised as familiar by the reporters themselves: the vagabond who pretends to be a prince, the buffoon who reveals the lie of his own testimony by refusing to swear, the garrulous performer who tells the authorities his life story, as well as a few fictions, but refuses to give his name. These are all familiar tropes of Irishness in English colonial representations of the nineteenth century, but here are transferred on to the 'coloured visitor' to Cork. For the Irish newspapers what is clearly appealing about the case of the 'Prince' is its theatricality, the comic performance of an obvious masquerade, the comedy of which is available to those of 'us' sufficiently rational and educated to see through the 'Prince's' touchingly artless manner of deception. Thus, the imprisonment and deportation of the 'Prince' are important, if unremarkable, proofs of the maturity and rationality of the state, and its capacity to define and defend its borders not just against illegal aliens, but also against its own colonial, black 'other'. In showing the effective operation of state mechanisms of admission and deportation, the case against 'Prince Shervington of Abyssinia' served to underline the association of legality with national identity. It did so not least in the ways in which the transience and whimsicality of the 'Prince' so obviously contrasted with the legal requirements for identification and registered settlement under the Aliens Order, so obviously contrasted, then, with the very foundations of the nation-state as the legal basis of citizenship and human rights. Here was a subject whose testimony before the law was inherently, self-avowedly, unreliable. Here was a subject who was by definition outside the law, and therefore subject to the penalty of the laws devised to regulate and express the very terms of nationhood.

What the newspapers highlighted for derision, of course, may be read instead as part of a self-conscious, perhaps even parodic, performance. Indeed, one might usefully consider the 'Prince's' incredible testimony, his evidently misleading claims, and refusal to give or verify his identity, as a deliberate rhetorical strategy of 'signifying', as Henry Louis Gates has characterised the figure of the 'signifying monkey' in Afro-American culture – 'he who dwells at the margins of discourse, ever punning, ever troping, ever embodying the ambiguities of language' – which for Gates is a 'trope-reversing trope, a figure of a figure'.[30] Declan Kiberd makes a similar argument about the rhetorical resistance and strategic masquerade of the 'stage Irishman' in Victorian England,[31] but in an ironic reversal of the trope of the stage Irishman, the case of the 'Prince' in Cork shows a newly arrived black immigrant resorting to such measures in order to obfuscate the determinacy of the laws of the Irish Free State. Ironically, too, the case was reported by Irish newspapers in a similar vein to the Victorian newspaper reports of Irish court appearances, delighting in the discovery of a comic racial foil to their implied vision of a settled Irish nation, defined and ordered by its adherence to law, and determined to police its own newly acquired borders. What we have in this first reported case of deportation from the state, then, is one example of how the discourse of Irish political modernity has been practised, or enacted, upon the figure of a black other, but, of course, it could only do so through the dis-articulation of race as a category within the seemingly liberal terms of the law. I want to show here that it is not the only example of such exploitation within the terms of a liberal modernity in recent Irish history.

The history of black British culture and representation since the Second World War which Gilroy traces in *There Ain't No Black in the Union Jack* is, of course, a history of settlement, community, and social conflict. The black presence in Ireland in the twentieth century, in contrast, has usually been characterised as one involving small numbers of individuals, often coming to Ireland for short periods of specialised education or training. There has been no evidence to date of a black community in Ireland, as such, nor a sense of permanent settlement of significant numbers of black people, until the mid-1990s.[32] For this reason, it has been relatively easy to dismiss the existence of racial tension or racial conflict in Irish society between 'black' and 'white' people, as John Ardagh does in the quotation above, especially as racist violence in Britain has been routinely explained as the consequence of an increasing, and threatening, population of black immigrants.[33] In contrast, as Mutwarasibo and Smith argue, Africans in Ireland, for example, 'would have been generally well accepted into Irish society, largely due to their small numbers and the temporary nature of their stay here'.[34] There is significant evidence, however, that this has not been the case.

There is the evidence from Irish courts of young African men charged with 'seduction', or 'having carnal knowledge', of young Irish women, cases usually brought by irate fathers. In one such case in 1948, the prosecuting barrister called for the jury to consider the 'slur on a white girl and a blow at the pride of a white man that a white girl should be seduced by a person of another colour', and to award damages on the basis that 'to the ordinary person in this country, at this stage, it still was something abhorrent that a white girl should be seduced by a coloured man'.[35] The judge regretted that such comments were made (they had no place in the courtroom, he argued), but the jury nevertheless ordered the Nigerian medical student to pay £700 in damages to the woman's family. There is evidence too of a recurrent struggle by African students against widespread prejudice and hostility in trying to find accommodation during their studies. This had become such a serious problem in 1969 that the *Irish Times* devoted a series of articles to it, entitled 'No Blacks – Sorry', in which it was reported that only twenty of the 300 approved landladies for student accommodation in Dublin would accept black students. In some instances where black students were not admitted, landladies cited the case of Shan Mohangi, a South African man convicted of murdering an Irish girl in Dublin in 1963.[36] In others, however, it was clear to one black student of Nigerian parentage that a more persistent, underlying racism was to blame: 'Irish people are brought up in such a way that they still think we swing in trees in Africa and that we are savages'.[37] There is also anecdotal evidence of racist violence in Irish society against black students. One such anecdote was reported directly to the Taoiseach, Eamon de Valera, in 1944, in a letter from a Nigerian man, J. F. A. Modebe, with whom the Taoiseach had recently had a meeting concerning the difficulties faced by African students in Ireland. Modebe writes that, subsequent to their meeting, he had been pelted with stones by 'unthinking youths' in Drumcondra, and reports that such incidents of 'fights between black and white boys in Ireland' are widespread. De Valera forwarded this letter to Archbishop McQuaid, expressing concern about its contents, but McQuaid's reply works to dismiss the letter: 'it is a sad document for he evidently feels that he is a member of a despised people . . . . But against his complaints, nevertheless, I can set the opinions of aliens who find our Catholic people unusually welcoming'.[38]

Comforting as his words of assurance may have been to de Valera, McQuaid's complacency was ill-founded, for racially motivated assaults on African students in Ireland persisted and reached a crisis point in 1964, when Nigerian newspapers issued warnings to their readers not to study in Ireland because of the alarming frequency of racist violence. The Nigerian embassy had begun to lodge official letters of concern and protest with the Minister for External Affairs, Frank Aiken, about the number and nature of racist attacks on Nigerian students in April 1963, asking then for the Minister to intervene 'so that this sort of thing could be nipped in the bud before it assumes unmanageable proportions'.[39] The letter cited as an example the case of a Nigerian man who had been assaulted by a Dublin bus conductor, and told 'Get out from the bus you nigger, you black face. Go to where you belong!' The Nigerian man then suffered a further injustice when he was fined for assault by the court, and the letter mentions 'several other manifestations of racial prejudice on the part of the police'. Further letters from the embassy in 1963 complained of other cases of such abuse and injustice, and enquired as to why the government had taken no action against racism. The letters grow more impatient, so that when the son of a Nigerian judge, Charles Fadipe, was assaulted on 14 June 1964, an attack in which he almost lost one eye, the embassy remarked caustically that 'The prospect of many Nigerian students having their eyes damaged or other parts of their bodies dismembered by unprovoked attackers before they leave Ireland is rather frightful'.[40]

The Fadipe case brought the issue of racist attacks in Ireland to public attention, both in Ireland and Nigeria. The *Morning Post* in Lagos reported the injuries suffered by Charles Fadipe as another instance 'of white attempts to stifle the black man'. The *Nigerian Outlook* was more specific in its criticism:

> Nigerian and other Afro-Asian students in the Irish Republic are being sub-jected to brutal attacks by the people of Ireland. A report from that country said yesterday that most of these attacks are being made in the very nose of Irish policemen who do not make arrests.[41]

In response to the attack on his son, Judge Fadipe and another son who was a law graduate, investigated reports of other such attacks and, on 21 August 1964, presented the Minister for Justice, Charles Haughey, and the Nigerian High Commissioner in London, with a list of twenty-five racially motivated attacks on African and Asian students in the past year.[42] On the same day, the *Daily Telegraph* in Lagos 'urged that Nigerian students should be withdrawn from Ireland'.[43] From the outset of these reports, the response of the Irish government had been to deny the severity and frequency of the attacks (Aiken claimed that only seven of the twenty-five cases had come to the attention of the Gardaí), and also to deflect attention away from the charge of racism. A memo from Seán Lemass, for example, seeking clarification from his secretary, reveals that the protests of the Nigerian embassy had not won his sympathy: 'It is my understanding that these [attacks] have been very few in number and that in each case colour hardly entered into the situation but rather the indiscreet behaviour of the student. Is this correct?'[44] This indeed was the general tendency of all statements issued by the Irish government during this time. Aiken attributed the attacks to 'midnight rowdyism',[45] of a kind witnessed in any major urban centre, while the Irish Ambassador in Lagos, Kevin Rush, blamed the African students themselves, as many of the attacks had occurred 'where no right-thinking student should be walking late at night'.[46] Charles Haughey also dismissed the allegations, and said that he knew of only three attacks, which were 'the work of thugs and hooligans, who would just as readily attack white people'.[47] Ministerial action concerning the reports of racist violence appeared to culminate in a meeting held between Frank Aiken and the Nigerian Ambassador to Ireland, Alhaji Abdul-Maliki, on 21 August 1964, in which the minister appears to have admonished the ambassador and the Nigerian government for not quelling Nigerian media reports of racism in Ireland, and for forgetting the 'assistance which has been given through educational institutions and voluntary organisations in Ireland to assist in the education and training of Afro-Asian students' and 'The Irish record of assistance to developing countries overseas and to their students and trainees here in Ireland', which 'should have made these charges against the Irish people as a whole unthinkable'.[48]

In Aiken's view, and it was a view reflected more widely in the government response to these accusations of racially motivated violence, racism did not exist in Irish society, as Ireland was at the forefront of development work in Africa, not least in Nigeria where many of the students who had been attacked came from. Two of his own children were involved in development work in Africa at the time.[49] Aiken had also been influential in the United Nations in representing Ireland as uniquely positioned within the west to befriend and support the emergent nations of Africa and Asia, and had spoken publicly about its historical affinity with other former colonies:

> We know what imperialism is and what resistance to it involves. We do not hear with indifference the voices of those spokesmen of African and Asian countries who passionately champion the right to independence of millions who are still, unfortunately under foreign rule. . . . More than eighty years ago the then leader of the Irish nation, Charles Stewart Parnell, proclaimed the principle that 'the cause of nationality is sacred, in Asia and Africa as in Ireland'. That is still a basic principle of our political thinking in Ireland today, as it is with those of my generation who felt impelled to assert in arms the right of our country to independence.[50]

It was this position that led the Irish government to seek out special relations with some of the newly independent countries, especially Nigeria, and perhaps Aiken was able to rely upon this special relationship to quell the protests of the Nigerian embassy about the attacks in Dublin. But, as Conor Cruise O'Brien pointed out at the time, it was a falsely complacent response to the rise of racism. O'Brien criticised Aiken's statement to the press concerning the violence against African students:

> The United States gives more help to Africans than any other country in this world, but that does not mean that there is no racialism in the United States. . . . This is a universal problem, and it does exist here. We cannot give ourselves medals for anti-racialism.[51]

Prionsias MacAonghusa, writing in the *Free Press*, criticised Lemass for not condemning racial attacks in Ireland as 'unChristian and unworthy of this country',[52] while the *Irish Times* editorial, although it laid some of the blame on Nigerian authorities, also argued that the Irish government had 'not gone far enough towards recognising the needs of a substantial student body that by definition is rootless and friendless in this country'.[53] But the government's petulant response found favour with other newspaper commentators. The *Evening Herald*, under the headline 'Ireland and Her Guests', declared that it was the 'solemn duty' of the Nigerian government to 'end this exaggeration and distortion of the facts', while Jack Butterly, writing for the same newspaper, argued that there was no 'colour' problem in Dublin, and that the violence was 'the inevitable result of a foreign element in fair numbers coming into a stable and settled community'.[54] This figure of a 'stable and settled community', into which comes the disruptive, or rootless, 'foreign element', should be familiar, of course, from the previous chapter, and largely such representations of the Nigerian students as immoral, or prone to scandal, served to bolster the myth of Irish cultural homogeneity. But the government and media responses to the racist attacks on African and Asian students also emblematise a particular phase, or historically specific juncture, in the history of 'race relations' in Ireland.

To acknowledge racism in Irish society, to take it seriously, would have been conceptually and ideologically incompatible with the international image of the country that Lemass and his government sought to project in the 1960s. This much is obvious, especially as the peacekeeping role Ireland had played in the Congo, and the benevolent relations it sought with countries like Nigeria, were partly premised upon avowed ideological commitments to anti-colonialism, and therefore also to anti-racism. But it ran deeper than this, for as is clear from Aiken's statement to the United Nations quoted above, for example, Irish solidarity with nationalist movements in Africa, and Irish commitments to missionary and developmental work, were founded upon a sense of historical pre-eminence. Ireland could 'show the way', as it were, both in political and spiritual terms. The *Irish Times*, in its editorial response to Aiken's statement on the racist attacks, articulated this sentiment as an ethical obligation, deriving from Irish historical experience, 'to give Afro-Asians the benefit of such experience of government and professions as we have had'.[55] This ethical obligation had been explained as the basis for Irish missionary involvement in Africa as early as the 1930s, in an article in *Studies* calling for Irish nuns to go to Uganda, for example, for Ireland could 'with entire disinterestedness . . . help to set up a type of Christian civilisation that in the long run will prove an example of the only way in which Europe can rightly interfere in African affairs'.[56] Political independence was the basis upon which Ireland could make a positive ethical or spiritual contribution to what were perceived to be less developed peoples in the world, but, correspondingly, the evangelisation and education of those peoples would also be critical yardsticks of Irish political maturity. A key indicator, then, of the success of political modernity in Ireland was its capacity to host and educate African and Asian students. Through this process, Ireland could figure itself as 'the west', as the developed world of enlightened, liberal modernity, but what remained (or was meant to remain) invisible was the extent to which the process continued to rely upon the figure of African dependence and underdevelopment. Racial difference is thus necessary to the figuration of Irish liberal modernity, yet at the same time, as David Goldberg has argued of the paradox of race within liberal modernity more generally, racism must be 'reduced to personal prejudices of individuals, to irrational appeals to irrelevant categories, to distinctions that delimit universal liberal ideals'.[57]

For the black student in Dublin, something akin to the experience described by Frantz Fanon in 'The Fact of Blackness' must have been evident in the disjuncture between the universal humanity espoused by Irish missionaries and politicians alike, the promise that black and white were simply, equally human, and the persistent, depressing reality of racist verbal and physical attacks, the refusal of admission to dance halls, the patronising collections of money in churches and schools for 'black babies', and the signs, or perhaps just the landlady's stare, which said 'Sorry – No Blacks'.[58] The promise of equality, of 'assistance', in these terms, must have come to appear as an invitation, as Homi Bhabha puts it, 'to occupy the past of which the white man is the future'.[59] The effective presentation of Irish political modernity in the 1960s depended, in its exploitation of the newly emergent nations in Africa as a testing ground, upon this paradoxical interplay of the discourse of universality, and the constitutive time-lag of a racially structured social order. For Fanon, according to the logic of such representations, blackness was always a belated form of whiteness. Like the 'black babies' depicted on collection boxes, resonant with Irish historical experiences of famine and poverty, and yet, resolutely black and resolutely now, the image of 'black Africa' more generally in Ireland was one of dependence and backwardness, as Tim Pat Coogan recalls:

> We were brought up believing that Africans as a class were as much in need of the civilising influences of the Irish religions as parched earth was of water. It was an image propagated by the missionary magazines with their pictures of a big, beaming Irish priest, generally robed in white, surrounded by a group of adoring, chubby little black children.[60]

Coogan provides a detailed defence of the achievements and sometimes heroic work of Irish missionaries against disease, child prostitution, political oppression, and lack of access to medical and educational facilities, among other problems, but it is also clear from his account that the representation in Ireland of this work relied upon the temporal and spatial disjuncture of black African and white Irish identities, upon 'blackness' remaining a displaced, belated form of Irish historicity. The consequence, according to one Kenyan student who came to Ireland in the late 1950s, was that black students were 'insecure in the streets or in any of the public places'.[61]

The Politics of Analogy: Nigeria and Ireland in the 1960s

The same Kenyan student claimed that Ireland had escaped publicity regarding racial discrimination and violence, not just because its black and Asian population was relatively small, but also because the Irish 'were more secretive about it than the British, who were frank'.[62] The myth that Ireland had had no experiences of racism, no meaningful encounters with racial difference, might be explained by this secrecy, were it not for the fact that, as shown above, incidents and complaints of racism did appear in national newspapers, and warranted government statements and diplomatic meetings. It is clear from the discussion above that racialised meanings were encoded in the very terms in which accusations of racism were managed by the state and the media, but I want to show further in this chapter that racialised meanings were also encoded and indeed decoded in literary and cultural texts in Ireland in the 1960s and 1970s. In this section, I focus on the ways in which the topicality of relations between Ireland and Africa in the 1960s brought issues of racism and cultural chauvinism into explicit contention in some literary texts, and that such texts envisaged participating in a public debate about racialised meanings in Irish culture, before proceeding in the next sections to examine more generally the figuration of blackness as a racialised trope in a number of other texts.

The relationship between Ireland and Nigeria, and specifically the complex nexus of Irish church and state interests involved in promoting relations with Nigeria, forms the target of Austin Clarke's satirical poem, 'Flight to Africa', published first in the collection of that name in 1963.[63] It was written, it would seem, in immediate response to Taoiseach Seán Lemass's visit to Nigeria in 1960, on the occasion of the Nigerian independence celebrations, and it abounds with that sense of 'driving energy', 'momentum', and wry testimony that Maurice Harmon argues characterises this period in Clarke's career.[64] Perhaps what is most useful about the poem, as evidence of a cultural response to issues of racism and race relations in Ireland in the 1960s, is its density of topical allusion, its 'thick description' of the interlocking layers of political and ecclesiastical power at work in Irish relations with Nigeria. The poem scorns the patronising assumptions behind Lemass's visit to Nigeria, with the pretence of a 'trade mission' thinly veiling Lemass's shrewd political calculation in allying himself with the spiritual mission of the Holy Ghost Fathers, with its 'hope of further bounties from heathens'. Clarke loads the poem with puns upon the analogy between Ireland and Nigeria, referring to Lemass as 'Our Chief', 'Hailing the flag of freedom, green/ And white like ours – with the Six Counties/ Cut off', and of the Nigerians, he writes that 'Once they rattled beads,/ Were slaves of cotton, Protestant creeds:/ Black brothers, now'. The tribal connotations of 'chief' and the Catholic connotations of 'rattled beads' should alert us to the poet's sardonic view of this Irish 'blessing' of Nigerian independence. The image of the curtailed flag, with the six counties cut off, returns at the end of the poem, too, when the poet wonders when 'will our North be *Notre-Dame*'d?' The 'Protestant North' is figured as the repressed other in the self-congratulatory ideology of Catholic evangelism, for while the heroes of the Irish war of independence are now 'Hallowers' in 'smoking-rooms', regaling each other with tales of having been 'knights who of old salaamed/ Mahoun', and devoted energetically to the Catholic quest to 'unburn the darkie', the North remains British and Protestant, and in the logic of Irish Catholic nationalism, therefore, unfree and unsaved. The freedom hailed by Lemass in Lagos, it seems, is a severely curtailed one, not least for him who, in travelling to and from Lagos has stopped at Lourdes on the way, and Rome on the way back. Even gestures of political solidarity, it seems, have to be made 'in piety', as a 'pilgrim on knees', the only way of gaining 'more votes at home'.

Lemass is not the main object of Clarke's satire, however. The poem begins with a scene taking place in Cork at the same time as the Taoiseach's visit to Nigeria. In Cork, the Papal Nuncio was attending a civic reception, accompanied by the Bishop of Cork, Dr Lucey. Lucey was renowned for making controversial comments, not least in his rants about foreign residents and workers in Ireland, and he used the occasion of the Nuncio's visit to Cork seemingly to upbraid the Taoiseach.[65] The Nuncio praised the work of the Taoiseach in Nigeria, and more importantly the Irish missionaries who were contributing so much to Nigeria's welfare.[66] In reply, Bishop Lucey articulated his disagreement:

> I am not one who takes kindly to emigration. I do not think that we can always afford in the spiritual world to send our boys and girls as priests and brothers and sisters abroad, for that is the part of the work of Christian charity, but the right place for an Irishman is in Ireland.[67]

It is this speech which the poet in 'Flight to Africa' describes as giving a 'culdee clout' to the Taoiseach for encouraging missionary work, which the Bishop unusually discourages as a form of emigration. It is the ironic reversal of roles, in which the national political leader is seemingly embracing spiritual missions overseas, and the Catholic bishop appears to be staunchly defending national isolationism, which both delights and incites Clarke here. 'The Church unbeds the State', the poet says early in the poem, an allusion itself to Lucey's claim that the church had the right to arbitrate in any matter of Irish politics,[68] but it is this interfusion of political and ecclesiastical interests which Clarke interrogates throughout the poem. 'Flight to Africa', however, is more than just 'a bemused observation on misfired zeal', as Craig Tapping argues.[69] It is a poem loaded with scepticism about the racial politics of that zeal, the implied racial schema behind Bishop Lucey's sense that Irish missionaries were being 'misspent' 'where skin is black', the implied cynicism of Lemass's missionary pilgrimage to hail a flag 'like ours', and the figure of the racial other – 'Mahoun' or 'darkie' – underlying both the Irish political and ecclesiastical 'investment' in Nigeria. Behind it all, Clarke's poem suspects, was an investment in national self-adulation, at the expense of the racial other.

Desmond Forristal's (unpublished) play, 'Black Man's Country' (1974), also makes clear the racial politics at stake in the language and imagery of Irish missionary activities in Africa.[70] 'Black Man's Country' is set in Nigeria, during the civil war, or Biafran war, of 1967–70, and it concerns a group of Irish missionaries caught at the front line in the battle between the warring forces. It was performed first at the Gate Theatre in Dublin on 30 April 1974, directed by Hilton Edwards. Father Desmond Forristal, a Catholic priest, had some experience of Biafra. He was a leading figure in the pioneering group of priests who, acting on Archbishop McQuaid's initiative, set up the Radharc film unit which proceeded to make an innovative and challenging series of documentaries about Irish and global social and political affairs.[71] As part of the Radharc team, he had travelled to Biafra and 'most of the new African countries' in the 1960s.[72] Irish interest in African political affairs intensified in the 1960s as the continent was transformed by nationalist movements demanding and winning independence from the waning European imperial powers. The story of small colonised nations fighting for the right to self-determination inevitably chimed with Irish political narratives, but it was chiefly through Catholic missionary work in Africa that this sense of affinity and analogy was made apparent. As Kevin Kenny argues:

> [T]he work of Irish Catholic missionaries in Africa also helped to define postcolonial Ireland's sense of itself and its role in the twentieth-century world. The *Missionary Annals* of the C.S.Sp. (Holy Ghost Fathers) and the *African Missionary*, published by the Society for African Missions, were filled with stories of heroic missionaries, surrounded by danger and suffused with religious courage, bringing Christianity to the 'Dark Continent', 'benighted Africa', and other exotic parts of the world. While these are stock images of romantic racialism, they also invoked the prevailing language of heroism and self-sacrifice in Irish political life, especially in the wake of Easter 1916. The Irish missionary was portrayed very much as a man of his time, willing to die for his faith; and missionaries helped resuscitate the idea of Ireland's historical mission as a 'land of saints and scholars', incorporating this idea into the new sense of Irish national identity articulated by the generation of 1916.[73]

Indeed, Irish missionary zeal, although it had important roots in the nineteenth century, appears to be roughly coterminous with the most significant period of nation-building in Ireland, with five new Irish missionary movements founded between 1916 and 1937, three of which were focused on Africa.[74]

Joseph McGlade's history of the Irish missions, published in 1967, describes these movements and their activities with the same rhetoric of romantic adventure, the same sense of heroic courage and devotion in the face of paganism on the 'Dark Continent', as Kenny observes in the quotation above. He also presents statistical evidence for the 'proportionately greater contribution' made by Ireland in Catholic missions, especially in Africa, showing a league table in which 'in the period 1933–57 Ireland moved from seventh to third place in the percentage of clergy supplied to Africa', for example, as well as claiming that 'There is at least one priest abroad on foreign missionary work for every priest at home in Ireland'.[75] McGlade celebrates this contribution to the growth of Catholicism in Africa as a credit to Ireland, and Irish adherence to the Catholic faith, but he is also in no doubt that Irish missionary activities piggybacked on the structures and apparatuses of British colonial administration. The concentration of Irish missions in Africa was entirely concomitant with the geographic location of British colonies and protectorates, and for the most part, even from the mid-nineteenth century, British colonial administrations were favourable to the work of Irish Catholic missions, which were largely preoccupied with establishing primary schools.[76] Indeed, McGlade voices grave concerns about the fate of the Irish missions and its church schools under the newly emergent nationalist governments in Africa: 'No Irishman is likely to dispute the right to political independence but the Irish missionary must be realistic and evaluate the results of this independence in its effects on the life of the Church. There is suspicion, if not growing hostility, to the white man in general, or to the European, in many of these independent areas; the Irish missionary is included in this attitude of mind'.[77] It is precisely this dilemma which Forristal explores in 'Black Man's Country', of Irish missionaries struggling to reconcile the conflicting demands of nationalist solidarity and racial difference.

The play begins as the Biafran war approaches, foreshadowed in the opening scene in which the central character, Father Joe Mitchell, argues with his servant, Cyprian, and an Ibo priest, Father Zachary Akuta, about the legitimacy of Ibo nationalism. 'There is no such place as Biafra', asserts Mitchell, 'Your nation is Nigeria'. When Zachary replies that 'It was the Irish also who taught us the idea of nationhood . . . who taught us that nationhood depends on the heart and will of a people, not on boundaries drawn on a map by British colonialists', Mitchell dismisses the argument by claiming 'There's no analogy between Ireland and what's going on here'.[78] For Cyprian and Zachary, the lesson of Irish history, taught to them through the Catholic schools staffed by Irish missionaries, is clearly an empowering one of the right of small nations to assert their own political identities. For Mitchell, however, even if he has preached this lesson himself, it is a history particular to Ireland and not available for analogy in Africa, an attitude which Zachary immediately discerns as racist: 'Is there any reason why your freedom is worth fighting for and ours is not? Is it because you are white and we are black?'[79] Father Mitchell is perhaps emblematic of an older generation of Irish missionary priests, dependent upon and accustomed to the ideologies and practices of colonial administration. In the opening scene, he remarks to Cyprian upon the necessity of his mother in Ireland having to tape up the Irish newspapers she sends him every week 'so that the bloody light-fingered Nigerians won't be able to pinch the sporting section'.[80] Later in the play, in an argument with Zachary, he alludes to the job of the Irish missionary as having coaxed the Nigerians down out of the trees.[81] But the play also marks a significant turning point for missionary work in Africa by pitting the attitudes of Father Mitchell against those of his younger Irish colleague, Father O'Brien. O'Brien's view is that the job of the missionary in post-colonial Africa is 'to build up the local church so that it is self-sufficient', and then judge the right time for the Irish to hand over the church to African priests. Mitchell dismisses this as unrealistic: 'I know that the Church couldn't survive here without the white missionaries'.[82] The Irish bishop in charge of Mitchell's diocese, however, passes over Mitchell when seeking a successor, and appoints Father Zachary as the new bishop, signalling that the tide has turned against the need, or desire, for Irish missionaries in Africa. In McGlade's account of Irish missionary history, Mitchell's attitude was perhaps the more common, as he criticises Irish missionaries for being 'relatively slow in helping to develop a native clergy and hierarchy'.[83] Forristal's play suggests two reasons for this in its characterisation of Mitchell: that of complicity among missionaries with the racist ideologies of colonialism; and also, the sense that native dependence upon missionary leadership gave those missionaries a sense of heroic purpose.

That missionary work has a heroic purpose is nowhere made more evident than in the scene in which Sister Eileen, a young and cheerful nun, is killed in an air raid on the mission, a death which is repeatedly figured as analogous with the martyrdom of Robert Emmet. As Kenny suggests, much of the literature of Irish missionary activity presents a narrative of heroic sacrifice akin to the nationalist iconography of martyrdom. Indeed, one of the most persistent and celebrated narratives of heroic struggle against the arduous conditions of disease, starvation, and poverty in Africa is the extraordinarily popular story of Edel Quinn, a young Irish woman who devoted her last years while suffering from terminal illness to missionary work.[84] If the analogy between Biafran and Irish nationalisms suggests itself repeatedly through 'Black Man's Country', ultimately the more persistent analogy in the play however is between the missionary and the coloniser. Both Zachary and O'Brien, in their respective arguments with Mitchell, serve to identify Mitchell's role with the values and practices of colonial power. The evangelising and 'civilising' role of the missionaries is shown to have had a powerful impact on Nigerian society. Mitchell recalls how the tyrannical nun, Mother Gertrude began the process by compelling her schoolgirls in the mission school to wear knickers, and 'Even today, nearly fifty years later, whenever she walks through Uzala market-place, aged grand-mothers clutch their skirts in panic and disappear behind grass-huts'.[85] At the end of the play, when a Nigerian soldier comes to arrest the Irish missionaries as suspected missionaries, he is chastened into submission by the same Mother Gertrude when she gleans from him that he has been taught in an Irish Catholic mission school by nuns of her order. The implication is clear that Irish missionary work has transformed the people, whether Biafran or Nigerian, into compliant Catholics, but the end of the play is equally clear about the future for the Irish missionar-ies. Mitchell and Gertrude are led away from the mission, while Cyprian is left to continue their work, and silently, poignantly, he moves to sit in the same chair that Mitchell occupied at the beginning of the play. The conclusion has obvious historical resonances. Irish missionaries were expelled from Eastern Nigeria in 1970 for their perceived role in supporting the Biafran insurgency, and Kenny suggests that the contro-versy prompted the Catholic church to move towards 'Africanisation', rather than continue missionary efforts. But the title of the play also indicates the broader implication regarding Irish missionary history, that although the representation of the missions in Ireland aligned them with nationalism, and with nationalist struggles against European imperialism, solidarity with African nationalism would inevitably be hampered and refuted by the interdependence of missionary work and the racial ideologies of colonialism.[86] Within that context, as Forristal's play shows, the story of Irish missionary work is also a story of Irish investment in the 'wages of whiteness', in the hierarchical advantages of whiteness in a world defined by what Fanon called the 'racial epidermal schema' of colonialism.[87]

'Black Man's Country' was not particularly successful on the Irish stage. The performances were generally commended, but the play was more noteworthy for the issues it raised about Irish missionary work in Africa than for its theatrical presentation. Indeed, its first run drew critical responses from a number of priests and nuns for its simplifica-tion of the Biafran war, and the fate of Irish missionaries during and after the war.[88] When the play had a second run during the Dublin theatre festival in October 1974, Hilton Edwards, the play's director, expressed disappointment that it received barely any critical atten-tion.[89] With the exception of the reaction of the Catholic church, the response to the play tended to focus on its documentary value, on how well Forristal had managed to produce a synopsis of the debates and issues involved in Irish missionary work in eastern Nigeria at the time of the war.[90] There was every reason why audiences and critics may have been drawn to the play for the topicality of its theme, for as Enda Staunton has suggested, 'Nigeria was the showpiece of Ireland's "reli-gious empire"'.[91] The expulsion of Irish missionaries in the aftermath of the Biafran war, however, signalled the questionable legitimacy of Ireland's claim to moral leadership in its role in African affairs. As we have seen above, Lemass's government, in particular his Minister for External Affairs, Frank Aiken, had represented Ireland in the 1960s as the moral pioneer of anti-colonialism, and the friend of emergent small nations, but the outcome of the Biafran war, and, of course, the resur-gence of violent conflict in Northern Ireland, seriously undermined the basis for this claim. Indeed, the priests and nuns who wrote to complain about Forristal's play were able to point to the contrast between 'the work of reconciliation accomplished by the Nigerian people [since the war and] Ireland in its present troubled situation'.[92] Forristal's play is more significant in this respect than its relative lack of theatrical success, for in showing the racial and colonial structures underlying the notion of an Irish 'spiritual empire' in Africa, with its 'exceedingly rich harvest of souls',[93] it exposes the ambivalence of Irish gestures of cross-racial solidarity.

Black Masks, or Racial Cross-Dressing

Brendan Behan had gestured towards a relationship between the terms 'black' and 'Ireland' in his play, *The Hostage*, in 1958, when he had a black character wave a flag bearing the words 'Keep Ireland Black' on the stage setting of a Dublin brothel. It occurs in a scene in which other characters are waving Irish and Russian flags, and another character is singing 'Land of Hope and Glory'.[94] It is largely read as a farcical scene, and a number of critics have argued that both the black character and his banner were included to make topical reference to English racial tensions, specifically as an ironic counter-point to the fascist slogan 'Keep Britain White'.[95] Against the comfortable 'whiteness' of Ireland, the notion of 'black Ireland', as in Carlyle, is treated as an impossible conjunction, worthy of comedy and farce. In *Richard's Cork Leg*, Behan's posthumous play which was revised and completed by the theatre director, Alan Simpson, and produced first in Dublin in 1972, Behan again included a black character, called 'Bonnie Prince Charlie'. His lines are attributed simply to 'Prince'. When he first appears early in Act One, the other characters, mainly the two prostitutes, Bawd I and Bawd II, speculate about his identity, recycling a series of tired racial stereotypes and anxieties.[96] Bawd II identifies him as a 'black Yank', dressed in a beautiful silk dressing gown. Bawd I instead thinks he's an Indian, and with Behan's fondness for malapropism, surmises that he is an 'Indian potentialtate', and then the 'Bag and Can': the 'Aga Khan'. This leads her to fantasise that they might become 'recruits for his harem': 'We could be white slaves on silk cushions, eating Hadji Bey's Turkish Delight and drinking gins and tonics'.[97] When the Prince passes the women, they bow to him, addressing him as 'Your Majesty, Your Highness, Your Holiness'. When the Prince dismisses them contemptuously from his path, however, their reaction changes, calling after him 'Go along, you black bastard', and 'the heathen whoremaster'.[98] At this point he exits, and as he turns the audience reads 'in bright orange-gold letters across the back of his gorgeous garment the words "Harlem Globe Trotters"'.[99] Within this short scene in which we're first introduced to the 'coloured gentleman', then, a series of popular signifiers of racial difference in Ireland are played out. Black men are princes or pimps; the sumptuous dressing gown might indicate royalty, but also sporting heroes from boxing, like Muhammad Ali, the millionaire race-horse owner, the Aga Khan, and basketball with the 'Harlem Globe Trotters'. These signifiers register that blackness is encountered in Irish culture as foreign, even 'heathen', and the response of the white Irish characters in the play oscillates sharply between veneration or desire, and castigation.

It appears from this first encounter with the Prince that he is perceived through prescribed images and stereotypes of blackness, fixed identifications for which black skin serves as metonym. What this scene also demonstrates, however, is the difficulty that the white Irish characters have in placing blackness, socially and culturally, and that difficulty draws our attention to blackness as a figure, as a trope. We encounter racial difference in this play as signification, which constantly exceeds any presumed essence or presence. The Prince reappears a short time later, and after the women have speculated that he might be 'a doctor in the Rotunda', he attempts to correct their misperceptions of him.[100] The stage directions indicate that he speaks '*with an Oxford or a Trinity or a Yale accent*', presumably to signal to the actor in English, Irish, or American productions to adopt an appropriate linguistic marker of social class. He declares that he is not a Prince at all, but 'an ordinary American', to which Bawd I replies 'Begod I never heard of an ordinary American before. That must be because you're black'.[101] This might be a joke at the expense of American exceptionalism, or a joke about the ways in which Americanness always seems to be hyphenated, especially as the Prince then professes to be 'a fully integrated American'. But it is a joke which plays upon a similar ironic conjunction of 'black' and 'ordinary American' to Carlyle's conjunction of 'black' and 'Ireland'.

The Prince now reveals that he is, in fact, the representative of Forest Lawn memorial parks, and is in an Irish graveyard to promote the company's services. Later, however, in the second act, the Prince offers a contradictory explanation of his identity, when he speaks in a 'very British' accent, and confesses to coming from Notting Hill in London. For Behan, writing the first draft of the play in 1960, Notting Hill would then have been synonymous with the race riots of 1958, although this black Notting Hill resident offers the Irish characters an apology for the abuses of English colonialism, and laments that the Irish didn't take up more English tastes, specifically 'cricket, early closing [and] blazers'.[102] Immediately after this apology, he professes to have been 'Lady Chatterley's Lover', and sings a song on this theme to the tune of 'Land of Hope and Glory'. The switching of identity, here signalled by the Prince's fluctuation across several registers of nationality, race, and class, is characteristic of farce, and specifically of Behan's farcical method. Its function, of course, is to dislodge fixed identifications. The black gentleman is signified through a series of stereotypical images, which may even serve to deconstruct the notion of presence altogether. There is a brief moment, however, when the comically confused personae of the black character seem to slip: the Prince doesn't understand the allusion to Matt Talbot, and asks 'Who dat?', at which point the stage direction indicates that he '*recovers*', and says 'I mean, who was he?'[103] This is the only point in the play when we might be invited to witness the black character as a presence, with the caricatured minstrel or plantation dialect used to denote the 'real' blackness behind the mimed accents of 'Oxford or Trinity or Yale'. This slippage might well undermine the deconstructive tendencies of Behan's farce. 'Who dat?' seems to fix the black character, in contrast to his performance of various roles and caricatures. As Henry Louis Gates argues, this is indicative of the problem of dialect (and the reason why Gates surmises that black writers from the Harlem Renaissance onwards found it difficult to use dialect), because 'dialect was a form apart, its meaning lurking beneath the surface of meaning'.[104] The space marked out for 'authentic' black presence, then, returns us to the domain of minstrelsy, which Gates defines as 'a white parody of black sentiment'.[105]

Is this, then, how we might characterise the figuration of blackness in *Richard's Cork Leg*, as 'white parody', as a form of minstrelsy? I've been paying close attention to the text of *Richard's Cork Leg* in this discussion so far, but the performance raises an important problem in the representation of racial difference in Irish theatre. When the play transferred to the Royal Court Theatre in London, the black gentleman was played by Olu Jacobs, the eminent Nigerian actor. When it opened in Dublin, however, the character was played by Barney McKenna from the Irish band, The Dubliners. Other members of the band acted all the male parts in the play, although not to the satisfaction of most of the reviewers. McKenna in particular was criticised in reviews for his acting abilities, and Mary MacGoris in the *Irish Independent* commented that he looked 'acutely unhappy'.[106] Reviewers did not comment, however, on the incongruity of a white man acting the part of a black character. McKenna was not blacked-up in any way, according to those involved in the production of the play.[107] The audience were instead invited to make a leap of faith between the verbal signification of the character's blackness through his description by the other characters and his slippage into minstrel dialect, and the obvious visual signification of whiteness. It was not the practice of the Abbey at the time to use 'blacking': indeed, just two months after *Richard's Cork Leg* opened, there was a production of Eugene O'Neill's *The Iceman Cometh*, in which the character of Joe Mott was played by Trinidadian actor, Horace James. Although blacking had been used in earlier times in the history of the Abbey, it was clearly not deemed possible or desirable by 1972, by which time Ireland was understood to be more 'liberal'.[108] None of the reviewers mentions minstrelsy, either, even though we have a white actor using the dialect of minstrelsy at one point.[109] The reviewer for the *Irish Times*, Seamus Kelly, refers to the character as 'a Notting Hill negro', although the other reviewers avoid mentioning the character altogether.[110] Despite the obvious epidermal discrepancy, then, between the actor and the character, one reviewer at least accepted that this character was black, even if this meant blackness was understood as a figure, and indeed as a figure of speech.

To read racial signification in *Richard's Cork Leg*, then, is to register not the absence of blackness *per se*, but its presence as trope. What is specifically absent is instead the black body, or rather the body as marker of blackness. We are directed not to the ways in which black subjects are made publicly visible, but to the aural and verbal traces of racial difference. This represents a somewhat different problem from the one encountered by many critical theorists who have considered the representation of blackness in contemporary white culture, for whom the dominant motifs are of visibility, the gaze, and pornographic objectification.[111] Yet, in terms of aural markers, as already noted, blackness is only denoted once by the character himself. What the play reveals, as a text and a performance, is that blackness does not have to be signified visually, or to appear as epidermal or corporeal presence, in order to be the object of ceaseless speculation. The racialising gaze of white Irish constructions of black otherness is coded in verbal forms in this play, and, I would argue, it is in verbal discourse that blackness is figured as a constantly reiterated presence in Irish culture. Racial difference occurs in *Richard's Cork Leg* as a familiar trope, as a verbal and aural trace, and yet depends for its meanings on the very epidermal and corporeal markers that are conspicuously, repeatedly deferred.

On the Limits of Cross-Racial Solidarity

The performance of racial stereotypes of blackness in *Richard's Cork Leg* raises some vital issues about the assumed racial dynamics of Irish theatre-going audiences. Although it is possible (but not without some qualifications) to argue that Behan's earlier inclusion of a black character in *The Hostage* could be understood within the economy of the play as a whole as a gesture of cross-racial and post-colonial solidarity, it is clear that in *Richard's Cork Leg*, the figure of the black Prince functions chiefly as a comic trope or comic foil. The character exists to make available to an Irish, white audience the predictable stereotypes of blackness already familiar from many facets of popular culture, from music-hall shows to the BBC television show (still running at the time), *The Black and White Minstrel Show*.[112] Effectively, the black Prince serves to delineate racial difference, and to reinforce the implicit writing of white Irishness. The switching of actors between the Dublin and London productions, from a white Irish musician to a black Nigerian actor, is an index of the degree to which Irish audiences were expected to be mono-racial, white, and therefore able to enjoy the fictions of blackness being produced in Barney McKenna's performance without being troubled by any sensitivities about the racial stereotyping of blackness. To generalise, even when Irish cultural productions performed the verbal and visual signs of racial difference, these were understood to be performed for 'ourselves alone', and therefore marked the implicit racialisation of Irish society.

Paul Durcan's poem, 'Black Sister', exposes the racial dynamics of Irish identity in the early 1970s more forcefully. Published in Durcan's first collection, *O Westport in the Light of Asia Minor*, in 1975, the poem draws upon images of Angela Davis, the radical black feminist who was accused in 1970 of participation in the attempt to free George Jackson in a shootout on the steps of a courthouse in California.[113] It draws also upon the discourses of Irish missionary and charity work in Africa, where sympathy for the plight of black people in Africa is shown to be thinly, precariously, separated from racial denigration and victimisation. Just as in *Richard's Cork Leg*, images of black majesty, beauty, and desirability slide quickly and inexorably into hostility and refusal. The poem consists of two stanzas, spoken by 'Acton', presumably an allusion to the historian Lord Acton, a home rule advocate, and renowned liberal politician who served under Gladstone. In the first stanza, 'black sister' is a conflation of a figure similar to Angela Davis and other images of black women:

> Black sister with an afro halo round your head
> And a handbag by your side and a string of beads,
> Watching for news from a newsreel in the dark
> Of the television lounge of a country hotel,
> You are lean, tall and fruitful as a young beech
> And seductive as the tree of knowledge
> But – forgive me, this *is* the millenium to inquire –
> Is that not you yourself stepping across the screen
> Out of missionary fields into a country courthouse
> Machine gun firing from your thigh, and freedom
> On your dying lips?
> But you are whispering to me tonight:
> 'Oh Acton let us be ambiguous tonight'[114]

'Black Sister' is idealised here in various forms: the angel with the afro halo, the originary woman, mother, and temptress in the garden of Eden, the natural beauty of missionary fields, strong and fruitful, the Amazonian woman-warrior, the political revolutionary, her politics suffused with sexual imagery. The iconography of the black freedom fighter is made problematic by the association of the machine gun with her thigh, suggesting phallic substitution, and by the fact that freedom can only be expressed on dying lips. Here, Durcan's poem arguably draws also upon the Irish canon of martyrdom and blood sacrifice, in its equation of death and freedom, and thus plays upon the renewed currency of such images in the nationalist movement in Northern Ireland.

Arguably too, the title of the poem, 'Black Sister', is indicative of the ironic conjunction of familiarity and distance, attraction and repulsion, since the familial 'sister' (like Clarke's allusion to 'black brothers') needs to be qualified by epidermal difference. In this first stanza, she encapsulates the range of idealised stereotypes of black femininity, which are made further ironic by the image of 'a handbag by your side and a string of beads', watching the news in a country hotel. Durcan plays here with the juxtaposition of media image against mundane reality, the screen icons of black feminism against the safe, docile clutches of handbag and beads. The speaker, Acton, connects the black woman sitting in a country hotel with the media image of militant black femininity, 'Is that not you yourself?', perhaps suggesting the elision of one black subjectivity into another, perhaps suggesting solidarity. As Cullingford observes in her analysis of the poem, the encounter between Acton and 'black sister' must of necessity be 'ambiguous'.[115] The second stanza opens up these idealised images, and the possibility of connection with Ireland, to devastating critical scrutiny:

> Instead you are cooped up in Ireland in a small hotel
> Waiting for your boy whose magic daddy
> Though no niggard to mission fields at Sunday Mass
> Is not standing for his son to hitch up with a black bitch
> Even if she's a Catholic virgin
> She's black; and a whore therefore.
> And electric mammy than whom there is no more fiercesome
> Drum-beater for black babies
> Collapsed when she glimpsed the sun dancing halo round your head.
> But you're a patient girl –
> While over dark deep well waters lit up by huge arc lights
> You whisper to me tonight:
> 'Oh Acton let us be ambiguous tonight'[116]

Ireland here is the dark scene of social repression, its social constraints sharply contrasted with the apparent militancy and heroism visible on the newsreel screen. The institutional Catholicism which orchestrates charity for 'black babies' is inseparable from virulent racism. That 'daddy' is no 'niggard' to missionary causes is Durcan's shrewdly simple way of suggesting such charity donations to Africa are entangled in racial divisions, and constitute an investment in Irish 'whiteness' as much as, if not more than, they imply analogy or empathy with black people. That 'black sister' is a 'Catholic virgin' might have enabled some scope for considering her one of 'us', but racial difference is the certain barrier against all such analogies or possibilities of inclusion: 'She's black; and a whore therefore'. Against the images of radical activism, of idealised beauty and strength in the first stanza, Durcan's second stanza offers us instead the grim mundanity of being 'cooped up', like an animal for the slaughter, in a small Irish country hotel, waiting submissively for tolerance, for liberalism, for inclusion, for the end of fear, division, and violence. Durcan's poem goes further than challenging what Cullingford describes as 'the political identification between Catholic nationalists and black freedom fighters'.[117] The whispered refrains between 'black sister' and Acton suggest love-making, the possibility of ambiguous conjunction, but Irish society is shown to have invested in a complex form of racialisation, of Ireland as well as others, at the heart of which is the fear of miscegenation. The sexual union of the boy with his black girlfriend is imaged in the phrase, 'hitch up', taken from the harnessing of a cart to a horse, just as 'black bitch' demonises her as animalistic, and beneath the 'standing' of an Irish boy and his family. The poem shows instead that there is no 'union' available between the terms 'black' and 'Ireland'. The aggressive dominance of Irish Catholic nationalism takes what it wants from the images of radical black politics, the mirror of its own grounding in the iconography of martyrdom and mother/whore Ireland, while the remainder is viciously repudiated.

In *Richard's Cork Leg*, the absence of the black body proves problematic for the racial politics of Irish society, but Durcan's poem exposes a further ambiguity in that black presence, corporeal and sexual presence, is rejected while the media image of an eroticised black body and indeed the missionary image of dependent black babies are clearly not. The poem shows, in other words, the complex inter-reliance of Irish forms of racism and Irish gestures of cross-racial solidarity. Here, as Homi Bhabha argues of colonial stereotypes, our attention should be drawn not to whether specific racial images are positive or negative, nor even to the hypocrisy of certain stereotypes, but 'to an understanding of the *processes of subjectification* made possible (and plausible) through stereotypical discourse'.[118] At stake in the cultural productions discussed in this chapter is no less than the articulation (in the Althusserian sense) of the racialised subjectivities of white Irishness, blackness, including indeed black-Irishness. There is a complex legacy to be explored here in terms of how white Irishness has historically been produced in Ireland (and considerable efforts have already been made to explore the construction of white Irishness in Britain and America), but there is an equally urgent and complex legacy to be explored in terms of the possibilities of black Irishness, and the possibilities of black cultural production in Ireland.

A Very Irish Hero

In John Kelly's *Bildungsroman* about growing up in Ireland of the 1970s, Phil Lynott is the subject of a chapter simply titled 'hero'. For a white kid in Fermanagh, desperate to escape the social constraints imposed by religious authorities, Lynott epitomised freedom:

> Philip Parris Lynott was a black Irishman and as cool as it got. He had a dog called Gnasher. He was good to his mother and his granny and he was into football. Teenage girls loved him. Teenage boys wanted to be like him. He mixed the imagery of cowboy, comic-book hero, gigolo, rake, romantic, hard man and old softie, and I wanted to be all of those things – depending on the company.[119]

Perhaps the most prominent example of black-Irish cultural production is the work of Phil Lynott, the lead singer and songwriter of 1970s folk-rock band, Thin Lizzy. Lynott was raised by his grandparents in Crumlin in Dublin city, having been born in Birmingham to his white Irish mother, Philomena, and his black Brazilian father, Cecil, who did not know of his son's birth, and subsequently would play little part in his upbringing.[120] As Gerry Smyth has argued, Lynott's upbringing gave him an ambivalent sense of belonging. On the one hand, he was brought up a working-class Dubliner, imbued with an 'acute sense of national and gender identity that had emerged during the traumatic revolutionary period earlier in the century, and which continued to inform Irish culture well into the modern era'.[121] On the other hand, he was an illegitimate black child in a country in which illegitimacy was severely stigmatised and which was 'almost universally white', and thus experienced both social and racial abuse. From an early age, Lynott took an interest in music, and particularly with emergent forms of popular folk and rock music. Thin Lizzy was not his first band, but it was the first to depart fully from the conventions of 'showband' music, and to achieve success as an Irish rock band on the international stage. It took three years for the band to establish itself outside Ireland, during which time Lynott and his fellow members, Eric Bell and Brian Downey, were developing a style which fused guitar sounds influenced by Jimi Hendrix with a strong note of Celticism and a penchant for folk ballads. The success of the band was secured only when they made a rock version of the traditional Irish rebel song, 'Whiskey in the Jar', which topped the Irish single charts in Christmas 1972, and did well in the British single charts in January 1973. Within a few years, they were legendary rock musicians, and Lynott especially acquired a cult following, which since his tragic early death from drug addiction, according to Smyth, 'tends to attract the same combination of nostalgia and adoration as Brendan Behan'.[122] As John Kelly's depiction of Lynott in the quotation at the beginning of this section shows, he had become an idol for thousands of Irish young people who saw him as a popular hero, a romantic rebel, who was both comfortably Irish and apparently free from the constraints of Irish society. Lynott is widely acknowledged as a major influence on the international success of later Irish bands like U2 and the Boomtown Rats, who in turn fuelled the development of a vibrant indigenous music industry. The more instructive context for this essay, however, is to examine the Irish music scene from which Lynott emerged.

Lynott had not been without precursors as a non-white musician in Ireland. In the 1960s, Earl Jordan, a black singer, had featured with the Derek Joy Showband and the Caroline Showband, while a South African student of Asian descent, Gene Dushy Chetty, was the lead singer with Gene and the Gents, and Roly Daniels, born in Jubbelpore in India, sang with the Memphis Showband. Jordan, Chetty and Daniels played with successful showbands, bands which performed across Ireland in small town ballrooms, serving up a familiar repertoire of classic and hit songs. Lynott insisted, however, on writing and performing his own songs, songs which, as we will see, attempted to fuse influences into a new musical form, one which would draw upon Irish roots but within the musical vocabulary of Anglo-American rock. Jordan, Chetty, and Daniels also dressed in the sharp suits and clean-cut look of the showbands, in contrast to Lynott who wore an afro hairstyle and dressed in the leathers and T-shirts of rock stars. More interesting than this contrast, however, is the persistence of racial cross-dressing and indeed racial cross-styling among a number of prominent white Irish bands of the time. In 1971, for example, The Plattermen, described as 'one of the most progressive bands in the country', had adopted 'Afro-Rock', and used instruments such as conga-drums, tom-toms, cowbells, tympani, and maracas, as well as the bodhran in their act.[123] They appeared alongside a touring three-piece Afro-Rock band of black musicians who wore grass skirts and tribal headdresses, led by 'Prince Nil-Afadi' who performed a fire-eating act on stage. Again, one could argue that what was taking place on stage in such events were acts of cross-racial solidarity, the tom-toms and the bodhran signifying an implicit cultural connection, but equally the tom-toms, grass skirts, and fire-eating performances were all too familiar as colonial icons of African primitivism.

The Royal Earls showband metamorphosed in 1972 into a band called Zulus, who took racial masquerading further. The Zulus dressed in animal skins, bore spears and shields on stage, wore afro-wigs, and

were blacked up. They were the complete minstrel act, and for publicity purposes named themselves Mungo, Tonka, Kiya, Ganora, Ohuru,
Zanadu, and Onosa.[124] In a similar vein, The Indians emerged from a
showband called Casino in 1971, dressed in warpaint and feathers (and
are still playing today using the same gimmick), adopted caricature
Indian names such as Little Thunder and Crazy Horse, and styled a
dance which their fans could imitate.[125] Both Zulus and The Indians
might be understood in the context of a competitive music business,
in which a distinctive gimmick could attract publicity and fame, but
the emergence of several bands which appropriated the icons and
metonyms of specifically racial difference suggests that race was a constitutive element in the ways in which Irish musicians and audiences
brokered their relationships with cultural production and meaning. As
Eric Lott argues of minstrelsy in nineteenth-century America, cross-
racial masquerades cannot simply be dismissed as deluded racist forms
of entertainment, for they are also unstable and contradictory forms
which borrow from black performative practices as well as ridiculing
them, and which invest desire and identification in simulated blackness as well as troping blackness as inherently comic and pathetic.[126]
Nevertheless, unlike black acts of 'passing', which may potentially
disrupt racial hierarchies and particularly discourses of white superiority, when white men perform in blackface or in racial masquerade, it is
likely that hierarchies are reinforced as the black body is made available
for consumption as a reproduced and commodified trope.[127]

It is in the problematic context of racial masquerading in the Irish
music scene that we might usefully situate Lynott's attempt to inter-
polate a black-Irish identity, and in which we might better understand
how Lynott's work could be figured as a response within the terms of
black cultural production in Ireland. Lynott and Thin Lizzy became
famous for their version of the folk ballad, 'Whiskey in the Jar', but in
fact they had intended to record this only as the B-side to 'Black Boys
on the Corner'. According to drummer Brian Downey, the band had
been in studio to record 'Black Boys on the Corner', when they began
'for a laugh' to work out a rock version of 'Whiskey in the Jar'. Their
manager Ted Carroll heard it and suggested it should be the B-side of
the single, but within a few days when executives from their record
company, Decca, had heard it, the band were told that 'Whiskey in the
Jar' was to be the A-side.[128] The switch was crucial to the success of the
band. 'Whiskey in the Jar' became their signature song, and in many
ways produced an image of the band which they would repeat in many
later songs, an image of tough, rebel masculinity, quick to violence and
distrustful of women, which borrowed both from the postwar 'angry

Figure 4.1   A publicity photograph of *Zulus* © British Library Board. All rights reserved (*New Spotlight* magazine 22 April 1972)

Figure 4.2   Phil Lynott, lead singer of *Thin Lizzy*, and, in his own words, 'the first black Irishman'. *Evening Standard*, Hulton Archive, courtesy of Getty Images

young man' figure which came to dominate Anglo-American rock music, and Irish nationalist iconography of the republican rebel. The unnamed narrator robs Captain Farrell of his money with a pistol and rapier, but when the narrator returns drunk on whiskey to his lover, Molly, she tricks him. When Captain Farrell arrives to arrest him, the narrator shoots him 'with both barrels', and ends the song lamenting the ball and chains with which he is imprisoned, the whiskey which made him drunk, and the woman who betrayed him. The song plays partly on the appeal of traditional Irish rebel lore, then, but the sharp sounds of Eric Bell's electric guitar and Lynott's raspy voice take Irish folk music into the idiom of 1970s rock.

'Whiskey in the Jar' was, however, a 'joke song' in the minds of the band, whereas according to Downey, Lynott was particularly proud of 'Black Boys on the Corner', and desperately wanted it to be the next single.[129] 'Black Boys on the Corner' produces a related image of aggressive masculinity – the male gang on the street corner shoot pool, roll dice, play cards, and 'pull chicks' – but it does so through a specifically black American vernacular. The hard rock sounds are much closer to the influence of Jimi Hendrix.[130] The song opens with a snatch of street conversation between two Afro-American voices: 'Hey, what you doin', man?' 'I think I'll go on down the corner'. The song itself articulates in several lines a note of black pride, or at least defiance, with its refrain of 'I'm a little black boy, and I don't know my place', which echoes the civil rights campaigns in the USA against racial segregation. The singer reports the speech of some of the 'boys' on the corner, one of whom declares 'I need none of your pity', while another threatens 'I'm a givin' a warnin'/ People been putting me down/ I'm so tired I'm yawnin''. The verses use quick, repetitive rhymes, not unlike the cadences of rap, and Lynott delivers the lines in an intonation which draws upon rhythm and blues music as much as rock. This is Lynott's closest attempt to give expression to black identity and black politics in his work, but of course he can only do so in the masquerade of Afro-American culture and politics. It may thus be argued that Lynott's work could be more properly understood in relation to the ways in which black British musicians and audiences drew upon Afro-American and Caribbean music and musical idioms. But this would be to deny the very real sense in which Lynott's musical persona and success was articulated through his Irishness as well as his blackness. It would equally be difficult to contextualise 'Black Boys on the Corner' purely in relation to the Irish social and cultural scene, since Lynott was one of the few black men in Dublin at the time, there was no collective black-Irish identity to which he could belong, and the song registers an Afro-American vocal and musical idiom. Instead, 'Black Boys on the Corner' demands to be understood as an expression of connection rather than belonging, of identification across the confines of one national culture or another. It constitutes an adoption of racial subjectivity which is specifically cross-cultural and transnational in a way which corresponded to Lynott's lived experience.

Taken together, 'Whiskey in the Jar' and 'Black Boys on the Corner' suggest a cultural strategy which tends towards adoption, fusion, and translation. Lynott invents himself in both songs as an interpellated, ventriloquised subject, either the voice of the Irish rebel or the collective voice of a black street-corner gang. This process of ventriloquism must not be misunderstood simply as imitation or pastiche, but as a distinct mode of address constitutive of Lynott's attempt at black-Irish cultural production. The mode of address is as significant as the persona adopted, oscillating sharply between identification with specifically Irish cultural voices, and specifically non-Irish cultural voices. In both songs we find what Paul Gilroy has noted as a distinct trend in black music, 'an amplified and exaggerated masculinity . . . that self-consciously salves the misery of the disempowered and subordinated'.[131] In Ireland of the 1970s, the appeal of such a balm had long historical roots. That this appeal was reconstructed by Lynott and Thin Lizzy through a complex negotiation of cross-cultural and cross-racial identities, and that Lynott became 'Ireland's first great rock poet'[132] within the complicated field of racial masquerade that sometimes constituted Irish music at this time, serves to remind us that narratives of Irish national achievement (such as that which pervades the history of Irish rock music) are never free from a more problematic historical engagement with the politics of class, race, sex, and gender, in Ireland as well as beyond it.

Coda: The Blacks of Europe

It would be remiss of any discussion of the conjunction of the terms 'black' and 'Irish' not to remark upon perhaps the most famous manifestation of that conjunction in Alan Parker's film of Roddy Doyle's *The Commitments* (1991), in which Jimmy invites his band members to identify with black soul music on the basis that 'The Irish are the blacks of Europe'. In Doyle's novel (1987), of course, Jimmy uses a different term, telling the band members that 'The Irish are the niggers of Europe'.[133] Jimmy proceeds to say that 'Dubliners are the niggers of Ireland. . . . An' the northside Dubliners are the niggers o' Dublin', thus making it clear that the use of the terms 'nigger' or 'black' are not specifically keyed to Ireland's experience of the racist practices and ideologies of colonialism, but more generically to the position of any marginalised or oppressed minority. 'Nigger' or 'black' are mobile metaphors for Jimmy, available as a trope for the experience of the colonised margins within a largely post-imperial Europe, the urban within a largely agrarian Ireland, or the working class within an increasingly bourgeois Dublin. Perhaps most significantly, Jimmy uses 'black' as a token not just of oppression but of the struggle against oppression. 'I'm black an' I'm proud', Jimmy asks his bemused white cohorts to repeat, after James Brown, while Joey the Lips later confesses that 'The biggest regret of my life is that I wasn't born black'.[134] For the aspiring Irish musicians of Doyle's novel, 'blackness' exemplifies dignity, sex appeal, and style, and is the epitome of counter-cultural chic, and yet, in ways which prefigure Paul Gilroy's critique of the appropriation of 'blackness' as marketable cultural icon in postmodern consumer society, 'blackness' is also their ultimate symbol of translocal cultural and commercial success.[135] Jimmy's exhortations on the virtues of black soul music, and of blackness as cultural icon, follow immediately upon his observation that 'Your music should be abou' where you're from an' the sort o' people yeh come from', which raises the question, then, of why black soul music from the racially segregrated ghettoes of urban America should be considered the most authentic, 'local' form through which Northside Dubliners might articulate their own experiences and identities.[136] Interestingly, in the course of discussing what constitutes the meanings and attractions of black soul as a form of cultural expression, Phil Lynott is mentioned briefly: 'Fuck off, said Jimmy. – He wasn't soul'. 'He was black', comes the reply.[137]

As Kevin Phinney suggests in his book on white cultural appropriations of black music in America, the politics of such cultural appropriations are difficult to disentangle: 'when whites adopt black influences as their own and express them artistically despite being raised apart from African Americans, where do they lead us? Does their music nudge society toward racial harmony or naked profiteering and ridicule?'[138] The same question might be asked of Doyle's fictional band, The Commitments: is the appropriation of black soul by a white Irish band a radical act of cross-racial, translocal solidarity, or another instance of minstrelsy and racial masquerade? The question is not particular to Doyle's novel, either, for as Declan Kiberd observes, *The Commitments* was only one iteration of a wider tendency within Irish culture in the 1980s and early 1990s to explore transcultural metaphors for Irish experiences, among which he cites the music of U2, the campaigns of Bob Geldof, Joseph O'Connor's novel, *Desperadoes* (1994), which analogises Irish and Nicaraguan experiences, and Brian Friel's *Dancing at Lughnasa* (1990), in which Irish religious and cultural rituals are likened to those of an Ugandan tribe.[139] The question of Irish identifications with post-colonial cultures in Asia, Africa, and Latin America also spawned a number of significant critical publications, and has arguably defined the course of Irish literary and cultural studies since the early 1990s. C. L. Innes published her study of the similarities between Irish and African literatures, *The Devil's Own Mirror*, in 1990, a classic text in Irish post-colonial criticism.[140] Carol Coulter published a pamphlet entitled *Ireland: Between the First and Third Worlds*, in which she identified Ireland with 'fellow former colonies' as the 'centre of fresh thinking about politics in the world today', as well as generating 'the most innovative art and culture'.[141] In 1992, the Centre for Research and Documentation in Belfast, led by Caitriona Ruane, published the proceedings of its conference held the previous year, entitled *Is Ireland a Third World Country?*, in which its contributors explored parallels, analogies, and points of solidarity between Ireland and various so-called 'Third World' countries.[142] A similar sense of Ireland's oddity within the 'First World' motivated Seamus Deane's *The Field Day Anthology of Irish Writing* (1991), which sought to deconstruct the English canon by 'reclaiming' and 'defining' an Irish literary tradition that would necessarily demonstrate, as a result of Irish experiences of colonialism and nationalism, 'the configurations of power within a society that consistently has refused to accept their force or yield to their allure'.[143]

That analogies between Ireland and 'Third World' countries, or between 'Irish' and 'black' peoples, became pervasive in Irish culture in the late 1980s and early 1990s is perhaps indicative of many different factors, some of which were related to domestic economic failures when compared to European trends, and the waning explanatory power of both Catholicism and nationalism within Irish society, and some of which were more broadly tied to global changes and events, such as the end of the Cold War and the horrific consequences of the famines in Ethiopia. The intention behind many such analogies was undoubtedly to construct a sense of solidarity between oppressed peoples, and to globalise resistance to racism and colonialism. As such, they might be included in any summary of the (admittedly thin) history of Irish anti-racist movements and alliances, such as those attempted by Robbie McVeigh and Steve Garner.[144] Garner, in particular, emphasises that anti-racism in Ireland needs to be international in character, since the nation-state is, in many ways, constitutively incapable of becoming the foundation for anti-racist struggle.[145] The problem for the construction of such a foundation, however, is that the very transversal movements and gestures necessary to the formation of a genuinely international anti-racism depend upon the figures of analogy and metaphor which may elide as much as they reveal. As David Lloyd argued in 'Race Under Representation', 'Metaphor is not merely the oscillation between sameness and difference but the process of subordinating difference to identity', a point he makes in examining the role of metaphor in the construction of racialised subjects.[146] In the twenty-first century, after more than a decade of dramatic economic and social change, with Ireland listed as the second richest country in Europe in 2007,[147] and with conspicuous evidence of racism in Ireland against black and Asian immigrants,[148] such claims of analogy and solidarity seem especially strained. The evidence presented in this chapter shows, however, that racism against black people in the Irish state and in Irish culture has a longer history, deeper roots, and a more problematic legacy than has hitherto been acknowledged.

Notes

1. Thomas Carlyle, 'Occasional Discourse on the Negro Question', p. 530.
2. Colin Graham, *Deconstructing Ireland*, pp. 1–31.
3. John Mitchel, *The Jail Journal*, p. 44.
4. Graham, *Deconstructing Ireland*, p. 2.
5. See Julie M. Dugger's discussion of the reception of Carlyle's ideas among the Young Ireland Movement, and the curious silence of the Young Irelanders on issues of race and slavery: 'Black Ireland's Race', pp. 461–85.
6. Luke Gibbons, *Gaelic Gothic*, p. 38.
7. Ibid., pp. 38, 41. I have quoted Gibbons's paraphrase of Matthew Frye Jacobson, *Whiteness of a Different Colour*.
8. Luke Gibbons, *Transformations in Irish Culture*, p. 3.
9. David Lloyd, *Ireland After History*, p. 105.
10. Gibbons, *Transformations*, p. 149.
11. Hyde's lecture is recorded in Minutes of the Irish Race Congress, Eamon de Valera Papers, UCD Archives, P150/1603.
12. *Speeches and Statements by Eamon de Valera, 1917–73*, p. 31.
13. Noel Ignatiev, *How the Irish Became White*. Ignatiev's work builds upon research on the construction of whiteness in the USA by David Roediger in *The Wages of Whiteness* and Theodore Allen in *The Invention of the White Race*. For an alternative view, which emphasises harmonious relations between the white Irish and black African Americans, see Graham Hodges, '"Desirable Companions and Lovers"', pp. 107–24. Ignatiev's work was criticised in some reviews for simplifying the factors which gave rise to Irish identifications with whiteness, and for depicting Irish whiteness as the product of collective self-determination on the part of the Irish-American community. See Diane Negra, 'The Stakes

of Whiteness', pp. 109–14; Eileen McMahon, '*How the Irish Became White*', pp. 571–2. See also Kevin Kenny, *The American Irish*, p. 68.

14. Lauren E. Onkey, *Blacking Up on Broadway*, p. 5. See also Eric Lott, *Love and Theft*, Lauren Onkey, '"A Melee and a Curtain"', Lauren Onkey, 'James Farrell's *Studs Lonigan* Trilogy and the Anxieties of Race', Catherine Eagan, "*I Did Imagine . . . We Had Ceased to Be Whitewashed Negroes*", Catherine M. Eagan, 'Still "Black" and "Proud"', Catherine M. Eagan, '"White," but "not Quite"'. See also Robert Nowatzki, 'Paddy Jumps Jim Crow'.

15. See, for examples, Declan Kiberd, 'White Skin, Black Masks', Brian Gallagher, 'About Us, For Us, Near Us', Tracy Mishkin, *The Harlem and Irish Renaissances*, Kathleen M. Gough, 'Polymorphous Playboys', Michael Malouf, *Other Emerald Isles*, and several essays in Joseph McMinn (ed.), *The Internationalism of Irish Literature and Drama*.

16. Bill Rolston, 'Are the Irish Black?', pp. 95–102.

17. Lloyd, *Ireland After History*, p. 106.

18. Michael Malouf, 'With Dev in America', p. 27.

19. See Ethel Crowley and Jim MacLaughlin (eds), *Under the Belly of the Celtic Tiger*; Paul Cullen, *Refugees and Asylum-Seekers in Ireland*; Bryan Fanning, *Racism and Social Change in the Republic of Ireland*; Gretchen Fitzgerald, *Repulsing Racism*; Dermot Keogh, *Jews in Twentieth-Century Ireland*; Ronit Lentin, *The Expanding Nation*; Jim McLaughlin, *Travellers and Ireland*; Robbie McVeigh and Ronit Lentin (eds), *Racism and Anti-Racism in Ireland*; and Steve Garner, *Racism in the Irish Experience*.

20. Rolston, 'Are the Irish Black?', p. 101.

21. John Ardagh, *Ireland and the Irish*, p. 342.

22. See note 19 above for these studies.

23. See the following newspaper reports on the court sessions of 22 June and 30 June at which the 'Prince' appeared in Cork District Court: 'Undesirable "Prince"', *Irish Independent*, 23 June 1925, p. 7; 'Failure to Register – Prince in Trouble', *Southern Star*, 27 June 1925, p. 2; 'A Prince in Cork', *Irish Times*, 27 June 1925, p. 8; and 'The "Prince of Abyssinia"', *Irish Times*, 1 July 1925, p. 5.

24. Initially, Sir Hari Singh's name had been protected in the fraud case and he was identified as 'Mr A.', but he was named in early December 1924, and there followed intense speculation about his whereabouts when it was revealed that he was wanted for questioning by British police. See 'The Elusive Mr A.', *Irish Times*, 8 December 1924, p. 7. The 'Prince of Abyssinia' defendant had been mistaken for 'Mr A.', or Sir Hari Singh, in Wales, and had got 'extensive mention in an English newspaper' according to the *Irish Independent*: see 'Undesirable "Prince"', *Irish Independent*, 23 June 1925, p. 7. Sir Hari Singh was also well known in Ireland as a race-horse owner, and was noted in Irish newspapers when he visited race meetings.

25. Evidence for the local celebrity acquired by the 'Prince' includes not just the newspaper coverage of the case itself, but also an allusion made by a man who appeared in court on 25 July 1925, accused of passing counterfeit coins: he described the charges against him as fictitious, and yet still he was 'sharing his apartments at present with the Prince of Abyssinia

(Laughter)', meaning, of course, that he was in jail: 'Counterfeit Coins', *Irish Times*, 25 July 1925, p. 5.

26. Cork District Court Order Book, June-July 1925: Tuesday 30 June, Case No. 439. National Archives of Ireland CC/97/60/31.
27. '"Prince" Goes to Jail', *Irish Independent*, 21 July 1925, p. 8.
28. Paul Gilroy, *There Ain't No Black in the Union Jack*, pp. 72–3.
29. Sir Kenneth Newman was the commissioner of the Metropolitan Police of London, and the quotation comes from Gilroy's epigraph, p. 72.
30. Henry Louis Gates, Jr, 'The "Blackness of Blackness"', p. 686.
31. Declan Kiberd, 'The Fall of the Stage Irishman', in his *The Irish Writer and the World*, pp. 21–41.
32. See Fidele Mutwarasibo and Suzanne Smith, *Africans in Ireland*.
33. This has certainly been the Powellite explanation, made famous by Enoch Powell in a speech in Birmingham in April 1968, known as the 'rivers of blood' speech, which was influential especially on Conservative Party policy on race relations in the 1970s and 1980s.
34. Mutwarasibo and Smith, *Africans in Ireland*, p. 2.
35. 'Nigerian Student to Pay £700 in Seduction Case', *Irish Times*, 6 November 1948, p. 3.
36. Mohangi was initially convicted of murder, and sentenced to death, but on appeal he was re-tried and convicted of manslaughter, for which he was sentenced to seven years' imprisonment. He was released in 1968 and returned to South Africa, so the case would still have been fresh in the minds of Dubliners in 1969.
37. 'Sorry – No Blacks – 2', *Irish Times*, 11 December 1969, p. 6.
38. National Archives of Ireland, Dept of Taoiseach files, Taois 97/9/453.
39. Letter to Minister Aiken from Nigerian Embassy, 22 April 1963, National Archives of Ireland, Dept of Taoiseach files, Taois 17660/95.
40. Letter to Minister Aiken from Nigerian Embassy, 16 June 1964, National Archives of Ireland, Dept of Taoiseach files, Taois 17660/95.
41. *Morning Post*, 2 July 1964 and *Nigerian Outlook*, 4 July 1964. Cuttings of these articles were included in an appendix to an aide memoire sent from the Minister for External Affairs, Frank Aiken, to the Taoiseach, Sean Lemass, 20 August 1964, National Archives of Ireland, Dept of Taoiseach files, Taois 17660/95.
42. 'List of Attacks on Nigerians Given', *Irish Times*, 21 August 1964, p. 6.
43. 'Nigerian Reports Annoy Government', *Irish Times*, 22 August 1964, p. 1.
44. Memo from Sean Lemass to secretary, 29 July 1964, National Archives of Ireland, Dept of Taoiseach files, Taois 17660/95.
45. 'Nigerian Reports Annoy Government', *Irish Times*, 22 August 1964, p. 1.
46. 'Minister to see Nigerian Ambassador', *Irish Times*, 21 August 1964, p. 1.
47. 'Nigerian Protest Over Attacks on Students', *Irish Times*, 21 July 1964, p. 12.
48. 'Nigerian Reports Annoy Government', *Irish Times*, 22 August 1964, p. 1. The text comes from a statement issued to the press by Aiken, after his meeting with the Nigerian Ambassador.
49. 'Minister to see Nigerian Ambassador', *Irish Times*, 21 August 1964, p. 1.
50. Quoted in F. S. L. Lyons, *Ireland Since the Famine*, p. 594.

51. Quoted in Prionsias MacAonghusa, 'Straight from the Shoulder', *Free Press*, 28 August 1964. Press cutting in National Archives of Ireland, Dept of Taoiseach files, Taois 17660/95.

52. Prionsias MacAonghusa, 'Straight from the Shoulder', *Free Press*, 28 August 1964. Press cutting in National Archives of Ireland, Dept of Taoiseach files, Taois 17660/95.

53. 'Editorial: Human Relations', *Irish Times*, 22 August 1964, p. 9.

54. Jack Butterly, 'Colour Bar? There is no real problem in Dublin', *Evening Herald*, 11 August 1964, and 'Our View: Ireland and her Guests', *Evening Herald*, 22 August 1964. Both were cuttings kept for the Taoiseach. National Archives of Ireland, Dept of Taoiseach files, Taois 17660/95.

55. 'Editorial: Human Relations', *Irish Times*, 22 August 1964, p. 9.

56. V. M. Crawford, 'Uganda Calls to Ireland', *Studies*, 97, March 1936, p. 108.

57. David Theo Goldberg, *Racist Culture*, p. 7.

58. Frantz Fanon, *Black Skin, White Masks*, pp. 109–40.

59. Homi Bhabha, *The Location of Culture*, p. 238.

60. Tim Pat Coogan, *Wherever Green is Worn*, p. 508.

61. 'Irish Accused of Colour Prejudice', *Irish Times*, 7 September 1964, p. 8.

62. Ibid., p. 8.

63. Austin Clarke, 'Flight to Africa', *Flight to Africa and Other Poems*, pp. 20–3.

64. See Maurice Harmon, *Austin Clarke*, pp. 184–5.

65. On Bishop Lucey's fondness for controversy, and his dislike of foreigners, see Michael Sheehy, *Is Ireland Dying?*, pp. 184–98.

66. 'Civic Reception for Papal Nuncio', *Irish Times*, 27 September 1960, p. 11.

67. Ibid., p. 11.

68. A claim which Lucey made in 1955 but later qualified. See J. H. Whyte, *Church and State in Modern Ireland, 1923–1970*, p. 312.

69. G. Craig Tapping, *Austin Clarke*, p. 217.

70. Desmond Forristal, 'Black Man's Country', script courtesy of Gate Theatre Archives, McCormick Library of Special Collections, Northwestern University, Evanston, Illinois. Thanks to Scott Krafft, Acting Head of the McCormick Library, for his kind assistance in locating and making available a copy of the script. As it was unpublished, all references to the play are to this script.

71. See Lance Pettitt's brief consideration of the Radharc film unit in *Screening Ireland: Film and Television Representation*, pp. 82–5.

72. 'Kay Kent Talks with Father Desmond Forristal', *Irish Times*, 30 April 1974, p. 10.

73. Kevin Kenny, 'The Irish in the Empire', *Ireland and the British Empire*, p. 115.

74. See Joseph McGlade, *A History of Irish Catholicism, Vol. vi*, p. 2. The five new Irish missionary movements were: St Columban's Foreign Mission Society (1918); the Missionary Sisters of St Columban (1922); the Missionary Sisters of the Holy Rosary (1924); St Patrick's Foreign Missionary Society (1932); and the Medical Missionaries of Mary (1937).

75. Ibid., pp. 28, 25.

76. Ibid., p. 33.
77. Ibid., p. 16.
78. Forristal, 'Black Man's Country', pp. 2–3.
79. Ibid., p. 3.
80. Ibid., p. 1.
81. Ibid., p. 47.
82. Ibid., pp. 10–11.
83. McGlade, *A History of Irish Catholicism*, p. 89.
84. Forristal indeed went on to write a biography of Edel Quinn in 1994, but there had already been several books on her life, evidence of the popularity of her life story of sacrifice in the service of the Catholic faith. See bibliographical entries under Bob Bloomfield, Evelyn M. Brown, Frank Duff, Desmond Forristal, Marius McAuliffe, Anselm Moynihan, Leon-Joseph Cardinal Suenens, and Mary Walls.
85. Forristal, 'Black Man's Country', p. 9.
86. Edmund Hogan disputes the argument that Irish Catholic missionaries were slow to cede control of the church in Africa to African priests for racist reasons, although Hogan's definition of what constitutes racism relies upon notions of biological determinism (that is, whether 'Africans' were innately less intelligent, or less capable of the discipline of celibacy, for example). Hogan argues that most Irish missionaries believed that 'Africans *were* capable of being educated to the highest standards, would in time be able to assume the responsibility of priesthood and religious vocation, and eventually the leadership roles in their own churches'. As discussed earlier in this chapter, the idea of a racially structured social order based upon a time-lag between European and African, or white and black, peoples forms a key part of both Fanon's and Bhabha's critiques of the racial theories of colonialism. See Edmund M. Hogan, *The Irish Missionary Movement*, pp. 164–8.
87. Fanon, *Black Skin, White Masks*, p. 113.
88. 'Letters to the Editor: Black Man's Country', *Irish Times*, 2 May 1974, p. 13.
89. 'Lack of Reviews for Gate Play Upsets Hilton Edwards', *Irish Times*, 10 Oct 1974, p. 9.
90. See 'An Irishman's Diary', *Irish Times*, 24 May 1974, p. 13, for an example of this type of response, under the sub-headline 'Good Reporting'.
91. Enda Staunton, 'The Case of Biafra', p. 512.
92. 'Letters to the Editor: Black Man's Country', *Irish Times*, 2 May 1974, p. 13.
93. McGlade, *A History of Irish Catholicism*, p. 20.
94. Brendan Behan, *The Complete Plays*, pp. 204–5.
95. See Ulick O'Connor, *Brendan Behan*, pp. 203–20; Richard Wall, 'Introduction', *An Giall/The Hostage*, pp. 1–21; Declan Kiberd, *Inventing Ireland*, pp. 513–29.
96. Behan, *The Complete Plays*, pp. 254–5.
97. Ibid., p. 254.
98. Ibid., p. 255.
99. Ibid., p. 256.
100. Ibid., p. 260.

101. Ibid., p. 260.
102. Ibid., p. 285.
103. Ibid., p. 262.
104. Henry Louis Gates, Jr, *Figures in Black*, p. 186.
105. Ibid., p. 180.
106. Mary MacGoris, 'Juvenile Brendan Unkind to Behan', *Irish Independent*, 15 March 1972, p. 7.
107. Thanks to Mairéad Delaney, archivist at the Abbey Theatre, who checked with Finola Eustace, who was one of the stage directors for the production in the Peacock Theatre.
108. Indeed, the substance of Oliver Marshall's criticism of the play in the *Irish Press* is that its 'rather dated quality' puts it out of step with 'these liberal days'. Oliver Marshall, 'The Peacock: Cork Leg Leads a Merry Dance', *The Irish Press*, 15 March 1972, p. 7.
109. Perhaps of more tangential interest is the fact that Barney McKenna was renowned for his banjo playing, and indeed is credited among others for bringing the banjo into Irish folk music, but it is an instrument associated historically with minstrel shows, and before this with slave plantations in America.
110. Seamus Kelly, 'Brendan Behan – Dubliners Combination at Peacock', *Irish Times*, 15 March 1972, p. 12. The play was also reviewed on 15 March 1972 in *Irish Independent* (p. 7), *The Irish Press* (p. 7), *Evening Herald* (p. 4), *Evening Press* (p. 4), and on 31 March 1972 in *Hibernia* (p. 19).
111. See for example bell hooks, *Black Looks* and Kobena Mercer, *Welcome to the Jungle*.
112. *The Black and White Minstrel Show* was one of the most popular variety shows on British television, achieving regular viewing figures during the 1960s of 16 million. It was broadcast as a regular Saturday night show from June 1958 to July 1978. It was possible for Irish viewers to receive BBC broadcasts from British transmitters, especially on the east coast and in areas bordering Northern Ireland.
113. Angela Davis had also been the subject of recent songs, 'Angela' by John Lennon and Yoko Ono, and 'Sweet Black Angel' by The Rolling Stones.
114. Paul Durcan, *O Westport in the Light of Asia Minor*, p. 57. Thanks to Paul Durcan, c/o Rogers, Coleridge and White Ltd, for kind permission to reproduce this poem in full.
115. Elizabeth Butler Cullingford, *Ireland's Others*, pp. 155–6.
116. Durcan, *O Westport in the Light of Asia Minor*, p. 57.
117. Cullingford, *Ireland's Others*, p. 155.
118. Bhabha, *The Location of Culture*, p. 67.
119. John Kelly, *Sophisticated Boom Boom*. I am very grateful to my colleague P. J. Mathews for this reference to Lynott.
120. For the story of Phil Lynott's upbringing, see Philomena Lynott, with Jackie Harden, *My Boy*, and also the bibliographical entries under Stuart Bailie, Ken Brooks, and Mark Putterford.
121. Gerry Smyth, *Noisy Island*, p. 39.
122. Ibid., p. 37.
123. *New Spotlight* (Dublin), 5 August 1971, p. 2.

124. *New Spotlight* (Dublin), 22 April 1972, p.36.
125. *New Spotlight* (Dublin), 21 December 1972, pp. 22–3.
126. See Lott, *Love and Theft*, pp. 3–5.
127. An argument made persuasively about Victorian and Edwardian cross-racial dressing in Gail Ching-Liang Low's *White Skin/Black Masks*.
128. See Putterford, *Phil Lynott*, p. 67; also Mark J. Prendergast, *Irish Rock*, p. 44.
129. Putterford, *Phil Lynott*, p. 67
130. Although Hendrix was a key icon for Lynott of a successful black rock musician, in an art form which was overwhelmingly white, Hendrix's reputation as a specifically black musician is not itself without its problems, as Paul Gilroy discusses in *The Black Atlantic*, pp. 93–4.
131. Ibid., p. 85.
132. Prendergast describes Lynott thus in his tribute to the rock star in *Irish Rock*, pp. 274–6.
133. Roddy Doyle, *The Commitments*, p. 9.
134. Ibid., p. 125.
135. Paul Gilroy, *Between Camps*, pp. 241–78.
136. Doyle, *The Commitments*, p. 9.
137. Ibid., p. 75.
138. Kevin Phinney, *Souled American*, p. 24.
139. Declan Kiberd, *Inventing Ireland*, p. 611.
140. C. L. Innes, *The Devil's Own Mirror*, passim.
141. Carol Coulter, *Ireland: Between the First and Third Worlds*, p. 22.
142. Caitríona Ruane et al. (eds), *Is Ireland a Third World Country?*
143. Seamus Deane (ed.), *The Field Day Anthology of Irish Writing, Vol. 1*, p. xx.
144. See McVeigh and Lentin, *Racism and Anti-Racism in Ireland*, pp. 211–25, and Garner, *Racism in the Irish Experience*, pp. 214–21.
145. Garner, *Racism in the Irish Experience*, pp. 198–224.
146. David Lloyd, 'Race Under Representation', p. 256.
147. On 24 June 2008, Eurostat, the statistical office of the European Commission, released its preliminary estimates for 2007 of GDP per inhabitant expressed in terms of Purchasing Power Standards. These showed Ireland as the second richest country in the EU after Luxembourg, with Luxembourg a specially inflated case because of the large number of cross-border workers who contribute to GDP but are not counted as inhabitants. See http://epp.eurostat.ec.europa.eu
148. See Fanning, *Racism and Social Change in the Republic of Ireland*, pp. 24–5.

Conclusion: Imagining the 'New Hibernia'

On the morning of 7 June 2004, just a few days before the citizenship referendum, two men wearing balaclavas hung a life-sized black doll from a railway bridge in Longford town. A bag was placed over the doll's head, and a sign hung around its neck which read 'Niggers go home – you'll never be Irish'.[1] As the journalist who reported the incident for the *Sunday Independent* observed, the mock execution, the effigy, and the balaclavas may all have been modelled upon 'the darkest days of the Klu Klux Klan [sic]', but the performance was unmistakably charged with the racist undertones of the referendum itself. Government ministers oscillated between depicting the proposed amendment as a purely pragmatic issue of closing loopholes in Irish citizenship law which were out of step with European standards, and trotting out unsubstantiated 'scare' stories about the apparent 'flood' of expectant mothers arriving from Africa solely in order to give birth and collect the passport. Whichever reason for approving the amendment was proffered, however, the referendum debate, such as it was, posed the same symbolic antithesis to Irish voters as had preoccupied the voters and volunteers at the foundation of the state: on the one hand, there were white Europeans deserving of prosperity, independence, and human rights, while on the other, there were black Africans seemingly undeserving of any of these things. As John Harrington argues in tracing the trajectory of discourses of 'citizenship' in post-independence Ireland, the Europeanism which had for so long represented for Irish liberals the aspiration towards cosmopolitan modernity was also a racialised identity forged in opposition to an idea of black Africa as 'a state of nature incapable of development'.[2] The overwhelming endorsement of the citizenship amendment was revealing evidence of the racial underpinnings of Irishness, and Irish commitments to Europeanness, in the twenty-first century. A few days after the referendum, the journalist John Waters, who had argued for a 'No' vote, and predicted that the government amendment would be defeated 'three to one', was compelled to face up to the hard truth of racism in Irish society: 'Last week I met a man who told me: "You're missing the point. This is about keeping the niggers out"'.[3]

At first glance, perhaps, the despicable gestures and words of racial hatred, sickeningly evocative of segregation and slavery in the American south, seem out of place in the new Ireland which emerged in the 1990s. During that decade, Irishness became fashionable, enviable, and global. So many of the symbols of the failed experiments of conservative, Catholic Ireland were transformed. The 'stiff-backed', sexless formality and parochialism of 'traditional Irish dancing' was re-invented in the raunchy, leather-trousered version which crossed the world as 'Riverdance', at the same time as the Irish priest, long a symbol of repressive social authority, lost his revered status as a result of successive cases of child abuse and sexual scandal. The Irish soccer team, competing in a sport which had been forbidden to GAA members as a 'foreign' game, and managed by the charismatic English football legend, Jack Charlton, garnered a huge wave of national support, and opened a new avenue for patriotic expression, proving that 'Irishness' could be articulated through the medium of an international sport and did not require its own exceptional forms. Arguably, some Irish rock bands had already shown this versatility and gift for reinvention in the 1980s, as Joe Cleary has recently shown in relation to The Pogues.[4] The Irish pub, symbolic in many works of literature and film (from *Ulysses* to *The Quiet Man*) of the closeted, secretive, male society which dominated every level of Irish politics, from Kildare Street to Listowel, became a themed, global franchise, to be found in Beijing, Montpellier, or São Paulo. The Irish economy, which in the 1980s had been hampered by debt, unemployment, and the 'brain drain' of emigration, became by the late 1990s a model of growth, prosperity, and high-skilled, high-tech employment, which had acquired its own epithet, 'the Celtic Tiger'. As the conflict in Northern Ireland stuttered towards peace and political settlement, so too, the notion that Ireland was trapped in the blind alleys of its own past gave way to the dream that Ireland might instead symbolise hope for other troubled regions. Even emigration, which for decades had been the ultimate sign of political and economic failure in Ireland, was reconceived during the Robinson presidency as the 'diaspora', a term which somehow seemed more a sign of global success than domestic ruin.[5]

In *The Generation Game*, one of Ireland's leading political and economic journalists, David McWilliams, argues that the next phase of Ireland's economic development, and the key to future success, is to harness the resources, skills, and clout of the global Irish diaspora to the demands of the Irish state. This is a vision McWilliams describes as a kind of re-union of 'the tribe', and which he compares to the relationship between Israel and Jewish peoples around the world: 'No two races have a Diaspora quite like us pair and in a globalised world, these exiles are an enormous resource for the homeland'.[6] According to McWilliams, the Irish are a 'globalised tribe', and it is time for the Irish in Ireland to learn how to manipulate this accident of historical circumstances to their advantage in planning future economic development. At the heart of McWilliams's vision of the 'New Hibernia', as indeed at the heart of Mary Robinson's embrace of the Irish diaspora as a concept, is an implicitly racial view of the state, its inhabitants, and its relations with other peoples around the world. This view is not uncommon: in fact, since the amendments to the Irish constitution made in the wake of the Good Friday Agreement in 1998, it is a constitutional commitment that 'the Irish nation cherishes its special affinity with people of Irish ancestry living abroad who share its cultural identity and heritage'.[7] Perhaps ironically, this commitment was given in the same revised text for Article Two of the constitution which guaranteed citizenship for all those born in the island of Ireland, the revision deemed responsible for the 'loophole' which gave rise to the citizenship referendum in 2004. Ancestry, together with a commitment to a singular 'cultural identity and heritage', was understood as the basis for the new dispensation in Irish citizenship, so that third-generation descendants of Irish emigrants in Birmingham, Boston, or Buenos Aires, were, after 2004, fully entitled to rights which could be legitimately denied to children born in Ballyfermot. This extraordinary entitlement privileges the imaginary existence of a 'globalised' race over the actual presence, labour, and contribution of all those within the boundaries of the state. To put it even more cynically, it affords rights to citizenship to those from wealthy, first-world countries whose grandparents had to leave Ireland half a century ago to find a home, and denies them to the poor, the oppressed, and the exiled who have recently arrived in Ireland seeking a home, a job, refuge, or a safe place to raise their children.

The citizenship amendment established racial identity as the foundation of Irish citizenship, and arguably lent credence and legitimacy to racist attacks upon immigrants, refugees, and minority groups in Irish society. Both government policy and social attitudes towards perceived 'racial others' were not incongruous with the appearance of a newly cosmopolitan, global brand of Irishness, however. John Harrington argues that inequality is integral to the new, 'post-nationalist' Ireland, that in its headlong embrace of neo-liberal economics, the state requires inequality in order for the ideology of micro-economic individualism to thrive, and he quotes the Minister for Justice who sponsored the citizenship amendment, Michael McDowell, dismissing 'the current rights culture and equality notion' as inflexible, and incompatible with 'A dynamic liberal economy like ours'.[8] Carmen Kuhling and Kieran Keohane also highlight the structural role of inequality in the new economy, and argue that racism and anti-cosmopolitanism in Irish society, especially as expressed in the referendum, are inseparable from the state's

> narrow economic orientation to migrant workers which views them as factors of production rather than as human beings with rich and vibrant cultural resources who could contribute not only to the globalised Irish economy but to the development of a cosmopolitan Irish society.[9]

Michael O'Connell, writing before the amendment was proposed, sets the rise of racism and anti-immigrant sentiment in contemporary Ireland against the context of the resurgence of right-wing populism across Europe, a trend to which Ireland was increasingly susceptible. 'There is no particular reason', O'Connell argued, 'to hope that Irish civic beliefs, humanity and tolerance are rooted more deeply than in those other countries (and in many cases, frankly, one might guess that the roots of such Irish values are far more shallow)'.[10] Like many other critics of the resurgence of racism in Irish state and society, O'Connell sees racist violence and attitudes as not merely the product of a temporary lapse in Irish historical memory, nor the signs of a time-lag between isolated, 'backward' communities and a supposedly cosmopolitan elite, but rather as phenomena which are deeply embedded in the social, cultural, and economic structures of contemporary Irish society. Racism, and the racial ideologies which underpin racism, will continue to thrive in the conditions governing the 'New Hibernia', it seems.

They will thrive because the ideological negotiations between neo-liberal economics and social justice rarely exceed the boundaries of the nation-state. As long as notions of public interest, integration, citizenship, and welfare are defined and valued within the terms of the imagined national community, they remain bound by the ideological legacies of nationalism, and, as I hope this book has shown, the history of state nationalism in Ireland is a history marked by racism and racialisation. This is also why the literary and cultural critique of state nationalism so often takes the form, as examined here, of an attack on the racial underpinnings of nationalism. The persistence of racial ideologies through successive phases of the cultural and political history of the Irish state is testament not just to the mutative power of race as an explanatory tool, but also to the functional significance of race within the social glue of the nation-state. Yet, as race is a cultural construct, and as such depends upon the aesthetic sphere for its authority and its affective power, it is also constantly vulnerable to cultural resistance, to alternative and dissident voices and perspectives. It is too early as yet to assess the success or significance of some of the most recent forms of cultural resistance or response to the 'crisis racism' of the past decade or so. Roddy Doyle's collaborations with Bisi Adigun and *Metro Eireann* are perhaps the most important developments in terms of a literary response to narratives of immigration and social change, and perhaps significantly, these writings (*Guess Who's Coming for the Dinner* (2001), *The Playboy of the Western World* (2007), and the stories in *The Deportees* (2007)) tend towards the adaptation or rewriting of iconic or classic texts to incorporate the figure of the immigrant or the 'new Irish'.[11] Charlie O'Neill's *HURL* (2003), produced by the innovative Barabbas theatre company, also challenges the iconic in dramatising the fictitious journey of 'Ireland's first multi-ethnic hurling team'.[12] Laima Muktupavela's *The Mushroom Covenant* (2002), a Latvian novel about the author's experiences of exploitative working conditions as a mushroom picker in Louth, has also been widely noted by Irish academics and cultural commentators, although it is perhaps revealing that no English (or Gaelic) translation exists as yet.[13] The stories told by these plays and fictional texts thus far is one of a problematic, if sometimes optimistic, engagement between immigrants and the host culture. To this list might also be added two earlier instances of a cultural response to contemporary racism, Clare Boylan's *Black Baby* (1988) and Donal O'Kelly's *Asylum! Asylum!* (1994), both of which explore the legendary 'hospitality' of the Irish from the perspective of racialised 'others', but which obviously pre-date the specific racialised dynamics of immigration in the 'Celtic Tiger' era.[14] Culture, of course, is made not just in theatres and publishing houses, but in streets, houses, schools, restaurants, playing fields, churches, community halls, in the very quotidian fabric of our lives, and it is certain that the legitimacy of race as a category of human understanding will continue to be invoked and denied on a daily basis in Irish culture. These are the 'culture wars' which will shape and define the 'New Hibernia', as much as the battle for competitiveness in the neo-liberal economic order, or the role of the diaspora in the Irish state. Communities make themselves, and reinvent themselves, constantly, through every facet of human culture and communication, through every story that is told of human connection and contact.

The lesson of attending to figures of race in Irish literature, culture and politics is not simply the centrality of race, often in muted and insidious forms, to Irish political and social discourses, but also the extent to which the validity and efficacy of racial ideologies has persistently been the subject of radical doubt within Irish culture. It is perhaps notable that the literary and cultural texts examined in this study more often take the form of social and political critique, and none is able to proffer utopian visions of cosmopolitan communities, but in the very doubts they articulate about the racial dynamics of Irish society they open up the cultural space in which community demands to be reimagined beyond the dubious and destructive allure of race. The future of a genuinely cosmopolitan Ireland will depend upon this capacity in Irish culture to imagine the concept of community, perhaps even nation, beyond the bounds of racial ideologies, and to realise an ideal of civic and social community which can harness the positive value of human dependencies beyond the terms of national or racial affiliation. Notions of the Irish diaspora as a 'globalised tribe', or the Europeanism which has so often presented itself as the liberal panacea to Irish parochialism, merely offer to extend the geo-political boundaries of racial identity, while retaining the same capacities for racist discrimination and violence as has always been inherent in the form of the nation-state. At the same time, the appeal to a global identity or indivisible world-citizenship is unlikely to garner cohesion or legitimacy in a world divided into self-governing bounded communities. The challenge is not new, as I have sought to show throughout this book, but this book is also about the hope that continued to resonate through the cultural history of Ireland in the past century, of a community able to accommodate the heterogeneous bonds, connections, and affiliations of all of its members, without prejudice, and of a community able to host those from outside its bonds, without injustice. It is a hope fraught with difficulty, but like Leopold Bloom's fragile vision of the 'Union of all' in a 'Nova Hibernia', or his half-remembered song of a home free from persecution, it is also a hope worth continually renewing.[15]

Notes

1. Lara Bradley, 'Racial Tensions Spark Fears of Midlands Ghetto', *Sunday Independent*, 11 June 2004, p. 9.
2. John A. Harrington, 'Citizenship and the Biopolitics of Post-nationalist Ireland', pp. 426–7.
3. John Waters, 'Presumed Guilty of Xenophobia', *Irish Times*, 14 June 2004, p. 14.
4. Joe Cleary, *Outrageous Fortune*, pp. 261–94.

5. See David Lloyd's discussion of the use of the term 'diaspora' to describe Irish emigration in *Ireland after History*, pp. 101–8.
6. David McWilliams, *The Generation Game*, p. 236.
7. Article 2, *Bunreact na hÉireann* (Constitution of Ireland), as enrolled on 27 May 1999, after the 19th Amendment of the Constitution Act, 1998, which allowed the state to be bound by the Good Friday Agreement between Britain and Ireland as agreed on 10 April 1998.
8. Harrington, 'Citizenship and the Biopolitics of Post-nationalist Ireland', p. 435.
9. Carmen Kuhling and Kieran Keohane, *Cosmopolitan Ireland*, p. 51.
10. Michael O'Connell, *Right-Wing Ireland?*, pp. 104–5.
11. For a discussion of Roddy Doyle's collaborations with *Metro Eireann*, see Maureen T. Reddy, 'Reading and Writing Race in Ireland', pp. 374–88.
12. *HURL* was produced first at The Black Box by the Barabbas company on 14 July 2003.
13. Laima Muktupavela, *The Mushroom Covenant* (Šampinjonu Derība).
14. See Clare Boylan, *Black Baby. Asylum! Asylum!* was first produced at the Abbey Theatre on 27 July 1994.
15. James Joyce, *Ulysses*, pp. 457, 462, 641.

Bibliography

Abizadeh, Arash, 'Does Liberal Democracy Presuppose a Cultural Nation? Four Arguments', *American Political Science Review*, 96, 3 (September 2002), pp. 495–509.

Agamben, Giorgio, *The Coming Community*, trans. Michael Hardt (Minneapolis, MN: University of Minnesota Press, 1993).

Agamben, Giorgio, *Homo Sacer: Sovereign Power and Bare Life*. Trans. Daniel Heller-Roazen (Stanford, CA: Stanford University Press, 1998).

Allen, Theodore, *The Invention of the White Race, Vol. 1: Racial Oppression and Social Control* (London: Verso, 1994).

Anderson, Benedict, *Imagined Communities: Reflections on the Origin and Spread of Nationalism* (London: Verso, 1991).

Ardagh, John, *Ireland and the Irish: Portrait of a Changing Society* (London: Penguin, 1995).

Arendt, Hannah, 'The Jew as Pariah', *Reflections on Literature and Culture*, ed. Susannah Young-ah Gottlieb (Stanford, CA: Stanford University Press, 2007).

Arendt, Hannah, *The Origins of Totalitarianism* (London: Harvest, [1951]1968).

Armstrong, Gordon S., *Samuel Beckett, W.B. Yeats, and Jack Yeats: Images and Words* (Cranbury, NJ: Associated University Presses, 1990).

Arnold, Bruce, *Jack Yeats* (New Haven, CT, and London: Yale University Press, 1998).

Bailie, Stuart, *The Ballad of the Thin Man: The Authorized Biography of Phil Lynott and Thin Lizzy* (London: Boxtree, 1996).

Balibar, Etienne and Immanuel Wallerstein, *Race, Nation, Class: Ambiguous Identities*, trans. Chris Turner (London: Verso, 1991).

Beckett, Samuel, *The Grove Centenary Edition: Volumes I & II, Novels*, ed. Paul Auster (New York: Grove Press, 2006).

Beckett, Samuel, 'Homage to Jack B. Yeats', *Jack B. Yeats: The Late Paintings* (Bristol: Arnolfini; London: Whitechapel Art Gallery; The Hague: Haags Gemeentemuseum, 1991), p. 9.

Behan, Brendan, *The Complete Plays* (London: Methuen, 1978).

Beiner, Ronald (ed.), *Theorizing Nationalism* (New York: SUNY, 1999).

Benhabib, Seyla et al., *Another Cosmopolitanism*, ed. Robert Post (Oxford: Oxford University Press, 2008).

Benhabib, Seyla, *The Rights of Others: Aliens, Residents and Citizens* (Cambridge: Cambridge University Press, 2004).

Berman, Hannah, *Ant Hills* (London: Faber and Gwyer, 1926).

Berman, Hannah, 'The Charity Box', *The Dublin Magazine*, 1 (August 1923), pp. 32–8.

Berman, Hannah, *Melutovna* (London: Chapman and Hall, 1913).

Bhabha, Homi, *The Location of Culture* (London: Routledge, 1994).

Bhabha, Homi, 'Unpacking My Library Again', *Journal of the Midwest Modern Language Association*, 28.1 (Spring 1995), pp. 5–18.

Birmingham, G. A., *Irishmen All* (London: Foulis, 1913).

Bloomfield, Bob, *Edel Quinn: A Heroine of the Apostolate* (Dublin: Catholic Truth Society, 1994).

Boylan, Clare, *Black Baby* (London: Abacus, [1988] 1998).

Brooks, Ken, *Phil Lynott and Thin Lizzy: Rockin' Vagabond* (London: Agenda, 2000).

Brown, Evelyn M., *Edel Quinn: Beneath the Southern Cross* (New York: Farrar, Straus, and Giroux, 1967).

Brown, Terence, *Ireland: A Social and Cultural History, 1922–1985* (London: Fontana, 1985).

Bruce, Vicki and Andy Young, *In the Eye of the Beholder: The Science of Face Perception* (Oxford: Oxford University Press, 1998).

Butler, Judith and Gayatri Chakravorty Spivak, *Who Sings the Nation-State? Language, Politics, Belonging* (Oxford: Seagull, 2007).

Carlyle, Thomas, 'Occasional Discourse on the Negro Question', *Fraser's Magazine for Town and Country* (London), xl (Feb 1849), pp. 527–38.

Carter, Robert, 'Genes, Genomes and Genealogies: The Return of Scientific Racism?', *Ethnic and Racial Studies*, 30, 4 (July 2007), pp. 546–56.

Chambers, Iain and Lidia Curti (eds), *The Post-Colonial Question: Common Skies, Divided Horizons* (New York: Routledge, 1996).

Cheng, Vincent J., *Joyce, Race and Empire* (Cambridge: Cambridge University Press, 1995).

Child, Francis James (ed.), *The English and Scottish Popular Ballads*, Vol. III (New York: Folklore Press, 1956).

Clarke, Austin, *Flight to Africa and Other Poems* (Dublin: Dolmen, 1963).

Cleary, Joe, *Outrageous Fortune: Capital and Culture in Modern Ireland* (Dublin: Field Day, 2007).

Cleary, Joe and Claire Connolly (eds), *The Cambridge Companion to Modern Irish Culture* (Cambridge: Cambridge University Press, 2005).

Collins, Michael, *The Path to Freedom* (Cork and Dublin: Mercier Press, 1996).

Colum, Pádraic, *A Boy in Erinn* (New York: Dutton, 1913).

Connolly, Claire (ed.), *Theorizing Ireland* (Basingstoke: Palgrave, 2003).

Connor, Steven, *The Book of Skin* (London: Reaktion, 2004).

Coogan, Tim Pat, *Michael Collins: A Biography* (London: Arrow, 1991).

Coogan, Tim Pat, *Wherever Green Is Worn: The Story of the Irish Diaspora* (New York: Palgrave, 2001).

Coon, Carleton Stevens, *The Races of Europe* (New York: Macmillan, 1939).

Coughlan, Patricia and Alex Davis (eds), *Modernism and Ireland: The Poetry of the 1930s* (Cork: Cork University Press, 1995).

Coulter, Carol, *Ireland: Between the First and Third Worlds* (Dublin: Attic Press, 1990).

Crawford, V. M., 'Uganda Calls to Ireland', *Studies*, 97 (March 1936), pp. 97–108.

Cronin, Mike, *Sport and Nationalism in Ireland: Gaelic Games, Soccer and Irish Identity Since 1884* (Dublin: Four Courts Press, 1999).

Crowley, Ethel and Jim MacLaughlin (eds), *Under the Belly of the Celtic Tiger* (Dublin: Irish Reporter, 1997).

Cullen, Fintan, *The Irish Face: Redefining the Irish Portrait* (London: National Portrait Gallery, 2004).

Cullen, Paul, *Refugees and Asylum-Seekers in Ireland* (Cork: Cork University Press, 2000).

Cullingford, Elizabeth, *Yeats, Ireland and Fascism* (New York: New York University Press, 1981).

Cullingford, Elizabeth Butler, *Ireland's Others: Gender and Ethnicity in Irish Literature and Popular Culture* (Cork: Cork University Press, 2001).

Cunard, Nancy (ed.), *The Negro Anthology* (London: Wishart, 1934).

Curtis Jr, L. Perry, *Apes and Angels: The Irishman in Victorian Caricature*, revised edition (Washington, DC, and London: Smithsonian Institution, 1997).

Cusack, Tricia, 'Migrant Travellers and Touristic Idylls: The Paintings of Jack B. Yeats and Post-Colonial Identities', *Art History*, 21, 2 (June 1998), pp. 201–18.

Daly, Mary, *Industrial Development and Irish National Identity, 1922–1939* (Dublin: Gill and Macmillan, 1992).

Daly, Mary, 'Irish Nationality and Citizenship Since 1922', *Irish Historical Studies*, xxxii, 127 (May 2001), pp. 377–407.

Daniel, T. K., 'The Scholars and the Saboteurs: The Wrecking of a South African Irish Scheme, Paris 1922', *South African-Irish Studies*, 1 (1991), pp. 162–75.

Davis, Alex, *A Broken Line: Denis Devlin and Irish Poetic Modernism* (Dublin: University College Dublin Press, 2000).

Davis, Richard, *Arthur Griffith and Non-Violent Sinn Fein* (Dublin: Anvil Books, 1974).

Davis, Richard, *The Self-Determination of Ireland Leagues and the Irish Race Convention in Paris, 1921–1922.* Tasmanian Historical Research Association. Reprinted from *Papers and Proceedings*, 24, 3 (September 1977), pp. 88–104.

Davison, Neil R., *James Joyce, Ulysses, and the Construction of Jewish Identity: Culture, Biography, and 'the Jew' in Modernist Europe* (Cambridge: Cambridge University Press, 1996).

Deane, Seamus, *Celtic Revivals: Essays in Modern Irish Literature, 1880–1980* (London: Faber, 1985).

Deane, Seamus (ed.), *The Field Day Anthology of Irish Writing, Vol. 1* (Derry: Field Day, 1991).

Deleuze, Gilles and Félix Guattari, *A Thousand Plateaus: Capitalism and Schizophrenia*, trans. Brian Massumi (London and New York: Continuum, 2004).

Derrida, Jacques, *Of Hospitality: Anne Dufourmantalle Invites Jacques Derrida to Respond*, trans. Rachel Bowlby (Stanford, CA: Stanford University Press, 2000).

de Valera, Eamon, *Speeches and Statements by Eamon de Valera, 1917–73*, ed. Maurice Moynihan (Dublin: Gill and Macmillan, 1980).

Doyle, Paul A., *Liam O'Flaherty* (New York: Twayne, 1971).

Doyle, Roddy, *The Commitments* (London: Vintage, [1987] 1998).

Doyle, Roddy, *The Deportees and Other Stories* (London: Jonathan Cape, 2007).

Duff, Frank, *Edel Quinn* (Dublin: Catholic Truth Society, 1958).

Duffy, Enda, *The Subaltern Ulysses* (Minneapolis, MN: University of Minnesota Press, 1994).

Dugger, Julie M., 'Black Ireland's Race: Thomas Carlyle and the Young Ireland Movement', *Victorian Studies*, 48, 3 (2006), pp. 461–85.

Durcan, Paul, *O Westport in the Light of Asia Minor* (Dún Laoire: Anna Livia Books/ Dublin Magazine Press, 1975).

Eagan, Catherine, '"I Did Imagine . . . We Had Ceased to Be Whitewashed Negroes": The Racial Formation of Irish Identity in Nineteenth-Century Ireland and America'. Boston College, MA, 2000. Unpublished PhD Dissertation.

Eagan, Catherine M., 'Still "Black" and "Proud": Irish-America and the Racial Politics of Hibernophilia', in *The Irish in Us: Irishness, Performativity, and Popular Culture*, ed. Diane Negra (Durham, NC, and London: Duke University Press, 2006), pp. 20–63.

Eagan, Catherine M., '"White," but "not Quite": Irish Whiteness in the Nineteenth-Century Irish-American Novel', *Eire-Ireland*, 36, 1 & 2 (Spring-Summer 2001), pp. 66–81.

Ellmann, Richard, *The Consciousness of Joyce* (London: Faber, 1977).

Ellmann, Richard, *The Identity of Yeats* (London: Faber, 1964).

Ellmann, Richard, *James Joyce: New and Revised Edition* (Oxford: Oxford University Press, 1983).

Fallon, Brian, *An Age of Innocence: Irish Culture 1930–1960* (Dublin: Gill and Macmillan, 1998).

Fanning, Bryan, 'Book Reviews', *Ethnic and Racial Studies*, 30, 5 (September 2007), pp. 943–4.

Fanning, Bryan, *Racism and Social Change in the Republic of Ireland* (Manchester: Manchester University Press, 2002).

Fanning, Ronan, Michael Kennedy, Dermot Keogh, and Eunan O'Halpin (eds), *Documents on Irish Foreign Policy, Vol. 1: 1919–1922* (Dublin: Royal Irish Academy, 1998).

Fanon, Frantz, *Black Skin, White Masks*, trans. Charles Lam Markmann (London: Pluto, 1996).

Faragó, Borbála and Moynagh Sullivan (eds), *Facing the Other: Interdisciplinary Studies on Race, Gender and Social Justice in Ireland* (Newcastle: Cambridge Scholars, 2008).

Fitzgerald, Gretchen, *Repulsing Racism: Reflections on Racism and the Irish* (Dublin: Attic Press, 1992).

Fitz-Gerald, William G. (ed.), *The Voice of Ireland: A Survey of the Race and Nation from All Angles by the Foremost Leaders at Home and Abroad* (Dublin and London: Virtue and Company, n.d. [1923]).

Ford, John. Dir. *The Quiet Man*. Perf. John Wayne, Maureen O'Hara, Barry Fitzgerald. Republic Entertainment Inc., 1952. DVD, Universal, 2006.

Forristal, Desmond, *Edel Quinn, 1907–1944* (Dublin: Dominican Publications, 1994).

Foster, R. F., *Modern Ireland, 1600–1972* (London: Penguin, 1989).

Foster, R. F., *W.B. Yeats: A Life, II: The Arch-Poet* (Oxford: Oxford University Press, 2003).

Foucault, Michel, *The Hermeneutics of the Subject: Lectures at the Collège de France 1981–1982*, ed. Frédéric Gros, trans. Graham Burchell (Basingstoke and New York: Palgrave, 2004).

Foucault, Michel, *History of Sexuality, Vol. 1: The Will to Knowledge* (London: Penguin, 1998).

Fox, Russell Arben, 'J.G. Herder on Language and the Metaphysics of National Community', *The Review of Politics*, 65, 2 (Spring 2003), pp. 237–62.

Friberg, Hedda, *An Old Order and a New: The Split World of Liam O'Flaherty's Novels*. Studia Anglistica Upsaliensia, 95 (Uppsala, Sweden: Acta Universitatis Upsaliensis, 1996).

Friel, Brian, *The Home Place* (London: Faber, 2005).

Gallagher, Brian, 'About Us, For Us, Near Us: The Irish and Harlem Renaissances', *Eire-Ireland*, 16, 4 (Winter 1981), pp. 14–26.

Gamble, David P., 'Physical Type and Mental Characters: Preliminary Notes on the Study of the Correlation between Racial Types and Types of Psychotic Reaction', *American Journal of Physical Anthropology*, 2, 2 (June 1944), pp. 195–220.

Garner, Steve, *Racism in the Irish Experience* (London: Pluto, 2004).

Garvin, Tom, *1922: The Birth of Irish Democracy* (Dublin: Gill and Macmillan, 2005).

Garvin, Tom, *Preventing the Future: Why Was Ireland So Poor For So Long?* (Dublin: Gill and Macmillan, 2005).

Gates, Jr, Henry Louis, 'The "Blackness of Blackness": A Critique of the Sign and the Signifying Monkey', *Critical Inquiry*, 9, 4 (June 1983), pp. 685–723.

Gates, Jr, Henry Louis, *Figures in Black: Words, Signs, and the 'Racial' Self* (Oxford: Oxford University Press, 1989).

Gates, Jr, Henry Louis (ed.), *'Race,' Writing and Difference* (Chicago: University of Chicago Press, 1986).

Gates, Kelly, 'Identifying the 9/11 "Faces of Terror": The Promise and Problem of Facial Recognition Technology', *Cultural Studies*, 20, 4–5 (July/ September 2006), pp. 417–40.

Gavin, Alice, 'The "Angle of Immunity": Face and Façade in Beckett's *Film*', *Critical Quarterly*, 50, 3 (2008), pp. 77–89.

Gellner, Ernest, *Nations and Nationalism* (Ithaca, NY: Cornell University Press, 1983).

Gibbons, Luke, *Gaelic Gothic: Race, Colonization, and Irish Culture* (Galway: Arlen House, 2004).

Gibbons, Luke, *The Quiet Man: Ireland into Film* (Cork: Cork University Press, 2002).

Gibbons, Luke, *Transformations in Irish Culture* (Cork: Cork University Press, 1996).

Gibson, Andrew, *Joyce's Revenge: History, Politics, and Aesthetics in Ulysses* (Oxford: Oxford University Press, 2002).

Gifford, Don, *Ulysses Annotated: Notes for James Joyce's Ulysses* (Berkeley, CA: University of California Press, 1988).

Gill, Jerry H., 'On Knowing the Dancer from the Dance', *The Journal of Aesthetics and Art Criticism*, 34, 2 (Winter 1975), pp. 125–35.

Gilroy, Paul, *Between Camps: Nations, Cultures and the Allure of Race* (London: Penguin, 2001).

Gilroy, Paul, *The Black Atlantic: Modernity and Double Consciousness* (London: Verso, 1993).

Gilroy, Paul, *Small Acts: Thoughts on the Politics of Black Cultures* (London: Serpent's Tail, 1993).

Gilroy, Paul, *There Ain't No Black in the Union Jack: The Cultural Politics of Race and Nation* (London: Routledge, 1987).

Girvin, Brian, *Between Two Worlds: Politics and Economy in Independent Ireland* (Dublin: Gill and Macmillan, 1989).

Goldberg, David Theo, *The Racial State* (Oxford: Blackwell, 2002).

Goldberg, David Theo, *Racist Culture: Philosophy and the Politics of Meaning* (Oxford: Blackwell, 1993).

Gough, Kathleen M., 'Polymorphous Playboys: Irish-Caribbean Shadow Dancing', *Modern Drama*, 48, 4 (Winter 2005), pp. 777–99.

Gould, Gerald, *The English Novel To-Day* (Freeport, NY: Books for Libraries Press, 1924).

Gould, Stephen Jay, *The Mismeasure of Man*, revised edition (London and New York: W. W. Norton and Co., 1996).

Graham, Colin, *Deconstructing Ireland: Identity, Theory, Culture* (Edinburgh: Edinburgh University Press, 2001).

Grant, Madison, *The Passing of the Great Race, Or The Racial Basis of European History* (New York: Charles Scribner's Sons, 1916).

Graves, Joseph L., *The Emperor's New Clothes: Biological Theories of Race at the Millennium* (New Brunswick, NJ: Rutgers University Press, 2001).

Greenslade, Liam, 'White Skins, White Masks: Psychological Distress among the Irish in Britain', in *The Irish in the New Communities: The Irish World Wide, Volume Two*, ed. Patrick O'Sullivan (London: Leicester University Press, 1992), pp. 201–25.

Groden, Michael, 'Joyce at Work on "Cyclops": Toward a Biography of *Ulysses*, *James Joyce Quarterly*, 44, 2 (2007), pp. 217–45.

Habermas, Jürgen, *Legitimation Crisis*. Trans. Thomas McCarthy (Boston, MA: Beacon, 1975).

Hammond, Peter et al., 'Discriminating Power of Localized Three-Dimensional Facial Morphology', *The American Journal of Human Genetics*, 77 (2005), pp. 999–1010.

Hand, Seán (ed.), *The Levinas Reader* (Oxford: Blackwell, 1989).

Harmon, Maurice, *Austin Clarke: A Critical Introduction* (Dublin: Wolfhound, 1989).

Harrington, John A., 'Citizenship and the Biopolitics of Post-nationalist Ireland', *Journal of Law and Society*, 32, 3 (September 2005), pp. 424–49.

Harte, Liam, 'Free State Interrogators: Liam O'Flaherty and Frank O'Connor', *Irish Studies Review*, 8, 2 (2000), pp. 233–8.

Herr, Cheryl, 'The Erotics of Irishness', *Critical Inquiry*, 17 (1990), pp. 1–34.

Herrnstein, Richard J. and Charles Murray, *The Bell Curve: Reshaping of American Life by Differences in Intelligence* (New York: Simon and Schuster, 1994).

Hezser, Catherine, '"Are You Protestant Jews or Catholic Jews?" Literary Representations of Being Jewish in Ireland', *Modern Judaism*, 25, 2 (May 2005), pp. 159–88.

Higgins, Aidan, *Langrishe, Go Down* (London: Minerva, 1993).

Hodges, Graham, '"Desirable Companions and Lovers": Irish and African-Americans in the Sixth Ward, 1830–1870', in *The New York Irish*, ed. Ronald Baylor and Timothy J. Meagher (Baltimore, MD: Johns Hopkins University Press, 1996), pp. 107–24.

Hogan, Edmund M., *The Irish Missionary Movement: A Historical Survey, 1830–1980* (Dublin: Gill and Macmillan, 1990).

Hogan, Robert and Richard Burnham, *The Years of O'Casey, 1921–1926: A Documentary History* (Newark, NJ: University of Delaware Press, 1992).

hooks, bell, *Black Looks: Race and Representation* (London: Turnaround, 1992).

Hooton, E. A., *Up from the Ape* (New York: Macmillan, 1931).

Hooton, E. A., 'Stature, Head Form, and Pigmentation of the Adult Male Irish', *American Journal of Physical Anthropology*, XXVI (30 March 1940), pp. 229–49.

Hooton, Earnest A. and C. Wesley Dupertuis, *The Physical Anthropology of Ireland* (with a section on The West Coast Irish Females by Helen Dawson). *Papers of the Peabody Museum of Archaeology and Ethnology, Harvard University, Vol. XXX, Nos 1–2* (Cambridge, MA: Peabody Museum, 1955).

Howes, Marjorie, *Yeats's Nations: Gender, Class and Irishness* (Cambridge: Cambridge University Press, 1996).

Hunt, Edward E., 'Anthropometry, Genetics and Racial History', *American Anthropologist*, 61 (1959), pp. 64–87.

Ignatiev, Noel, *How the Irish Became White* (London: Routledge, 1995).

Ingman, Heather, 'Translating between Cultures: A Kristevan Reading of the Theme of the Foreigner in Some Twentieth-Century Novels by Irish Women', *Yearbook of English Studies*, 36, 1 (2006), pp. 177–90.

Innes, C. L., *The Devil's Own Mirror: The Irishman and the African in Modern Literature* (Washington, DC: Three Continents Press, 1990).

Jablonski, Nina G., *Skin: A Natural History* (Berkeley and Los Angeles: University of California Press, 2006).

Jacobson, Matthew Frye, *Whiteness of a Different Colour: European Immigrants and the Alchemy of Race* (Cambridge, MA: Harvard University Press, 1998).

Jameson, Fredric, *Marxism and Form: Twentieth-Century Dialectical Theories of Literature* (Princeton, NJ: Princeton University Press, 1974).

Johnston, Denis, *The Moon in the Yellow River*, in his *Selected Plays* (Gerrards Cross, Bucks: Colin Smythe, 1983).

Joyce, James, *The Critical Writings of James Joyce*, ed. Ellsworth Mason and Richard Ellmann (Ithaca, NY: Cornell University Press, 1989).

Joyce, James, *James Joyce's Letters to Sylvia Beach, 1921–1940*, ed. Melissa

Banta and Oscar A. Silverman (Bloomington and Indianapolis: Indiana University Press, 1987).

Joyce, James, *A Portrait of the Artist as a Young Man* (London: Granada, 1977).

Joyce, James, *Selected Letters of James Joyce*, ed. Richard Ellmann (New York: Viking, 1975).

Joyce, James, *Ulysses: The 1922 Text*, ed. Jeri Johnson (Oxford: Oxford University Press, 1993).

Kelly, John, *Sophisticated Boom Boom* (London: Jonathan Cape, 2003).

Kennedy, Seán, 'The Artist Who Stakes His Being Is from Nowhere', *Samuel Beckett Today/ Aujourd'hui: After Beckett, D'Aprés Beckett*, ed. Anthony Uhlmann, Sjef Houppermans, and Bruno Clement (Amsterdam: Rodopi, 2004), pp. 61–74.

Kenny, Kevin, *The American Irish: A History* (New York: Longman, 2000).

Kenny, Kevin (ed.), *Ireland and the British Empire* (Oxford: Oxford University Press, 2004).

Keogh, Dermot, *Jews in Twentieth-Century Ireland* (Cork: Cork University Press, 1998).

Keogh, Dermot, 'The Treaty Split and the Paris Irish Race Convention, 1922', *Etudes Irlandaises*, 12 (December 1987), pp. 165–70.

Keogh, Dermot, *Twentieth-Century Ireland: Nation and State* (New York: St Martin's Press, 1995).

Keogh, Dermot and Andrew McCarthy, *Limerick Boycott 1904: Anti-Semitism in Ireland* (Cork: Mercier, 2005).

Keown, Gerard, 'The Irish Race Conference, 1922, Reconsidered', *Irish Historical Studies*, xxxii, 127 (May 2001), pp. 365–76.

Kiberd, Declan, *Inventing Ireland: The Literature of the Modern Nation* (London: Jonathan Cape, 1995).

Kiberd, Declan, *Irish Classics* (London: Granta, 2000).

Kiberd, Declan, *The Irish Writer and the World* (Cambridge: Cambridge University Press, 2005).

Kiberd, Declan, 'Strangers in Their Own Country', in Declan Kiberd and Edna Longley, *Multi-Culturalism: The View from the Two Irelands* (Cork: Cork University Press, 2001), pp. 45–74.

Kiberd, Declan, 'White Skin, Black Masks: Celticism and *Négritude*', *Eire-Ireland*, 31, 1 & 2 (Spring-Summer 1996), pp. 163–75.

Kiberd, Declan and Edna Longley, *Multi-Culturalism: The View from the Two Irelands* (Cork: Cork University Press, 2001).

Killian, Dian, Arlent Wilner, Avy Trager, Victoria Boynton, Stephen Spencer, and Karen J. Hali, 'What's White Got to Do With It? Teaching Whiteness, Part II', *Modern Language Studies*, 32, 1 (Spring 2002), pp. 133–73.

Kirby, Peadar, Luke Gibbons, and Mike Cronin (eds), *Reinventing Ireland: Culture and the Celtic Tiger* (London: Pluto, 2002).

Kissane, Noel, *The Irish Face* (Dublin: National Library of Ireland, 1986).

Kuhling, Carmen and Kieran Keohane, *Cosmopolitan Ireland: Globalisation and Quality of Life* (London: Pluto, 2007).

Lee, J. J., *Ireland 1912–1985: Politics and Society* (Cambridge: Cambridge University Press, 1989).

Lentin, Ronit, *The Expanding Nation: Towards a Multi-Ethnic Ireland* (Dublin: Department of Sociology, Trinity College Dublin, 1999).

Lentin, Ronit, 'Ireland: Racial State and Crisis Racism', *Ethnic and Racial Studies*, 30, 4 (July 2007), pp. 610–27.

Lentin, Ronit and Robbie McVeigh, *After Optimism? Ireland, Racism and Globalisation* (Dublin: Metro Eireann Press, 2006).

Levy, Daniel, 'The Cosmopolitan Figuration: Historicizing Reflexive Modernization', in *Ulrich Beck's Kosmopolitisches Projekt*, ed. Angelika Poferl and Natan Sznaider (Baden-Baden: Nomos Verlagsgesellschaft, 2004), pp. 177–87.

Lewis, Pericles, 'The Conscience of the Race: The Nation as Church of the Modern Age', *Joyce through the Ages: A Nonlinear View*, ed. Michael Patrick Gillespie (Gainesville, FL: University Press of Florida, 1999), pp. 85–106.

Lloyd, David, *Anomalous States: Irish Writing and the Post-Colonial Moment* (Dublin: Lilliput, 1993).

Lloyd, David, *Ireland after History* (Cork: Cork University Press, 1999).

Lloyd, David, 'Race under Representation', *Culture/Contexture: Explorations in Anthropology and Literary Studies*, ed. E. Valentine Daniel and Jeffrey M. Peck (Berkeley, CA: University of Los Angeles Press, 1996), pp. 249–72.

Lloyd, David, 'Republics of Difference: Yeats, MacGreevy, Beckett', *Third Text*, 19, 5 (September 2005), pp. 461–74.

Lloyd, Michael, *The Face of Ireland* (London: Batsford, 1937).

Lott, Eric, *Love and Theft: Blackface Minstrelsy and the American Working Class* (Oxford: Oxford University Press, 1995).

Low, Gail Ching-Liang, *White Skin/Black Masks: Representation and Colonialism* (London: Routledge, 1996).

Lynd, Robert, *Rambles in Ireland* (London: Mills and Boon, 1912).

Lynott, Philomena, with Jackie Harden, *My Boy: The Philip Lynott Story* (Dublin: Hot Press Books, 1995).

Lyons, F. S. L., *Ireland Since the Famine* (London: Fontana, 1973).

McAuliffe, Marius, *Envoy to Africa: The Interior Life of Edel Quinn* (Dublin: Franciscan Herald Press, 1975).

MacConaill, Michael A., 'The Correlations of Length, Breadth and Height in Forty Mixed Crania'. MSc thesis, June 1928, Queen's University of Belfast.

MacConaill, Michael A., 'Normal Proportions of European Calvaria', *American Journal of Physical Anthropology*, XIV, i (Jan-Mar 1930), pp. 23–32.

MacConaill, Michael A., 'The People of Rachrai', *Proceedings of the Belfast Natural History Society*, 1922–3, pp. 4–7.

MacConaill, Michael A., 'The Physical Anthropology of Ireland', *Man*, 56 (March 1956), pp. 47–8.

MacConaill, Michael A., 'The Physical Forms of Irishmen', *Studies*, 45, 1 (Spring 1956), pp. 92–101.

MacConaill, Michael A., 'Post-Natal Development of Hair and Eye Colour with Special Reference to Some Ethnological Problems', *Annals of Eugenics*, VII, iii (1936), pp. 218–25.

McCormack, W. J., *Blood Kindred: W.B. Yeats – The Life, The Death, The Politics* (London: Pimlico, 2005).

McCormack, W. J., *From Burke to Beckett: Ascendancy Tradition and Betrayal in Literary History* (Cork: Cork University Press, 1994).

MacÉinrí, Piaras, '"A Slice of Africa": Whose Side Were We On? Ireland and the Anti-Colonial Struggle', *Race and State*, ed. Alana Lentin and Ronit Lentin (Newcastle: Cambridge Scholars Press, 2006), pp. 257–74.

McGlade, Joseph, *A History of Irish Catholicism, Vol. vi: The Missions – Africa and the Orient* (Dublin: Gill and Son, 1967).

MacGreevy, Thomas, *Jack B. Yeats: An Appreciation and an Interpretation* (Dublin: Waddington, 1945).

McLaughlin, Jim, *Travellers and Ireland* (Cork: Cork University Press, 1995).

McMahon, Eileen, 'How the Irish Became White', *American Historical Review*, 102, 2 (April 1997), pp. 571–2.

MacManus, Francis, *The Fire in the Dust* (London: Jonathan Cape, 1950).

MacManus, Seumas, *The Story of the Irish Race: A Popular History of Ireland* (New York: Devin-Adair/ The Irish Publishing Co., 1922).

McMinn, Joseph (ed.), *The Internationalism of Irish Literature and Drama* (Savage, MD: Barnes and Noble, 1992).

McVeigh, Robbie and Ronit Lentin (eds), *Racism and Anti-Racism in Ireland* (Belfast: Beyond the Pale, 2002).

McWilliams, David, *The Generation Game: Boom, Bust and Ireland's Economic Miracle* (London: Macmillan, 2008).

Malchow, H. L., *Gothic Images of Race in Nineteenth-Century Britain* (Stanford, CA: Stanford University Press, 1996).

Malik, Kenan, *Strange Fruit: Why Both Sides Are Wrong in the Race Debate* (Oxford: Oneworld, 2008).

Mallarmé, Stéphane, *Oeuvres Complètes* (Paris: Gallimard, 1945).

Malouf, Michael, 'Other Emerald Isles: Caribbean Revisions of Irish Cultural Nationalism', Columbia University, 2004. Unpublished PhD dissertation.

Malouf, Michael, 'With Dev in America: Sinn Féin and Recognition Politics, 1919–21', *Interventions*, 4, 1 (2002), pp. 22–34.

Manganaro, Marc, *Culture, 1922: The Emergence of a Concept* (Princeton, NJ: Princeton University Press, 2002).

Mathews, P. J., *Revival: The Abbey Theatre, Sinn Fein, The Gaelic League and the Co-operative Movement* (Cork: Cork University Press, 2003).

Mays, Michael, *Nation States: The Cultures of Irish Nationalism* (Plymouth, UK: Lexington, 2007).

Meaney, Gerardine, 'Regendering Modernism: The Woman Artist in Irish Women's Fiction', *Women: A Cultural Review*, 15, 1 (2004), pp. 67–82.

Meijer, Miriam Claude, *Race and Aesthetics in the Anthropology of Petrus Camper* (Amsterdam: Rodopi, 1999).

Mercer, Kobena, *Welcome to the Jungle: New Positions in Black Cultural Studies* (London: Routledge, 1994).

Miles, Robert, *Racism* (London: Routledge, 1989).

Miller, David, 'The Ethical Significance of Nationality', *Ethics*, 98 (July 1988), pp. 647–62.

Miller, David, *On Nationality* (Oxford: Clarendon Press, 1995).

Miller, J. Hillis, *Fiction and Repetition: Seven English Novels* (Cambridge, MA: Harvard University Press, 1982).

Miller, J. Hillis, *Topographies* (Stanford, CA: Stanford University Press, 1995).

Mishkin, Tracy, *The Harlem and Irish Renaissances: Language, Identity, Representation* (Gainesville, FL: University of Florida Press, 1998).

Mitchel, John, *The Jail Journal*, ed. Rev. T. Corcoran (Dublin: Browne and Nolan, n.d.).

Montague, John, 'An Occasion of Sin', in his *Death of a Chieftain and Other Stories* (Dublin: Wolfhound, 1998), pp. 128–44.

Moon, Krystyn R., *Yellowface: Creating the Chinese in American Popular Music and Performance, 1850s-1920s* (New Brunswick, NJ: Rutgers University Press, 2005).

Moore, Margaret, *The Ethics of Nationalism* (Oxford: Oxford University Press, 2001).

Moran, D. P., *The Philosophy of Irish Ireland* (Dublin: James Duffy, 1905).

Morton, W. R. M., 'Thomas Walmsley', *The Anatomical Record*, 114, 2 (1952), pp. 266–9.

Moynihan, Anselm, *Edel Quinn* (Cork: Dominican Bureau, n.d.).

Muktupavela, Laima, *The Mushroom Covenant* (Šampinjonu Derība) (Riga: Daugava, 2002).

Mutwarasibo, Fidele and Suzanne Smith, *Africans in Ireland: Developing Communities* (Dublin: African Cultural Project, 2000).

Nadel, Ira B., *Joyce and the Jews: Culture and Texts* (Gainesville, FL: University Press of Florida, 1989).

Nally, T. H., *The Aonac Tailteann and the Tailteann Games: Their Origin, History and Ancient Associations* (Dublin: Talbot Press; London: T. Fisher Unwin, 1922).

Nancy, Jean-Luc, *The Inoperative Community*, ed. Peter Connor, trans. Peter Connor et al. (Minneapolis, MN: University of Minnesota Press, 1991).

Negra, Diane, 'The Stakes of Whiteness', *Minnesota Review*, 7 (Fall 1996), pp. 109–14.

Nolan, Emer, *James Joyce and Nationalism* (London: Routledge, 1995).

North, Michael, *Reading 1922: A Return to the Scene of the Modern* (Oxford: Oxford University Press, 1999).

North, Michael, 'Virtual Histories: The Year as Literary Period', *Modern Language Quarterly*, 62, 4 (December 2001), pp. 407–24.

Nowatzki, Robert, 'Paddy Jumps Jim Crow: Irish-Americans and Blackface Minstrelsy', *Eire-Ireland*, 41, 3 & 4 (Fall-Winter 2006), pp. 162–84.

O'Brien, Edna, *The Country Girls* (London: Penguin, 1963).

O'Brien, James H., *Liam O'Flaherty* (Lewisburg, PA: Bucknell University Press, 1973).

O'Brien, John A., *The Vanishing Irish: The Enigma of the Modern World* (London: W. H. Allen, 1954).

O'Brien, Kate, *The Last of Summer* (London: Virago, 1990).

O'Connell, Michael, *Right-Wing Ireland? The Rise of Populism in Ireland and Europe* (Dublin: Liffey Press, 2003).

O'Connor, Ulick, *Brendan Behan* (London: Abacus, [1970] 1993).

O'Flaherty, Liam, *The Black Soul* (Dublin: Wolfhound, 1996).

O'Flaherty, Liam, *The Informer* (Dublin: Wolfhound, 1999).

O'Flaherty, Liam, *Insurrection* (Dublin: Wolfhound, 1998).

O'Flaherty, Liam, *Mr Gilhooley* (Dublin: Wolfhound, 1998).

O'Flaherty, Liam, *The Puritan* (Dublin: Wolfhound, 2001).

O'Flaherty, Liam, *Thy Neighbour's Wife* (Dublin: Wolfhound, 1992).

Ó Gráda, Cormac, *Jewish Ireland in the Age of Joyce: A Socioeconomic History* (Princeton, NJ: Princeton University Press, 2006).

Ó Gráda, Cormac, 'Lost in Little Jerusalem: Leopold Bloom and Irish Jewry', *Journal of Modern Literature*, 27, 4 (Summer 2004), pp. 17–26.

Ó Maitiú, Séamas, *W&R Jacob: Celebrating 150 Years of Irish Biscuit Making* (Dublin: Woodfield Press, 2001).

Onkey, Lauren E., *Blacking Up on Broadway: Racial Identity in Irish American Theater* (Muncie, IN: Ball State University, 2000).

Onkey, Lauren, 'James Farrell's *Studs Lonigan* Trilogy and the Anxieties of Race', *Eire-Ireland*, 40, 3 & 4 (Fall-Winter 2005), pp. 104–18.

Onkey, Lauren, '"A Melee and a Curtain": Black-Irish Relations in Ned Harrigan's The Mulligan Guard Ball', *Jouvert*, 4.1 (Fall 1999): http://social.chass.ncsu.edu/jouvert/v4iI/onkey.htm

O'Rahilly, T. F., *Early Irish History and Mythology* (Dublin: Dublin Institute for Advanced Studies, 1946).

Paul, Diane, *Controlling Human Heredity: 1865 to the Present* (Atlantic Highlands, NJ: Humanities Press, 1995).

Pettitt, Lance, *Screening Ireland: Film and Television Representation* (Manchester: Manchester University Press, 2000).

Phillips, Terry, 'A Study in Grotesques: Transformations of the Human in the Writing of Liam O'Flaherty', *Gothic Studies*, 7, 1 (May 2005), pp. 41–52.

Phinney, Kevin, *Souled American: How Black Music Transformed White Culture* (New York: Billboard, 2005).

Platt, Len, *Joyce, Race and Finnegans Wake* (Cambridge: Cambridge University Press, 2007).

Plock, Vike Martina, 'A Feat of Strength in "Ithaca": Eugen Sandow and Physical Culture in Joyce's *Ulysses*', *Journal of Modern Literature*, 30, 1 (2006), pp. 129–39.

Plunkett, James, 'A Walk through the Summer', *The Trusting and the Maimed* (London: Hutchinson, 1959), pp. 33–51.

Prager, Jeffrey, *Building Democracy in Ireland: Political Order and Cultural Integration in a Newly Independent Nation* (Cambridge: Cambridge University Press, 1986).

Prendergast, Mark J., *Irish Rock: Roots, Personalities, Directions* (Dublin: The O'Brien Press, 1987).

Prendergast, P. J. and T. C. Lee, 'Walking on Water: The Biomechanics of Michael A. MacConaill (1902–1987)', *Irish Journal of Medical Science*, 175, 3 (2006), pp. 69–75.

Price, David H., *Anthropological Intelligence: The Deployment and Neglect of American Anthropology in the Second World War* (Durham, NC: Duke University Press, 2008).

Putterford, Mark, *Phil Lynott: The Rocker* (London: Omnipress Books, 2002).

Pyle, Hilary, *Jack B. Yeats: A Biography* (London: André Deutsch, 1989).

Quick, Jonathan, 'Molly Bloom's Mother', *ELH*, 57, 1 (Spring 1990), pp. 223–40.

Raymond, Josephine Hunt, *The Remembered Face of Ireland* (Chicago: Wilcox and Follett, 1946).

Reddy, Maureen T., 'Reading and Writing Race in Ireland: Roddy Doyle and Metro Eireann', *Irish University Review*, 35, 2 (Autumn-Winter 2005), pp. 374–88.

Regan, John M., *The Irish Counter-Revolution, 1921–1936: Treatyite Politics and Settlement in Independent Ireland* (Dublin: Gill and Macmillan, 1999).

Reizbaum, Marilyn, *James Joyce's Judaic Other* (Stanford, CA: Stanford University Press, 1999).

Rhees, Rush (ed.), *Ludwig Wittgenstein: Personal Recollections* (Oxford: Oxford University Press, 1981).

Ripley, William Z., *The Races of Europe: A Sociological Study* (New York: D. Appleton and Co., 1899).

Roediger, David R., *The Wages of Whiteness: Race and the Making of the American Working Class*, revised edition (London: Verso, 1998).

Rolston, Bill, 'Are the Irish Black?', *Race and Class*, 41, 1 & 2 (1999), pp. 95–102.

Rolston, Bill and Michael Shannon, *Encounters: How Racism Came to Ireland* (Belfast: Beyond the Pale, 2002).

Ruane, Caitríona, Thérèse Caherty, Andy Storey, Mary Garvin, and Máire Molloy (eds), *Is Ireland a Third World Country?* (Belfast: Beyond the Pale, 1992).

Russell, George (Æ), *The Inner and the Outer Ireland* (Dublin: Talbot Press, 1921).

Russell, George (Æ), *The Interpreters* (London: Macmillan, 1922).

Saint-Amour, Paul K., 'Bombing and the Symptom: Traumatic Earliness and the Nuclear Uncanny', *Diacritics*, 30, 4 (Winter 2000), pp. 59–82.

Saint-Amour, Paul K., '"Christmas Yet to Come": Hospitality, Futurity, the *Carol*, and "The Dead"', *Representations*, 98 (Spring 2007), pp. 93–117.

Schnapper, Dominique, *Community of Citizens: On the Modern Idea of Nationality*, trans. Severine Rosee (New Brunswick, NJ: Transaction, 1998).

Scruton, Roger, 'Wittgenstein and the Understanding of Music', *British Journal of Aesthetics*, 44, 1 (January 2004), pp. 1–9.

Shaw, Bernard, *Back to Methuselah: A Metabiological Pentateuch* (London: Penguin, 1939).

Sheehy, Michael, *Is Ireland Dying? Culture and the Church in Modern Ireland* (London: Hollis and Carter, 1968).

Sheeran, Patrick F., *The Novels of Liam O'Flaherty: A Study in Romantic Realism* (Dublin: Wolfhound, 1976).

Smith, Dan, 'Ethical Uncertainties of Nationalism', *Journal of Peace Research*, 37, 4 (July 2000), pp. 489–502.

Smyth, Gerry, *Noisy Island: A Short History of Irish Popular Music* (Cork: Cork University Press, 2005).

Stallworthy, Jon (ed.), *Yeats: Last Poems* (Basingstoke and London: Macmillan, 1968).

Stanfield, Paul Scott, *Yeats and Politics in the Nineteen-Thirties* (London: Macmillan, 1988).

Staunton, Enda, 'The Case of Biafra: Ireland and the Nigerian Civil War', *Irish Historical Studies*, XXXI (1999), pp. 513–34.

Stibbe, E. P., *An Introduction to Physical Anthropology* (London: Edward Arnold, 1930).

Stoddard, Lothrop, *The Rising Tide of Color against White Supremacy* (New York: Charles Scribner's Sons, 1920).

Stuart, Francis, *Pigeon Irish* (London: Victor Gollancz, 1932).

Suenens, Leon-Joseph Cardinal, *Edel Quinn: Envoy of the Legion of Mary to Africa* (Dublin: C. J. Fallon, 1957).

Synge, J. M., *Collected Works, Volume 3: Plays, Book One*, ed. Ann Saddlemyer (Gerrards Cross, Bucks: Colin Smythe, 1982).

Tapping, G. Craig, *Austin Clarke: A Study of His Writings* (Dublin: The Academy Press, 1981).

Turpin, John, 'Visual Culture and Catholicism in the Irish Free State, 1922–1949', *Journal of Ecclesiastical History*, 57, 1 (January 2006), pp. 55–77.

Ussher, Arland, *The Face and Mind of Ireland* (London: Victor Gollancz, 1949).

Wall, Richard, 'Introduction', *An Giall/The Hostage* (Washington, DC: Catholic University of America Press, 1987), pp. 1–21.

Wall, Richard, *Wittgenstein in Ireland* (London: Reaktion, 2000).

Walls, Mary, *I Knew Edel Quinn* (Dublin: Catholic Truth Society, 1969).

Walmsley, T., J. M. Mogey, and D. P. Gamble, 'The Peoples of Northern Ireland', *Ulster Journal of Archaeology*, 3rd Series, 2 (1939) (pp. 89–97); 5 (1942) (pp. 98–118); 6 (1943) (pp. 112–25); 9 (1946) (pp. 107–27).

Welch, Robert (ed.), *The Oxford Companion to Irish Literature* (Oxford: Oxford University Press, 1996).

White, Richard, 'Herder: On the Ethics of Nationalism', *Humanitas*, 18, 1 & 2 (2005), pp. 166–81.

Whitty, Noel, 'Law and the Regulation of Reproduction in Ireland: 1922–1992', *University of Toronto Law Journal*, 43 (1993), pp. 851–88.

Whyte, J. H., *Church and State in Modern Ireland, 1923–1970* (Dublin: Gill and Macmillan, 1971).

Wills, Claire, *That Neutral Island: A Cultural History of Ireland during the Second World War* (London: Faber, 2007).

Wittgenstein, Ludwig, *The Blue and Brown Books: Preliminary Studies for the 'Philosophical Investigations'*, second edition (Oxford: Blackwell, 1969).

Wittgenstein, Ludwig, *Philosophical Investigations*, trans. G. E. M. Anscombe (Oxford: Basil Blackwell, 1968).

Yeats, Jack B., *Life in the West of Ireland, Drawn and Painted by Jack B. Yeats* (Dublin and London: Maunsel and Co., 1912).

Yeats, Jack B., 'Modern Aspects of Irish Art', Series F, No. 8 (Dublin: Cumann Leigheacht an Phobail, 1922).

Yeats, Jack B., *Sligo* (London: Wishart, 1930).

Yeats, W. B., *Autobiographies* (Dublin: Gill and Macmillan, 1955).

Yeats, W. B., *The Collected Works of W.B. Yeats, Vol. 5: Later Essays* (New York: Charles Scribner's Sons, 1994).

Yeats, W. B., *Memoirs*, ed. Denis Donoghue (London: Macmillan, 1972).

Yeats, W. B., *Yeats's Poems*, ed. A. Norman Jeffares (Dublin: Gill and Macmillan, 1989).

Young, Robert J. C., *The Idea of English Ethnicity* (Oxford: Blackwell, 2008).

Zneimer, John, *The Literary Vision of Liam O'Flaherty* (Syracuse, NY: Syracuse University Press, 1970).

Index